Teamwork from the Inside Out Fieldbook

Teamwork from the Inside Out Fieldbook

Exercises and Tools for Turning Team Performance Inside Out

Susan Nash and Courtney Bolin

MEDICAL LIBRARY
NORTH MEMORIAL HEALTH CARE
3300 OAKDALE AVENUE NORTH
ROBBINSDALE, MN 55422-2900

Davies-Black Publishing
Palo Alto, California

Published by Davies-Black Publishing, a division of CPP, Inc., 3803 East Bayshore Road, Palo Alto, CA 94303; 800-624-1765.

Special discounts on bulk quantities of Davies-Black books are available to corporations, professional associations, and other organizations. For details, contact the Director of Book Marketing and Sales at Davies-Black Publishing; 650-691-9123; fax 650-623-9271.

Visit the Davies-Black Publishing Web site at www.daviesblack.com.

07 06 05 04 03 10 9 8 7 6 5 4 3 2 1
Printed in the United States of America

Library of Congress Cataloging-in-Publication Data
Nash, Susan M.
Teamwork from the inside out fieldbook : exercises and tools for turning team performance inside out / Susan M. Nash and Courtney Bolin.
p. cm.
"A workbook and companion to the original book Turning team performance inside out"—P. xxi.
Includes bibliographical references.
ISBN 0-89106-172-X (pbk.)
1. Teams in the workplace. 2. Performance. 3. Leadership. I. Bolin, Courtney. II. Nash, Susan. Turning team performance inside out. III. Title.
HD66 .N367 2003
658.4′02—dc21

2002192505

FIRST EDITION

In memory of Vada Overall for teaching me the beauty of being unique
—Courtney Bolin

To my family, those alive and those who have passed on,
who have helped me live my dreams
—Susan Nash

Contents

Exercises

Chapter 4

Chapter 5

Chapter 6

Chapter 7

Chapter 8

Chapter 9

Acknowledgments

Bringing the further applications of type and temperament into the world of teams required an extensive expert, emotional, and physical support structure.

First, we wish to thank Linda Berens of Temperament Research Institute for her pioneering work in teaching whole type theory and for maintaining the integrity of the many applications of type and temperament. Her willingness to provide a set of ears, give objective feedback, and invest time in our work has been essential as we have developed this methodology.

Next we would like to thank the U.K. Temperament group for their input in developing the Teamwork from the Inside Out concepts, particularly Tessa Bradon, Mark Burdon, and Jacky Hughes, who unselfishly invested their time, considerable intelligence, and emotional dedication to supporting this work.

We also want to thank our many clients, without whom we would be unable to develop the applications and deepen our understanding. We particularly want to thank Ellen Dember, Karen Neely-Jones, Pat Schoof, Michael Knight, and Ben Cushman.

We wish to thank Davies-Black Publishing for their professionalism and dedication to the publication of this book, particularly Lee Langhammer-Law and Connie Kallback.

Finally, and most importantly, we wish to thank our families for their patience with our constant discussion and analysis as we have pursued this cause! Without the support, encouragement, tolerance, and love of Derek, Antony, and Laura, this book would not exist.

About the Authors

Susan Nash is an international expert on the applications of type and temperament theory in business. Founder and owner of EM-Power, Inc., a million-dollar consulting firm serving such clients as KPMG, Oracle, Seagate, and Network Associates, she is also a licensed certification provider of MBTI® programs and regularly runs Master Classes throughout the world. Formerly Director of Training with Williams-Sonoma, she is author of six books including *Turning Team Performance Inside Out.*

Courtney Bolin is principal of Behind the Bottom Line, a consulting firm that provides organization development and training services for businesses looking to unleash the competitive advantage of human potential. Her career has included positions with Andersen Consulting (now Accenture) and Exodus Communications, and her clients include San Diego State University, SGI, Cisco Systems, PETCO Animal Supplies, Inc., and CARES (Center for AIDS Research, Education, and Services).

How to Use This Fieldbook

The *Turning Team Performance Inside Out Fieldbook* is designed as a workbook and companion to the original book, *Turning Team Performance Inside Out.* The book documents a methodology for raising team performance known as the "Inside Out" approach and provides a thorough understanding of the concepts behind that approach. However, clients we have worked with, responding to the book, have told us, "The theory is great, but it comes to life as you work with our teams. Is there any way you can document the exercises and examples that you use to help us identify working style and provide more application with the theory?"

This fieldbook represents our response to them. In addition to further explanation of concepts presented in the book, it provides a wide variety of exercises that you can complete by yourself or with the entire team.

Who Can This Fieldbook Help?

This fieldbook is for:

- Team leaders who are struggling to make team performance a fact, not a fantasy
- Managers who wish to raise performance levels of their departmental teams
- Senior executives who wish to help their direct reports and functional teams increase productivity
- CEOs who wish to achieve greater alignment in their executive teams
- Consultants who are working with teams in raising team performance
- Professional coaches working within organizations
- Leaders who are trying to turn a diverse group of individuals—athletes, doctors, hobbyists, and so on—into a functional team
- Team members who are looking for tools and techniques to raise team performance

What's in This Fieldbook?

The *Turning Team Performance Inside Out Fieldbook* includes an introduction that will help prepare you to use the fieldbook and key information divided into two main parts: "Meet the Players" and "Building Your Dream Team."

- The introduction sets the scene by presenting warm-up exercises and defining the Inside Out approach. It also includes awareness-building exercises that will help get you ready to tackle part 1.
- Part 1, "Meet the Players," comprises three chapters whose goal is to help you and the other team members discover how you work best in a team, taking you through the following steps:
  - **Chapter 1:** assessing temperament
  - **Chapter 2:** determining the functions you use to gather information and make decisions
  - **Chapter 3:** selecting your "best-fit" working style
- Part 2, "Building Your Dream Team," includes six chapters describing how to start building team effectiveness using the Inside Out approach:
  - **Chapter 4:** assessing your current team performance level against the backdrop of working style and deciding which chapter to work on first
  - **Chapter 5:** building an integrated and cohesive strategy for your team to provide purpose and direction
  - **Chapter 6:** establishing clear roles and responsibilities for your team to increase accountability and reduce confusion
  - **Chapter 7:** raising trust in your team, thereby increasing your communication effectiveness and reducing conflicts
  - **Chapter 8:** exploring ways to react rapidly to change in order to capture opportunities your team would otherwise miss
  - **Chapter 9:** defining what constitutes effective leadership and implementing ways to raise leadership and ultimately team effectiveness

How to Navigate This Fieldbook

The material in this hands-on fieldbook is organized around several informational and instructional categories designed to create a learning experience that is interactive, inspiring, informative, and clear. Look for the icons identifying each category, described as follows.

Game Plan
An overview of what you will achieve within each chapter

Exercises
Activities, either individual or team focused, that can be used to "try on" material and put concepts to work

---

Foul!
An alert to clear up a perception that may not be accurate

Coaching Point
A note or reminder about what to do or look for as you try on material

---

Team Huddle!
A series of discussion questions used to emphasize learning points

---

Time Out!
A clarification or side note

Team Dynamics from the Inside Out
Observations on how working style and temperament affect team dynamics in raising the team "SCORE"

Scorecard
A series of questions to help you review outcomes from each chapter

Where to Start

The following approach is recommended to optimize your use of this fieldbook.

1. Read the introduction and complete the introduction exercises.

These exercises will begin to raise awareness of human differences. Complete these exercises with your team before continuing with the rest of the book.

2. Profile team members in part 1, "Meet the Players."

The most complex step in the Inside Out approach involves profiling each individual team member's temperament, cognitive processes, and working style. We recommend completing this section next. We have included charts, examples, case studies, and exercises to help reinforce these concepts.

3. Begin profiling your team in part 2, "Building Your Dream Team."

We recommend next profiling your team, not only to understand the team dynamics, but also to assess how well your team is currently performing.

4. Continue in part 2 by intervening to build your Dream Team.

Based on your team profile and the way you assess the current performance of your team, we recommend picking the "SCORE" category in which your team appears to need the most help. Use the exercises to stimulate discussion and identify ways to improve team performance.

If you have already profiled your team and know the working styles and temperaments of the team members—using either a professional facilitator or the original book—feel free to dip in and out of this fieldbook as you wish to experiment with the exercises.

Important Note on Exercises

Most exercises in this fieldbook are meant for all members of the team. Each team member should follow the instruction steps and, in most cases, share his or her results with the whole team. Exercises intended to be completed by the whole team working as a group are designated as "Team Exercises." Exercises in chapter 9, "Providing Effective Leadership in the 21st Century," are aimed at team leaders, though other members of the team can learn from them as well.

What Else?

Make the fieldbook your own: write in the spaces provided, complete the exercises, and make notes of your learning. Remember, any behavior change needs constant reinforcement—use this book as one of the resources in your toolkit for achieving team excellence!

Introduction

GAME PLAN

Teamwork represents a critical business strategy to help organizations achieve diverse and challenging business goals. Team performance, however, is no longer limited to your current functional group. Companies are using a variety of structures including cross-functional, project, and virtual teams to accomplish organizational goals. Organizations look to these teams to bring about increases in performance with fewer resources. Yet, too often, they are affected by conflicts, misunderstandings, and frustration, with the result that team performance does not reach its potential. With the concepts above in mind, we have created this fieldbook to help you

- Find out what makes you and your fellow team members "tick"
- Identify how well your team is currently performing
- Improve communication between team members, thereby raising team productivity
- Build your Dream Team

Teams Are Made Up of Individuals

The premise of this fieldbook is that the way individuals view and approach the world has a fundamental influence on the way they act in teams. Exercise 1 will serve to illustrate how individual team members view the world differently.

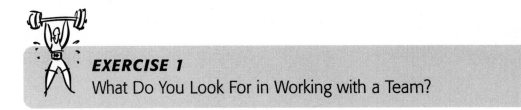

EXERCISE 1
What Do You Look For in Working with a Team?

1. Review the statements in each of the four boxes below.
2. Pick *one* box in which the phrases best reflect what is most important for you in working with your team and write down your ideas about them.
3. Be prepared to tell your teammates in two or three sentences why those phrases appeal to you.

Box 1 • Having fun, freedom, and variety • Doing it with style • Making an impact	**Box 2** • Being competent and inquisitive • Respecting expertise • Finding a better way
Box 3 • Achieving results • Taking responsibility • Belonging and contributing	**Box 4** • Being the best you can be • Having a purpose and meaning • Making a difference

Source: Susan Nash, Tessa Bradon, and Jacky Hughes.

Which box did you choose? Why?

____

____

____

____

____

____

Team Huddle!

Now discuss the results as a team, asking these questions:

- What were the surprises in listening to team members talk about their choices and why they made them?
- How many team members gravitated toward each phrase?
- What correlation do you see between the phrases they chose and the way they behave in the team?

Coaching Point

Team members are attracted to different phrases for varying reasons. By understanding what appeals to each team member and how this influences their approach to teamwork, we can begin the process of building a productive team from a position of greater insight.

End of Exercise

Understanding Ourselves

As you saw in exercise 1, team members can approach teamwork from various perspectives: the work they like, the people they like to work with, what they want out of the team, and how they express these wants and needs. With this diversity of interest and intent and the conflicts these differences can engender, the team may not be performing as well as it might.

Yet, to a certain extent, the way we respond in any situation tends to be unconscious. When we raised the topic of self-knowledge with a fifty-year-old client from IBM, he asked, "Do you honestly think people reach the age of fifty without knowing themselves?" Our answer: "Absolutely!" Understanding what is important to us and how we operate is not as obvious as you might think. Looking inside and trying to sort out the collage of abilities, skills, strengths, and weaknesses that make up our personality can be quite a challenge. Consider the complexity of developing an accurate perception of your own strengths and weaknesses.

Defining Strengths and Weaknesses

A tool we use to help define strengths and weaknesses is the "Strengths and Weaknesses Window," as shown in figure 1. Two of its quadrants cover strength/weakness areas of which we are aware:

Quadrant 1: Conscious Competence. Here we are aware of certain talents, skills, and abilities.

Quadrant 2: Conscious Incompetence. Here we are aware—perhaps painfully—of some of our weaknesses and shortcomings.

However, there are two other areas that others may see but that we are not tuned in to:

Quadrant 3: Unconscious Incompetence. Here are our most plaguing weaknesses; we don't know about them, but we don't know that we don't know!

Quadrant 4: Unconscious Competence: Here are some of our key strengths, although we take them for granted because they are natural to us.

FIGURE 1 Strengths and Weaknesses Window

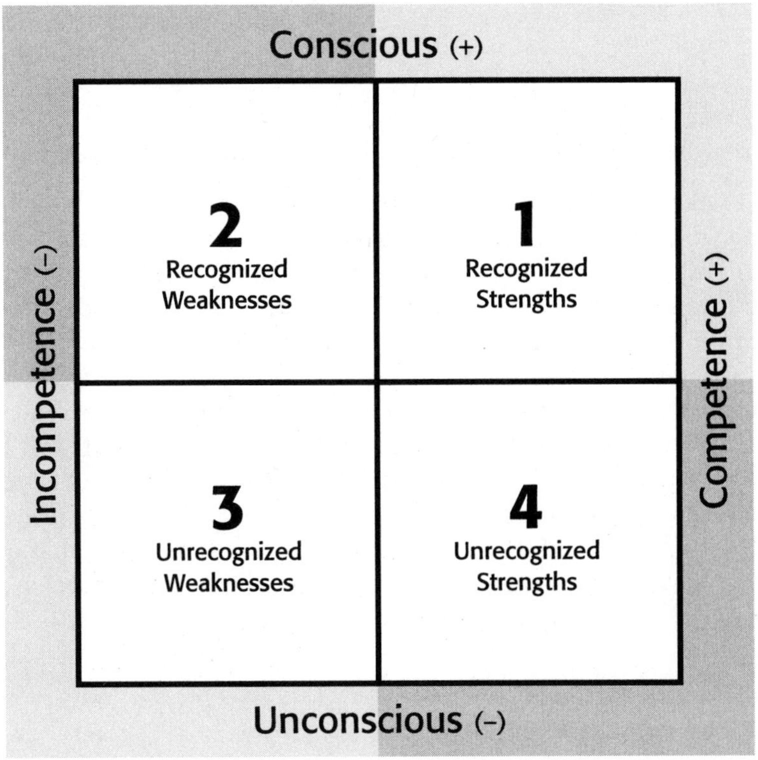

How you see yourself can differ significantly from how your teammates see you. The implications of this possible lack of self-knowledge for team performance are considerable. If you naturally do something well (quadrant 4), you may become frustrated with other team members because they don't have such natural competence in the same area. In contrast, if you are working in an unconscious area of weakness (quadrant 3), you may unknowingly irritate your team members. We see teams fail all the time due to these types of personality rifts. There are immense individual and team benefits when team members more consciously understand their strengths and weaknesses.

EXERCISE 2
Defining Your Strengths and Weaknesses

1. Use the blank Strengths and Weaknesses Window template on page 6 to assess your innate abilities, skills, and aptitudes by quadrant.
   - **Quadrant 1: Conscious Competence**
     Think about a significant work achievement. What was that achievement? What made this an important success for you? What did you specifically say or do that contributed to this achievement? What strengths might have enabled your accomplishment? Try to list at least three specific strengths in quadrant 1.
   - **Quadrant 2: Conscious Incompetence**
     Think about a work task that was not as successful as you had hoped. Why was it a disappointment? What did you specifically say or do that might have contributed to this occurrence? What possible weaknesses can you infer from your analysis? List them in quadrant 2.
   - **Quadrant 3: Unconscious Incompetence**
     Talk to three people whom you like and respect. Ask them for their honest feedback on what they perceive to be your greatest weakness or challenge. List at least one challenge in quadrant 3 that they mention but that you *did not* note in quadrant 2.
   - **Quadrant 4: Unconscious Competence**
     Ask the same individuals what attributes, characteristics, or competencies they value most about you. List at least three strengths in quadrant 4 that they observe but that you *did not* note in quadrant 1.

Strengths and Weaknesses Window

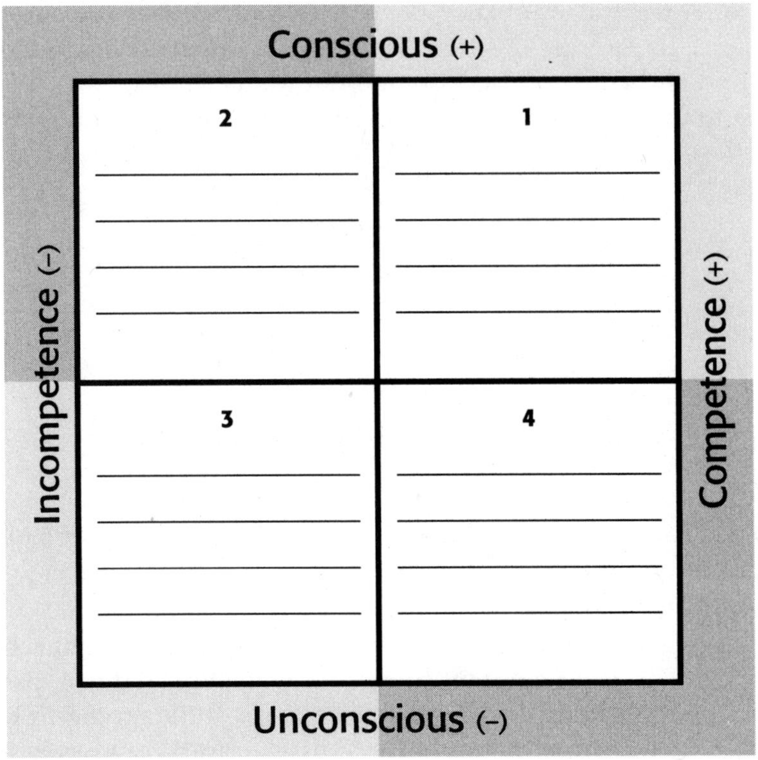

2. Present the results of your strengths and weaknesses assessment to the team.

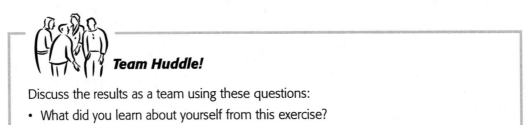

Team Huddle!

Discuss the results as a team using these questions:

- What did you learn about yourself from this exercise?
- What did you learn about other team members?
- What implications could this learning have for team performance?

Coaching Point

Members bring different strengths and weaknesses to the team. If we base our drive to raise team productivity on each individual's innate talents and skills, we will increase our chances of success.

End of Exercise

By studying personality using the methods in this fieldbook, we begin to become aware of who we are, in terms not just of strengths and weaknesses, but of all that lies behind them. This study will at the same time deepen our understanding of other team members.

Organizational Teams in the 21st Century

Despite society's emphasis on individuality, the critical work of business today is undertaken by teams, whether real or virtual. The success of organizations can be closely linked to how well these teams of diverse individuals perform, and it is clear that some teams truly do excel.

Characteristics of High-Performing Teams

As illustrated in figure 2, the following key elements known collectively as "SCORE" have been found to characterize high-performing teams.

S: Cohesive Strategy

C: Clear Roles and Responsibilities

O: Open Communication

R: Rapid Response

E: Effective Leadership

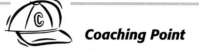

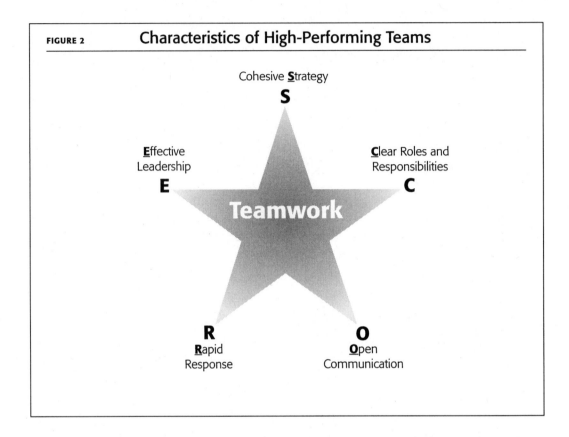

FIGURE 2 Characteristics of High-Performing Teams

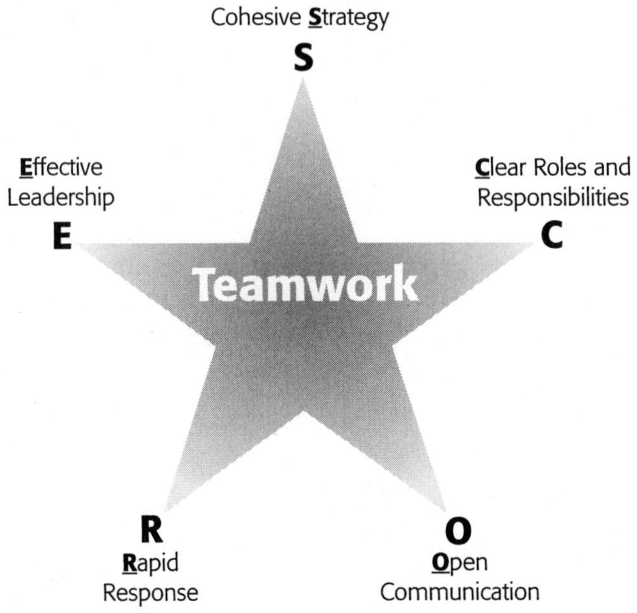

As we endeavor to raise team performance, we can use two contrasting approaches: the "Outside In" and the "Inside Out."

The "Outside In" Approach to SCORE

The Outside In approach involves assessing the team performance within each of the SCORE characteristics and then introducing techniques to improve functioning within each area. Consider the following scenario. Two members of a technology team are constantly at odds. To improve the quality of their interaction, their team leader sends them both to a communication skills program. Despite this intervention, after a short period the conflict escalates. In essence, the two "techies" view the world very differently and, despite their new listening skills, each cannot believe what he or she is hearing from the other!

If we do not consider team members' core needs and abilities when working on team effectiveness, either: (1) individuals will continue to respond in their habitual ways because they do not understand how their approach is affecting team performance, or (2) if they do change their behavior, the result will likely be short-lived as each person reverts to his or her subconscious patterns of action.

The "Inside Out" Approach to SCORE

The Inside Out approach is based on the premise that team members' driving forces and personalities fundamentally influence team performance; therefore, this is the place to start. By beginning with an understanding of who you are, what drives you, and what drives other team members' behavior, you will be able to understand the synergy (or lack of synergy) of the personalities forming your team.

In our work with over forty organizations and over five thousand individuals, we have found again and again that by understanding the core theory of personality style and temperament, individuals and teams can recognize the gifts and pitfalls each player brings to the table, diagnose potential problems, and capitalize more effectively on individual and team strengths. In addition, understanding which roles and activities energize each team member can result in reduced stress and higher overall team productivity. Therefore, the steps involved in the Inside Out approach include the following:

1. Profile each team member's personality.
2. Create a team profile.
3. Assess your current team SCORE.
4. Create a plan of attack to raise your team SCORE and create your Dream Team.

Building the Team—a Process, Not an Event

Building an effective team requires interventions at all stages of team development. Plus, even when the team is performing well, if a new team member joins or a member of the team changes, the whole team-building process starts over again. By integrating personality type and temperament theory with the characteristics of high-performing teams, this fieldbook provides a unique approach to raising long-term team productivity.

Coaching Point

Remember, building an effective team is a process, not an event! The "what" is easy, but the "how" can be a challenge.

Before beginning the process, you might want to jot down a few thoughts on what you want to achieve.

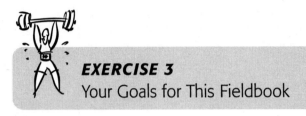

EXERCISE 3
Your Goals for This Fieldbook

What do you want to achieve using this fieldbook? By when?

____

____

____

____

End of Exercise

Good luck!

PART ONE

Meet the Players

In chapters 1–3, we will be focusing on individual team members' personalities as described through a series of lenses:

- Chapter 1: from the perspective of their driving forces (their temperament)
- Chapter 2: by assessing the cognitive processes they use to gather data and make decisions
- Chapter 3: by reviewing each team member's combined preferences as described by the *Myers-Briggs Type Indicator*® instrument (referred to here as "working style")

The Inside Out approach demonstrates that by understanding the team profile in terms of temperament, cognitive processes, and working style, it is possible to assess team strengths, diagnose potential team issues, and from there create a plan of attack to improve team effectiveness and performance.

Coaching Point

We recommend assessing each team member's personality before trying to raise team performance, so that you can use the information to influence team performance from the inside out.

1

Keys to Diagnosing Temperament

GAME PLAN

As you begin to assess your own and fellow team members' behavior, this chapter will help you

- Select the temperament that seems the best fit for you
- Identify possible temperaments for your team members
- Understand all four temperaments' contributions to the team
- Recognize temperament in action

Defining Temperament

In understanding human behavior, we start with what drives our behavior—our temperament. Let's begin with an exercise to explore your associations with *temperament.*

EXERCISE 4
Your Definition of Temperament

What thoughts come to mind when you hear the word *temperament?* List your ideas in the space below.

____

____

____

While *temperament* may conjure up thoughts of distemper, having a temper, or one's attitude, its definition as it pertains here to individuals at work and at home is different. It is the pattern of needs, values, and behaviors that underlie our way of acting and being in the world. As human beings, we are all unique individuals. Our genetics coupled with our family background, culture, education, and life experiences intermingle to create our individual character. Even identical twins are unique in their own way.

However, four underlying personality patterns have been consistently and cross-culturally recognized for over twenty-five centuries, as illustrated on the following chart. Though independently recognized and named, the basic themes are remarkably similar.

Temperaments Through Time

Idealist	**Guardian**
• Choleric (Hippocrates)	• Melancholic (Hippocrates)
• Ethical (Aristotle)	• Proprietary (Aristotle)
• Doctrinaire (Adickes)	• Traditional (Adickes)
• Inspired/Nymph/Water (Parcelsus)	• Industrious/Gnome/Earth (Parcelsus)
• Hyperaesthetic (Kretschmer)	• Depressive (Kretschmer)
• Religious (Spranger)	• Economic (Spranger)
• Bear (Native North Americans)	• Mouse (Native North Americans)
• Apollonian (Keirsey/Bates)	• Dionysian (Keirsey/Bates)
• Intuition/Feeling (Myers)	• Sensing/Judging (Myers)
Rational	**Artisan**
• Phlegmatic (Hippocrates)	• Sanguine (Hippocrates)
• Dialectical (Aristotle)	• Hedonic (Aristotle)
• Skeptical (Adickes)	• Innovative (Adickes)
• Curious/Sylph/Air (Parcelsus)	• Changeable/Salamander/Fire (Parcelsus)
• Anaesthetic (Kretschmer)	• Hypomanic (Kretschmer)
• Theoretic (Spranger)	• Aesthetic (Spranger)
• Buffalo (Native North Americans)	• Eagle (Native North Americans)
• Promethean (Keirsey/Bates)	• Epimethean (Keirsey/Bates)
• Intuition/Thinking (Myers)	• Sensing/Perceiving (Myers)

Source: Adapted from information from Linda V. Berens and David Keirsey presented in Linda V. Berens, *Understanding Yourself and Others* (2000).

Foul!

If people have the same temperament, that does not mean they are identical. They will share core needs and show similarities in behavior, but their actions may look very different, as the template of their shared temperament will be colored by their own individual experiences.

End of Exercise

Our temperament is the essence of our being; it permeates our likes, dislikes, talents, behaviors, approaches, and paradigms. If we understand our own and other team members' temperaments, we can shorten the process of identifying our strengths and weaknesses. We don't necessarily have to make a mistake to identify potential blind spots and we can, to an extent, predict the work and types of projects that we will find most fulfilling.

Temperament Characteristics

David Keirsey, the synthesizer of modern temperament theory, selected an animal as a metaphor for each temperament. He believed the innate patterns of behavior and preferences demonstrated by each animal are representative of the characteristics associated with each human temperament.

EXERCISE 5
Animal Characteristics

In the space below list four or five things you know about, or associations you have regarding, each of the following animals.

Animal	Notes
 Fox	
 Beaver	

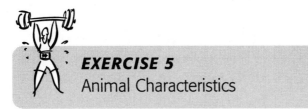

Animal		Notes
	**Owl**	
	**Dolphin**	

Source: Adapted from Linda V. Berens, Linda K. Ernst, Judith E. Robb, and Melissa A. Smith, *Temperament and Type Dynamics: The Facilitator's Guide* (1995).

End of Exercise

Table 1 is an expanded list of the general characteristics of the four animals. Explore each set, paying special attention to major patterns, and keep your own behaviors, needs, and values in mind as points of comparison.

Table 1 Characteristics of Four Animals

Animal	Characteristics
Fox	• Identified as a fast-reacting, quick, and resourceful animal • Has excellent sensory perception: can hear a mouse squeak from up to 100 feet! • Leaves a scent mark because it wants others to know it has been there • Is alert to the environment—notices any change of movement in the landscape • Is playful with other foxes • Takes advantage of opportunities—eats any animal it finds and can catch • Is adaptable—changes location easily based on environmental shifts or alterations in the food supply • Has beautiful, well-groomed fur

Table 1 Characteristics of Four Animals (cont'd)

Animal	Characteristics
Beaver	• Identified as a busy, industrious, hardworking animal • Has a multigenerational family structure: mates for life, is protective of family, and lives in family groups • Builds strong dams to protect its lodge, with a unique building technique to keep water entrances from freezing over in winter • Builds in a consistent manner and continually enlarges and repairs dams and lodges as needed • Uses its large, flat tail for packing down materials and slapping the water to warn others of danger • Is conservational: uses all parts of trees it cuts down and stockpiles food for winter use • Cooperates and rarely fights with other beavers • Will change location but with ample consideration of adequate water, forest, and seclusion
Owl	• Identified as a wise, knowledgeable, composed animal • Has expansive vision: sees 100 times better than humans; head rotates almost 360 degrees • Scans everything from a high perch, then silently swoops down to precisely pick out prey • From its high perch, sees things coming in the forest before other animals • Anticipates food supply and staggers young accordingly • Can precisely locate prey in the dark or underneath groundcover with its acute hearing • Is one of the few universal animals—complex varieties are present in every region of the world • Is independent: leaves the nest at a young age after receiving the critical teachings

Table 1 Characteristics of Four Animals (cont'd)

Animal	Characteristics
Dolphin	• Identified as a sociable, fun, and playful animal • Seeks interaction with other dolphins and other species • Stays within its group—some species members die if separated from the group • Uses advanced communication employing complex sounds (phonations) and echolocation • Calls other dolphins and family groups by a specific and unique "name" • Aids the pregnant and injured of its own species and reportedly has a healing quality for humans who swim with it • Uses consensus decision making to change direction • Practices hunting skills as play • Aids other dolphins against predators • Uses nose to nudge and guide but can also use it to kill a shark if attacked

EXERCISE 6
Choosing a Mascot

With which animal do you most closely identify? What are the characteristics that most appeal to you, and why? Write your answers in the appropriate box below.

Fox	Beaver	Owl	Dolphin

These animal "mascots" correspond to the four temperament names we will be using here: Artisan, Guardian, Rational, and Idealist.

Fox: the Artisan temperament Driven by the need to respond in the moment; free-thinking and adaptable	**Beaver: the Guardian temperament** Driven by the need to be responsible; builds results and needs to be part of the group
Owl: the Rational temperament Driven by the need for knowledge and competence; independent and focused on the big picture	**Dolphin: the Idealist temperament** Driven by the need to have a purpose; relationship focused and empathetic

End of Exercise

As we take a closer look at the characteristics of each temperament, the symbolic meaning of each mascot will become increasingly clear!

Temperament: Driving Forces and Behaviors

We talk about temperament as a pattern, a set of underlying values and core needs. Our temperament is expressed in our language, approach, and activities. While we can observe such behaviors, we may not always be aware of our own or others' core needs and values. The descriptions below and in table 2 provide a picture of each temperament from both the visible and more internal perspectives.*

Artisans

Artisans live one day at a time, seizing the day and all the freedom they can get. They are the natural crisis managers, problem solvers, and performers. They are opportunistic, act in the moment, and want to see the immediate, tangible results of their actions. Artisans enjoy team roles that are fast paced and dynamic, with few rules. They want to have fun and make an impact. Their acute sensory awareness and observation of physical clues (tactical intelligence) enable them to respond quickly and tune in to what other team members want.

**Note:* Much of the contemporary knowledge about temperament is credited to the work of Linda V. Berens and Temperament Research Institute.

Guardians

Guardians are driven by responsibility and duty, wishing to serve and protect those whom they care about. They are the pillars of society and need membership and a sense of belonging in a group. Guardians gravitate to roles where they are able to build, and be part of, a team. They enjoy a more structured, formalized approach and want to contribute to tangible outcomes. With their past perspective they are able to transfer learnings from previous experience to current activities. Their ability to manage large amounts of sensory data (logistical intelligence) enables them to organize and institute repeatable processes.

Rationals

Rationals seek knowledge and competence in all their endeavors. They seek to understand the operating principles of the universe around them to create their own destiny. Rationals like roles that offer them autonomy and independence and that call for use of their strategic-visioning and critical-thinking skills. They like designing and analyzing new abstract approaches to problems and systems. With their infinite time orientation and big-picture thinking (strategic intelligence) they are able to provide clearly articulated frameworks and models to improve team performance.

Idealists

Idealists are soul-searchers who are constantly on a quest for purpose and significance in their lives. They want to do something meaningful for this world and are on a journey to help people develop and optimize their potential. Idealists need roles that serve a broader purpose; demand strong, open communication; and offer them a chance to achieve their vision and make a difference. With their empathy, interpersonal skills, and ability to appreciate the big picture they are able to build bridges between disparate viewpoints (diplomatic intelligence) and create a cohesive team culture.

In table 2 the characteristics of each temperament are summarized so that you can compare and contrast the different look and feel of each temperament. (For more in-depth descriptions see chapter 1 in the book *Turning Team Performance Inside Out.*)

Table 2 Characteristics of Each Temperament

Characteristics	Artisans	Guardians	Rationals	Idealists
Estimated % of World Population*	Approximately 40%	Approximately 40%	Approximately 10%	Approximately 10%
Driving Forces/ Core Needs	• Be noticed or make an impact • Get a result • Act swiftly and practically in the moment	• Be part of a group or team • Act responsibly and dutifully • Contribute to a concrete goal or accomplishment	• Be an expert • Demonstrate knowledge and competence • Retain autonomy and control in activities	• Be unique • Develop own and others' potential • Have a greater purpose and meaning for actions
Work Approach	• Seek to make an impact with their style and skills • Act as tactical troubleshooters and "firefighters"	• Get the right thing to the right place in the right quantity at the right price at the right time • Put in repeatable processes	• Think logically, independently, strategically • Improve systems and redesign processes	• Build bridges between groups • Mentor and unleash potential
Time Preference/ Focus	• The present: the here and now	• The past: what was done before	• The future: infinite time orientation	• The future: life's a journey forward
Communication Style	• To the point • Concise—less is more	• Linear and sequential (1,1a, 1b, 2, 2a, 2a.1, etc.) • Structured: beginning, middle, end	• Abstract around models • Critically questioning	• Empathetic • Flowing and effusive
Language	• Concrete • Informal/casual, slang • Creative and humorous • Economical	• Concrete • Respectful and appropriate to the group • Conventional • Detailed	• Abstract • Precise and articulate • Free of redundancy • Relevant facts and data	• Abstract • Impressionistic • Colored with hyperbole • Global language
Word Usage: Favorite Words/ Expressions	• "Fun" • "Excitement" • "Challenge"	• "Do you remember when?" • "What's your experience?" • Comparisons, "better/worse than"	• "Why?" • Conditional: "if X, then Y"	• "Purpose" • "Connection" • "Meaning"

**Source:* David Keirsey.

Table 2 Characteristics of Each Temperament (cont'd)

Characteristics	Artisans	Guardians	Rationals	Idealists
Organization	• Tactical • Pragmatic	• Hierarchical • Cooperative	• Macro to micro • Pragmatic	• Integrated—everything connects with something else • Cooperative
What Appeals in a Job	• Flexibility • Solving tactical problems • Tangible results • Challenge • Excitement and stimulation	• Making a contribution • Tangible results • Structure • Improving a process • Security/stability	• Intellectual stimulation • Improving a system • Leading edge • Opportunity for independent thought • Challenge	• Contributing to the overall goal • Making a difference • Genuine relationships • Theories that can be related to people • Being special
As Kids	• Tend to be fearless; experiment with external environment	• Tend to look after others and mature more quickly	• Tend to be intensely logical; will request reasons at an early age	• May appear to like living in their own fantasy world
Humor Type	• Physical, tactile	• Dry/tongue in cheek	• Word play/ cerebral	• Self-deprecating
Stress Response	• May escalate situation or retaliate	• May blame others and complain about current situation	• May become preoccupied with perceived incompetence or failures	• May feel the world is against them
Examples	Winston Churchill, JFK, Larry Ellison, Michael Jordan, Barbra Streisand	Queen Elizabeth, Colin Powell, John D. Rockefeller, Mother Teresa, Barbara Walters	Margaret Thatcher, Thomas Jefferson, Bill Gates, Ayn Rand, Cybill Shepherd	Gandhi, Martin Luther King, Walt Disney, Ann Morrow Lindbergh, Jane Fonda
Quote	"The right man is the one who seizes the moment." —Goethe	"The buck stops here." —Harry Truman	"I do not think much of a man who is not wiser today than he was yesterday." —Abraham Lincoln	"Happiness is when what you think and what you say and what you do are in harmony." —Mohandas Gandhi
Gift to the World	Making the best of the present moment	Bringing the best of the past to the present and future	Designing a better future	Bringing hope for a better future

Now that you have reviewed the characteristics of each temperament, use the following exercise to help determine which temperament you and other team members gravitate toward most.

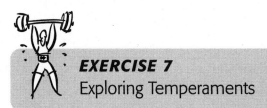

EXERCISE 7
Exploring Temperaments

1. Write your name in what you perceive to be your "best-fit" temperament box on the following page along with the characteristics of that temperament you feel represent you.
2. You may also be gravitating toward a second temperament; write your name in that box also with the representative characteristics of that temperament.
3. Note for your other team members the temperament you think they might be, by putting their names in the corresponding temperament boxes.
4. Jot down some key words that you associate with each temperament or draw a visual symbol to help you identify it.

If you are not sure which temperament you are at this point, you may want to rank the temperaments from 1 to 4, 1 being most like you. Keep exploring!

Artisan	**Guardian**
Rational	**Idealist**

Coaching Points

- Whether you see yourself in one of these temperament patterns or not, you are in the right place. If you see yourself clearly in one temperament—great! Keep learning about it and others. Think about what that means in terms of your actions and interactions.
- If you see yourself in more than one temperament, don't feel lost. Most of us see a bit of ourselves in all four groupings. Don't feel that temperament is a box you are being stuffed into. We are complex beings, and these categories are a simplified set of similarities. They are patterns that in no way will be able to completely define you.
- Keep thinking about which temperament you identify with most, and as we continue through the initial chapters, your selection should become clearer.

We have created visual symbols capturing the essence of each temperament, as follows.

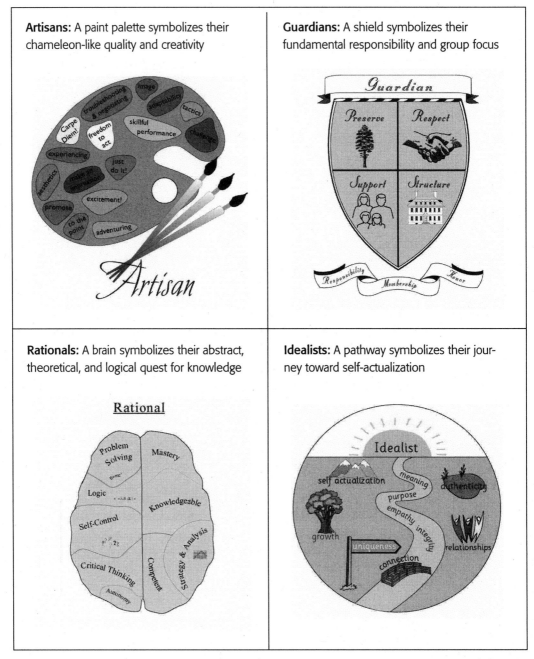

Artisans: A paint palette symbolizes their chameleon-like quality and creativity

Guardians: A shield symbolizes their fundamental responsibility and group focus

Rationals: A brain symbolizes their abstract, theoretical, and logical quest for knowledge

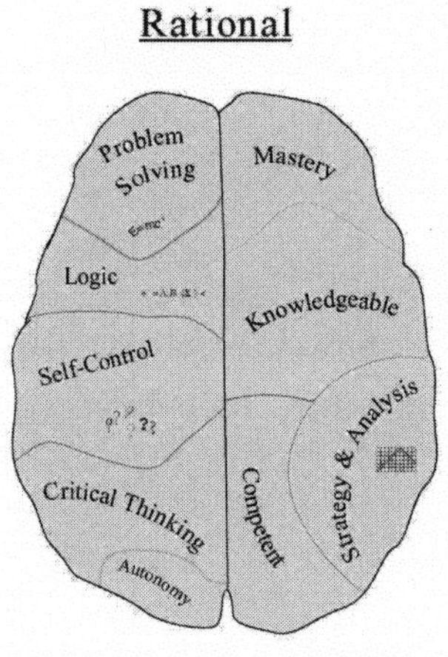

Idealists: A pathway symbolizes their journey toward self-actualization

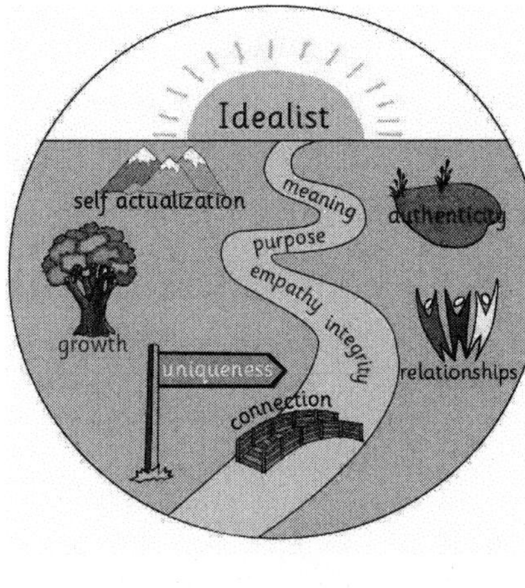

End of Exercise

Temperament at Work

Two examples of what temperament can look like in business situations are provided in table 3. The first scenario, an outdoor experiential treasure hunt, involves a number of teams created to collect a random assortment of items from a designated area, within a specific time. Rewards are associated with each clue uncovered. The pressure created by this exercise elicits temperament powerfully, as individuals soon cast off their work culture and fall into their natural temperament pattern.

The second scenario, an organizational assessment, involves interviewing four top executives from the same company to identify training requirements for each of their functional areas. In this instance, each leader's perspective is influenced by his or her own temperament or worldview (not necessarily what the group really needs!).

Table 3 Temperament at Work

Temperament	In an Outdoor Experiential Treasure Hunt	In an Organizational Assessment
Artisan	**Approach** • Let's go! • Who's winning? • Let's just get to it—don't waste time looking at the instructions. We have a deadline! • Who cares what they are doing? We'll do our own thing. You go there, we'll go here. • Let's do what it takes to get the job done.	**VP of Manufacturing says...** • We do our own thing here. • We don't comply with corporate standards when they don't fit our situation. • We'll do what it takes to make and ship products today. • We take it a day at a time. • The best training for us is "on the job"—none of that theoretical stuff!
Guardian	**Approach** • What are the rules? • How do we keep the group together and make sure no one gets left out? • How can we optimize resources? • What are the time frames? • What can we do? What can't we do? Let's read the instructions.	**VP of Finance says, "We need..."** • More adherence to processes and procedures • Detailed, step-by-step process improvement • Continuous improvement • Instruction on how to use equipment properly • To work with experienced people who have done the work themselves

Table 3 Temperament at Work (cont'd)

Temperament	In an Outdoor Experiential Treasure Hunt	In an Organizational Assessment
Rational	**Approach** • There must be some underlying principle behind this treasure hunt. • Let's analyze the instructions and look for another way to approach this exercise. • What categories do the clues fit into? Can we group categories somehow? • What else could we do to win this game? • Let's devise a strategy for winning.	**VP of Sales says, "We need to learn..."** • How to clearly articulate our unique selling proposition • How to concisely explain our strategic direction to customers • To communicate our strong conceptual vision • Skills to categorize accounts and prioritize carefully • Technological competence in all aspects of our products
Idealist	**Approach** • Maybe we could collaborate with other groups instead of competing. • How about we help others find the clues, build some trust, and then work together further? • What's the purpose of this exercise? • Let's consider the people. • In what other ways could we complete this exercise?	**President says, "The purpose of this consulting will be..."** • To build collaboration across cross-functional boundaries • To release the talent of our team; to make sure each person is able to capitalize on his or her own strengths • To help establish a clearer vision and purpose for the group • To reduce the extent of the "turf wars" that are occurring • To get to know each other better

Take a few minutes to assimilate the information from table 3 and move on to exercise 8.

EXERCISE 8
Exploring Temperaments at Work

Answer the following questions to explore your own temperament:

- Which approach would you have taken in the treasure hunt scenario, as presented on page 27? Why?

- What do you think is important when training people?

- Which temperament do you gravitate toward most? Why?

End of Exercise

Temperament in Action

Now that you have explored the four temperament patterns, you should have a good sense of what each temperament might look like in action. Use the following case studies to hone your skills in identifying temperament.

EXERCISE 9
Identifying Temperaments in Case Studies

1. Review the profiles of the eight individuals in four jobs.
2. Highlight key words and phrases that may be indicators of a certain temperament.
3. With the rest of the team, identify which temperament appears to be the best fit for each individual and note why.

Case Studies

Subcontract Trainers

Jennifer

Jennifer is a subcontract trainer for a training company. She has written two books and has a Ph.D. degree in organization development. Jennifer's strengths when preparing and presenting programs include her ability to research and provide relevant data to support any concepts introduced. Her logical presentation also impresses participants throughout the world.

Jennifer enjoys the intellectual independence of the work as she controls her own schedule and chooses which clients she works with. She is continually learning new theories as the training company introduces new models and training methodologies. In addition, because stress management is her core competency, she has been able to license her program to the training company, which has established her as an expert within the organization.

Temperament:____________________

Why? ____

Tony

Tony is a subcontract trainer working for the same training company. He has fun performing the work because every day is different. He gets to visit cool places and he is constantly on the move. As a trainer, he keeps classes entertaining—sometimes he can be a little over the top, but clients like that about him. Plus, he is great at adding fun exercises, cartoons, and technological tricks that make the content relevant and hands-on for the groups.

Tony's ability to tell stories and jokes to liven up the most boring content makes him popular with participants. He also enjoys the freedom he has as a subcontract trainer—he can take time off when he wants. Additionally, he loves seeing those great evaluations and competing with other trainers for the best scores!

Temperament:____________________

Why? ____

Sales/Account Managers

Karen

Karen works for a marketing company selling design solutions to businesses. She loves the work because she gets to meet lots of people; her strengths in selling originate from her ability to build strong long-term relationships. She enjoys the marketing field because she learns about different companies and helps them make a difference in positioning their products and services to their customers.

Prior to working in this field, Karen worked for the police force, but she left because she found that work unrewarding and felt it had little meaning. When selling, she is very effective at identifying needs by asking questions, using empathy to see the situation from the customer's perspective, and immediately seeing possibilities to tailor marketing services to a client's needs.

Temperament:________________________

Why?

____

____

Sharon

Sharon works in Silicon Valley selling office products to both small and large high-tech companies. She succeeds with the work because she is very organized, always follows up when she says she will, and understands customers' needs. She likes the role because she can see results, and she feels like she is contributing to the overall team.

Due to a company reorganization, Sharon is now based at home. This has proven to be a challenge, as she misses the structure and day-to-day contact with team members. The clients like working with Sharon because she remembers the details from previous orders and excels at recommending improvements to internal processes based on her experience. She is also very economical and gives them a fair price!

Temperament:________________________

Why?

____

____

IT VP/Directors

Tim

Tim has spent over 25 years in VP/Director-level positions in IT organizations. He excels at establishing processes and procedures in companies as they grow, building an effective team, and living up to his responsibilities. His ability to establish consistency in services has always been appreciated by his internal customers. However, on occasion, when they have wanted to introduce new software/systems, they have discovered that Tim can be a little reluctant to change if the new addition was not included as part of the corporate policy and did not make sense.

Tim is great at stepping into the gap at the last minute when others have not met the deadline to ensure a rollout will progress smoothly. As a manager, he finds it key to define job requirements, hire the right people, and then provide them with the structure to perform their roles efficiently.

Temperament:____________________________

Why?

____

____

Adam

Adam is VP for a global network solutions company. He really enjoys the role because he is able to develop the people on his team and influence the future direction of the IT organization. He has a clear picture for the end result he is trying to achieve, but sometimes when he tries to explain it to his team, his words seem too general.

While building the team from 20 people to over 400, Adam has consistently invested in professional development and team-building activities. The positive, collaborative departmental culture is very different from the rest of the organization, which tends to be more pragmatic and competitive, but it results in long-term employee retention and high employee satisfaction. The challenges he has faced as a manager include dealing with conflict, which he always finds stressful, and making tough decisions that he knows will make certain team members unhappy.

Temperament:____________________________

Why?

____

____

CEOs

Alison

Alison founded a retail company that specializes in selling naturally produced lotions and oils, after recognizing the opportunity during her trips around the globe. On those journeys she would get to know the local people and talk to them about how they took care of their skin and hair naturally. She took that idea and ran with it, focusing on a distinct brand identity with an aesthetic look and feel.

Alison runs the business in a hands-on, informal style, using a clear set of values in dealing with suppliers, materials, and manufacturing processes. This has gained her wide exposure in the press. She loves the touches, smells, and colors associated with her brand, and this is her passion. She has created a fun culture with lots of energy and the opportunity for employees to speak their mind. Alison's greatest challenge is in not getting bored with the organization now that it has reached a certain size and needs to introduce more structure.

Temperament:__________________________

Why?

____

____

Bob

Bob was hired at a retail company as a CEO to prepare the company for growth and to allow the founder to focus on product development. His strength as a CEO lies in clearly articulating the business model for the organization to potential investors. He can see market opportunities and develop a clear strategy for positioning the company in this marketplace. He enjoys the role because it provides him autonomy and enables him to use his core competency, which is assembling and directing an effective executive team to deliver on goals.

Bob's ability to develop a viable financial model for expanding the business profitably was crucial in obtaining outside investment. His greatest challenges as a leader are dealing with team members when they are not logical and refraining from correcting team members' word choices.

Temperament:__________________________

Why?

____

____

Team Huddle!

Discuss the exercise using the following questions:

- How easy was it to recognize the clues for each temperament?
- What problems, if any, did you have in recognizing different temperaments?

4. Now look at the answers in the appendix on pages 303–4 to see how you did.

End of Exercise

Temperaments and Their Contribution to the Team

Now that you have begun to build your knowledge of each temperament, use the following exercise to look at all four temperaments. The purpose of this exercise is twofold:

- It allows you to see how each temperament can bring different strengths to working on the team.
- It can give you further insight into which temperament might be the best fit for you; the temperament that we find easiest to analyze is often our best-fit temperament.

EXERCISE 10
Temperament Contributions to the Team

TEAM EXERCISE

Divide your team randomly into four groups, and have each group complete the following steps:

1. Consider the characteristics required to build a high-performing team:
   - Cohesive Strategy
   - Clear Roles and Responsibilities
   - Open Communication
   - Rapid Response
   - Effective Leadership
2. Choose one of the characteristics of high-performing teams to discuss (a different characteristic for each team). For example, one group could discuss how to establish clear roles and responsibilities, another how to promote open communication, and so on.
3. Identify two strengths and two challenges each temperament would contribute to the group's assigned characteristic: starting with Artisans, then Guardians, then Rationals, and then Idealists. "Cohesive Strategy" has been filled in as an example.

Temperament Perspective Grid

Characteristics of a High-Performing Team	Artisans	Guardians	Rationals	Idealists
Cohesive Strategy	**Strengths** • Bring a realistic perspective of the current situation • Lighten up the planning process with humor **Challenges** • May think more in terms of current tactics and details • May want quick, tangible results	**Strengths** • Encourage team involvement toward organizational goals • Use past data as a tool in guiding future direction **Challenges** • May view setting a team purpose as impractical • May want to focus on improving weaknesses rather than capitalizing on new opportunities	**Strengths** • Bring a natural, strategic perspective to the planning process • Bring an excellent view of trends and future opportunities **Challenges** • May struggle with creating realistic time frames—everything is possible • May wordsmith purpose and mission statements too much	**Strengths** • Bring a natural focus on team purpose and identity • Will tend to focus on the strengths of the team **Challenges** • May be unrealistic in defining the team purpose and direction • May get offended if team members are not as committed to the process as they are
Clear Roles and Responsibilities				
Open Communication				
Rapid Response				
Effective Leadership				

4. To debrief the exercise, answer the following questions:

- For which temperaments did you find it easier to respond? The temperament for which you find responses effortlessly often indicates your best-fit temperament.
  ☐ **Artisan** ☐ **Guardian** ☐ **Rational** ☐ **Idealist**

- For which temperament did you struggle most to complete responses? This difficulty can be an indicator of the temperament that you have the most trouble working with on a team.
  ☐ **Artisan** ☐ **Guardian** ☐ **Rational** ☐ **Idealist**

- Which temperaments were easy/hard for your teammates to relate to in responding to the situations?
  ☐ **Artisan** ☐ **Guardian** ☐ **Rational** ☐ **Idealist**

5. Compare your answers on the grid to those on pages 305–7.

End of Exercise

Self-Assessment

Hopefully, the exercises and examples you have completed so far have helped you identify your best-fit temperament. If not, don't worry—the individual discovery process isn't over yet!

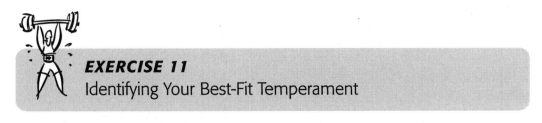

EXERCISE 11
Identifying Your Best-Fit Temperament

1. Reflect on the temperament discovery process you have completed in this chapter. What is your best-fit temperament?

☐ **Artisan** ☐ **Guardian** ☐ **Rational** ☐ **Idealist**

Why?

____

____

____

2. If you are still struggling to determine your best-fit temperament, try doing the following:
   - Ask those close to you and whom you respect to say which temperament they think you are and why.
   - Think about their comments—what do you agree/disagree with?
   - Think back to a time when you felt positive, motivated, and competent. What were you doing that you enjoyed?
   - Conversely, think back to a time when you felt unmotivated, deenergized, and unsuccessful. What was the cause of those feelings?

Don't worry if you are still not sure—completing the exercises in chapters 2 and 3 can help. You can also read more literature on the subject, especially chapter 1 in *Turning Team Performance Inside Out* and Linda V. Berens, *Understanding Yourself and Others: An Introduction to Temperament* (2000).

End of Exercise

Coaching Point

Remember, it is equally important to determine others' temperaments. Without that knowledge it is harder to adapt, and you will be unable to maximize team performance.

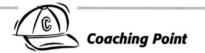

EXERCISE 12
Other Players' Temperaments

What temperaments other than your own do you see in your teammates?

Name:____________________________ Temperament:____________________________

Why?

____

____

____

Name:____________________________ Temperament:____________________________

Why?

____

____

____

Name:____________________________ Temperament:____________________________

Why?

____

____

____

End of Exercise

Coaching Point

Note the following guidelines when trying to determine the temperament of someone other than yourself:

- The best judge of an individual's temperament preference is that individual.
- Make sure you consider why you do what you do: people with different temperaments often do the same thing but are driven by different motivations.
- It is fine to share your ideas about a person's temperament with him or her, but explain what temperament is and don't assert your opinion as the definitive truth. Such behavior leaves people feeling labeled and simplified. Each person needs to go through a self-selection process to determine his or her own temperament.
- The temperament signals that you observe from another person might be part of the adaptive behavior you often see from individuals in a work setting. Be careful: what you see is not always what you get!
- There are four versions of each temperament, so be aware that in some situations two temperaments may look similar to each other! See chapter 2 to gain greater clarity.

Wrap-Up

The concept of identifying and understanding different temperaments and their inherent contribution to the team can be an invaluable tool in optimizing team performance. The information included in this chapter is designed to give you numerous opportunities to try on your own and other temperaments. However, four temperaments are obviously not enough to categorize all aspects of human behavior. In the next chapter, we will delve deeper into our personalities with a look at psychologist Carl Jung's "cognitive processes."*

**Note:* Beginning the discovery process with a look at temperament was pioneered by Linda V. Berens, Linda K. Ernst, and Melissa A. Smith in *The Guide for Facilitating the Self-Discovery Process* (1998, 2002).

SCORECARD

Before moving on to chapter 2, answer the following questions:

- ☐ Have you identified your temperament?
- ☐ Have you completed the exercises on temperament?
- ☐ Have you reviewed the other temperament descriptions so that you are familiar with the differences and complexities of each temperament?
- ☐ Have your teammates identified their temperaments?

2

Keys to Diagnosing Cognitive Processes and Functions

GAME PLAN

As you continue to assess your behavior and that of your team members, this chapter will help you

- Understand how you gather information and make decisions
- Try on all four information-gathering and decision-making functions
- Decide which functions appear to be the best fit for you
- Recognize the cognitive processes and the eight functions in action

Why Do We Need to Identify More Than Temperament?

Temperament theory provides insight into the patterns of personality. It serves as a sketch of the general characteristics of a person. However, to get a clearer picture, we also need to look at the dynamic forces of personality—our mental processing, or the specific ways we gather information and make decisions. Without examining the more in-depth theory and application of mental processes, many people claim the "wrong" temperament. They are drawn to a certain temperament for its attributes but do not look deeper to understand the dynamic processes that motivate and affect the varying expression of those attributes. For instance, sometimes an Idealist can look more like a Guardian when using the function known as Harmonizing—one that some Guardians and some Idealists access in specific situations. Examining the dynamics of the functions will provide us with a more specific understanding of why we and our fellow team members act in a specific way on a day-to-day basis.

Coaching Point

This chapter is one of the most abstract sections of the book, as it attempts to help you raise your consciousness of actions you perform unconsciously. However, this increased awareness is a critical basis for deepening your understanding of the human interaction in your team that we will explore throughout the rest of this book.

Defining Cognitive Processes and Functions

Carl Jung's work covered an impressive array of subjects, but the theory to which we refer in this fieldbook comes from his research and conclusions based on "typical habits of the mind": similar patterns of behavior that explain how individuals take in ("perceive") information and make decisions ("judge"). If we can understand the types of data different team members gravitate toward and the varying criteria each person uses to make decisions, then we can begin to understand the underlying dynamics at work in our team.

Cognitive processes are the specific ways in which individuals take in, and make decisions about, information. Jung believed that all our time is spent either gathering information or making decisions, which he identified, respectively, as perceiving and judging. He defined the two perceiving cognitive processes we now call Sensing and Intuition and the two judging cognitive processes, Thinking and Feeling.

Foul!

The use of the word *judging* in this context is not related to being judgmental! It is simply the process of making decisions.

Functions are defined as the normal ways we gather information and make decisions. There are two functions associated with each cognitive process:

- For Sensing (S): Experiencing and Recalling
- For Intuition (N): Brainstorming and Visioning
- For Thinking (T): Systematizing and Analyzing
- For Feeling (F): Harmonizing and Valuing

Time Out!

The letter denoting the Intuition process is *N* in the *Myers-Briggs Type Indicator®* instrument. The letter *I* is used to denote Introversion.

These relationships are diagrammed in figure 3 below.

FIGURE 3 **Cognitive Processes and Their Functions**

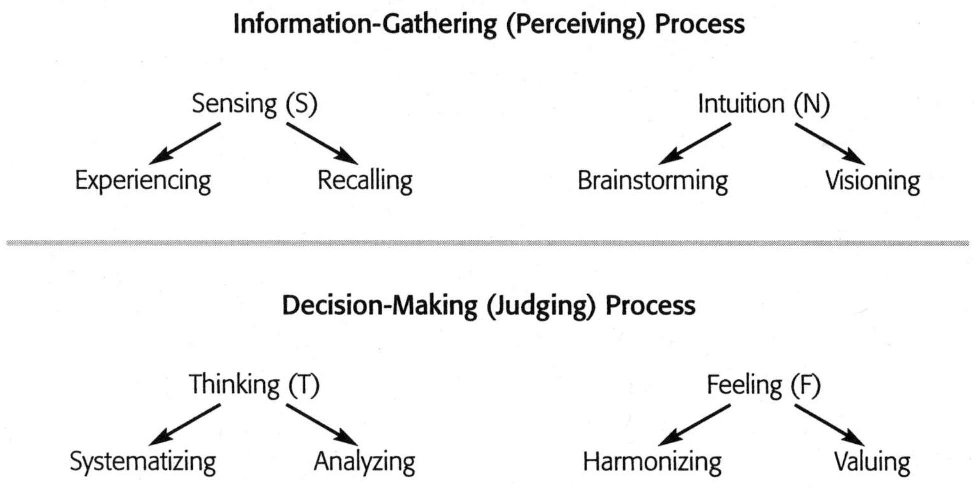

Coaching Point

Whew! Don't be discouraged by the seeming complexity of the processes and functions or the deluge of new vocabulary. We will break this information down into digestible bits as we proceed.

Jung observed that different individuals prefer one function over another when gathering information or making decisions. The following exercise will serve as a demonstration.

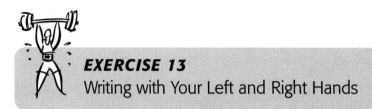

EXERCISE 13
Writing with Your Left and Right Hands

1. Write your name in the space below using your "preferred" hand (the one you normally write with—right or left).

2. Now, write your name in the space below using your "weaker" hand (the one you rarely write with).

What differences did you notice? How did it feel?

___

___

___

You probably found that writing with your preferred hand was natural, fast, and smooth—maybe even unconscious. By contrast, you may have found that writing with your nonpreferred (weaker) hand was more time consuming, difficult, and awkward. As an underdeveloped skill, it requires more focus to carry out.

Much like signing your name with your preferred hand, your preferred functions appear to be more fluid, require less energy to use, are quicker, demand less conscious thought, and are more comfortable. Like signing your name with your other hand, your nonpreferred functions may manifest awkwardness, take longer, require more energy, and demand more conscious thought.

Coaching Point

Jung believed that we each have a preference for one function for gathering information and one function for making decisions, in the sense that one or the other is more natural and, as a result, more consistently used. However, he also recognized that every individual potentially has access to all eight functions to a greater or lesser extent.

Time Out!

Did you know that the word *function* comes from the Latin word *fungare,* which means to enjoy? When we use our preferred function, as you saw with writing with your normal hand, it is easy and often enjoyable.

End of Exercise

Gathering Information (Perceiving)

Now that we have provided the overview of the eight functions, let's begin to learn about the information-gathering (perceiving) processes.

Learning About Sensing and Intuition

The two perceiving cognitive processes, Sensing and Intuition, describe how people gather or perceive information. People who prefer the Sensing process tend to gather information primarily through their senses such as sight, sound, smell, touch, and taste. They also tend to trust whatever can be measured or documented and what is real and concrete. As a result, they may initially appear to doubt intuitive insights.

People who prefer the Intuition process gather information through ideas, patterns, possibilities, hypotheses, and inferred meanings. They also tend to trust abstract concepts, generalities, and potentialities, minimizing the importance of concrete evidence.

Foul!

The word *Sensing* has nothing to do with being sensitive! It simply pertains to gathering data through our senses. The word *Intuition* has nothing to do with clairvoyance. It refers to gathering data using less obvious, more abstract information.

In working with companies, we find that a strong clue to determining one's preference for Sensing or Intuition is the tendency to recognize and talk about concrete or abstract information.

EXERCISE 14
Recognizing Concrete or Abstract Information

1. Study the picture below for 30 seconds.

Photo: Tom Hogan.

2. In the next 30 seconds write down everything you notice in the picture. Don't think! Just do it! Leave the column on the right blank for now. We'll return to it in step 4.

Observations	Concrete/Abstract

3. Information can be divided broadly into concrete and abstract information. See the table below for the differences between concrete and abstract.

Concrete	Abstract
• Information that can be directly observed (sun, bushes, shops)	• Information that can be inferred (summertime in town center)
• Tangible information (houses, road, sky)	• Conceptual information (summer, English design)
• Specific information (car, signs)	• General information (transportation)
• Empirical information (data from direct observation and experiment)	• Theoretical information (from knowledge/ concepts—more speculative)

4. Review your list of observations in step 2; in the right-hand column designate each observation as either concrete ("C") or abstract ("A"). How many of each did you note?

   Concrete ______ Abstract _______

5. Based on your notes, check the type of processing that seems most natural for you.

   ☐ **Concrete = Sensing** ☐ **Abstract = Intuition**

Time Out!

Guardians and Artisans tend to process more concretely, while Rationals and Idealists tend to process more abstractly. (Don't worry about matching your perceiving process with your temperament now. Just choose the process you seem to use primarily.)

End of Exercise

Learning About the Information-Gathering (Perceiving) Functions

The two perceiving cognitive processes, Sensing and Intuition, are further divided into four functions, Experiencing, Recalling, Brainstorming, and Visioning, as shown in figure 4. They are described in detail in table 4.

FIGURE 4 **Perceiving Processes and Their Functions**

Information-Gathering (Perceiving) Process

Sensing (S) → Experiencing, Recalling

Intuition (N) → Brainstorming, Visioning

Table 4 Descriptions of Information-Gathering (Perceiving) Functions

	Perceiving Functions			
	Sensing		Intuition	
Characteristics	Experiencing	Recalling	Brainstorming	Visioning
Concrete or Abstract	• Concrete	• Concrete	• Abstract	• Abstract
Description	• Gathering concrete data in the here and now • Seeing options in the moment • Reading sight, sound, smell, taste, and body language cues immediately	• Gathering sensory data and using them to compare and contrast with past sensory experiences • Viewing past data almost like watching a videotape • Using past data to understand what is "real" in a given situation	• Inferring patterns and meanings from current information • Reading between the lines • Thinking out loud: hypothesizing and exploring possibilities	• Assimilating data unconsciously, which then comes into consciousness as a complete picture • Incubating ideas until they are clear • Coming up with "Aha!" and "shower" solutions
Approach to Life	• Zealous hunger for experiences and adventure	• Prudence, valuing the lessons learned in the past	• Constant enthusiasm for new ideas	• Intensity, seeking to understand the meaning of things
Primary Users	• Artisans	• Guardians	• Some Rationals and Idealists	• Some Rationals and Idealists
Time Orientation	• Present	• Past	• Unlimited	• Future
Work Signals	• Jumping into action • Reading and commenting on minute changes in body language	• Appearing more cautious as data are processed • Talking about what worked and didn't work in the past	• Appearing positive and upbeat about possibilities • Constantly asking, "What if?"	• Appearing to step back before suggesting the complete idea or solution • Saying things such as "I just know"
Advantages at Work	• Being alert to small changes in the environment • Being able to seize opportunities	• Protecting group memory • Preventing the reinvention of the wheel and repeating the same mistakes	• Stimulating new ideas and possibilities • Achieving problem breakthroughs with high energy	• Initiating innovative solutions • Simplifying the complex

Table 4 Descriptions of Information-Gathering (Perceiving) Functions (cont'd)

	Perceiving Functions			
	Sensing		Intuition	
Characteristics	Experiencing	Recalling	Brainstorming	Visioning
Possible Challenges	• Jumping in too quickly without the big picture • Constantly seeking new sensory stimuli when bored	• Struggling when beginning new tasks or projects without experience • Appearing negative, talking about what cannot be done	• Being reluctant to settle on one solution as multiple possibilities emerge • Seeking continual change	• Being reluctant to accept others' viewpoints • Waiting for the solution to come to mind and delaying projects
Focus	• What is here and now	• What was	• What could be	• What will be

Important note: The descriptions in this table are defined and characterized by how they would appear as a "first" function, that is, the one used most often and most comfortably. Each function would look different as a second, third, or fourth function, that is, as a backup function. See pages 94–95 for more on first and backup functions.

EXERCISE 15
Trying On Information-Gathering (Perceiving) Functions

TEAM EXERCISE

As a team, work through the next four activities following these three steps:

1. Have one person read the instructions for each function and have team members individually write down their responses.
2. Then, as a group, discuss your responses to each question. Consider carefully the differences you observe between how different team members respond to the questions.
3. Rate your ability to use each function on the following scale:

   High: "I instantly recognized those behaviors and know I do that."

   Medium: "I do this somewhat but not all the time."

   Low: "I did not understand the behaviors—I am not really like that."

Coaching Point

Remember, if you get bored with the activity or don't understand what is being requested, this could be an indicator that the function is not one that you use easily!

Experiencing

As a group, stop what you are doing and focus on the here and now. Do not allow your mind to wander into conjectures or possibilities or to recall past data. Observe intensely the sights around you. Listen carefully for all sounds, smell the air, and tune in to every detail of the physical environment. Are there any distractions in the meeting room? What is the decoration like in the room? Is anyone fidgeting?

How did this exercise feel? How easy was it? How often do you use this function without being prompted? Rate your ability to use this function naturally below.

☐ *High* ☐ *Medium* ☐ *Low*

Coaching Point

If you notice being extremely distracted by external factors such as noise, smells, or visual stimuli, this is a good indicator that you use Experiencing—so rate it as high!

Recalling

Think of a previous team meeting that you attended (preferably more than one month ago). As you think of that meeting, put yourself back on that meeting day. Where was the meeting held? How did you get to the meeting? What did you wear? Where did you sit? Why did you sit there? How did the meeting start? What happened next? Replay the sequence of events and recall the outcome. How is this meeting similar to or different from that previous meeting?

How did this exercise feel? How easy was it? How often do you use this function without being prompted? Rate your ability to use this function naturally below.

☐ *High* ☐ *Medium* ☐ *Low*

Coaching Point

If you could not remember much about the previous meeting, rate Recalling as low! If you can remember past events almost like watching a rolling videotape, rate this function as high!

Brainstorming

Think of the subject matter of this fieldbook—personality types, temperaments, and teams. List as many alternative applications as you can for this material in the world at large. List all ideas. Think outside the box. What are some completely new approaches you could use? Anything goes . . .

How did this exercise feel? How easy was it? To what extent do you like to talk through possibilities when looking for new ideas? How often do you use this function without being prompted? Rate your ability to use this function naturally below.

☐ *High* ☐ *Medium* ☐ *Low*

Coaching Point

If a team member comes up with an answer like "establishing peace in the Middle East" or "hostage negotiation," don't roll your eyes! These are the kinds of answers suggested by individuals who rate Brainstorming as high!

Visioning

You may recognize the experience of working on a project, report, or problem and then having an "Aha!" breakthrough. You gathered information and then most likely stepped away. Then it all came to you and you knew how it would look completely. To what extent do you rely on these "shower" solutions and epiphanies?

How did this exercise feel? How easy was it? How often do you use this function without being prompted? Rate your ability to use this function naturally on the scale below.

☐ *High* ☐ *Medium* ☐ *Low*

> ***Coaching Point***
>
> You can't try on this function in the moment because Visioning requires a gestation period. Make sure you think back to times when you suddenly knew the answer but could not necessarily articulate where the solution came from.

Which perceiving function did you gravitate toward most?

(Sensing)		(Intuition)	
☐ **Experiencing**	☐ **Recalling**	☐ **Brainstorming**	☐ **Visioning**

End of Exercise

Information-Gathering (Perceiving) Functions Questionnaire

If you are still struggling to identify your best-fit perceiving function, use the following questionnaire to help you in your further exploration. If you feel comfortable with your selection, you can move on to the next section, observing how the perceiving functions are manifested at work, on pages 61–62.

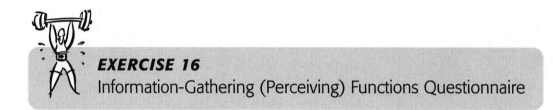

EXERCISE 16
Information-Gathering (Perceiving) Functions Questionnaire

To assess the functions that you use to gather information, give some thought to the following questions, using a scale of 1–4.

Function: Experiencing

	1	2	3	4
1. Are you *acutely* tuned in to the external environment (sound, sight, smell, taste, touch, movement, etc.)?	Always ○	Sometimes ○	Seldom ○	Never ○
2. Do you pride yourself on your physical acuity, rarely, if ever, having a physical accident due to clumsiness?	Always ○	Sometimes ○	Seldom ○	Never ○
3. Do you see options in the moment? If you are put in a difficult situation, can you see solutions?	Always ○	Sometimes ○	Seldom ○	Never ○
4. Can you read minute changes in body language? Do you see changes in facial expressions?	Always ○	Sometimes ○	Seldom ○	Never ○
5. Do you pride yourself on quickly picking up on what the other person wants and knowing how you could provide it for him or her?	Always ○	Sometimes ○	Seldom ○	Never ○
Total Experiencing	☐	☐	☐	☐

Function: Recalling

	1	2	3	4
1. When starting a new project do you immediately think back to a similar situation you experienced before?	Always ○	Sometimes ○	Seldom ○	Never ○
2. Does your memory play like a videotape, that is, do you clearly remember details and occurrences?	Always ○	Sometimes ○	Seldom ○	Never ○
3. Are you able to judge what is real and what is fake?	Always ○	Sometimes ○	Seldom ○	Never ○
4. Do you naturally compare and contrast the current data with the past to determine such things as better or worse, higher or lower, etc.?	Always ○	Sometimes ○	Seldom ○	Never ○
5. When assessing risks, to what extent do you put in safeguards, knowing something will go wrong?	Always ○	Sometimes ○	Seldom ○	Never ○
Total Recalling	☐	☐	☐	☐

Function: Brainstorming

	1	2	3	4
1. Do you naturally think of numerous possibilities when starting a project?	Always ○	Sometimes ○	Seldom ○	Never ○
2. Do you have a desire to bounce your ideas off someone?	Always ○	Sometimes ○	Seldom ○	Never ○
3. When you start with an idea do you verbally brainstorm "what if"/"what else" scenarios?	Always ○	Sometimes ○	Seldom ○	Never ○
4. When discussing plans and strategies do you consider unusual possibilities or methods to accomplish them?	Always ○	Sometimes ○	Seldom ○	Never ○
5. Do you easily read between the lines and see hidden patterns and meanings?	Always ○	Sometimes ○	Seldom ○	Never ○
Total Brainstorming	☐	☐	☐	☐

Function: Visioning

	1	2	3	4
1. If you are asked to come up with an idea on the spot, do you need to take a mental step back to reflect and allow the idea to gel?	Always ○	Sometimes ○	Seldom ○	Never ○
2. How often do you wrestle with a problem, only to have a complete solution come to you in the middle of the night or when you are not consciously working on the problem?	Always ○	Sometimes ○	Seldom ○	Never ○
3. When you come up with an idea, does it come as a flash of inspiration, a "shower" solution?	Always ○	Sometimes ○	Seldom ○	Never ○
4. Do you trust your vision to the extent that you take certain risks that others would not?	Always ○	Sometimes ○	Seldom ○	Never ○
5. Are you sometimes frustrated by your inability to articulate the steps you took in coming up with a solution?	Always ○	Sometimes ○	Seldom ○	Never ○
Total Visioning	☐	☐	☐	☐

Total your scores for each function. Your lowest total should give you some indication of your main information-gathering function, but use your best judgment in this decision.

(Sensing)		(Intuition)	
Experiencing	**Recalling**	**Brainstorming**	**Visioning**
☐	☐	☐	☐

End of Exercise

Information-Gathering (Perceiving) Functions at Work

As the use of cognitive processes tends to be unconscious and occur rapidly, recognizing the function in action can be a challenge. The following case studies provide examples of how these functions are manifested in the working world.

Experiencing

Dennis, the CEO of a restaurant chain, will walk into one of his restaurants and instantly notice an untidy display, what is lacking in the presentation of an entrée, and whether the room temperature is just right. He delights in experimenting with new flavors and dishes and enjoys the challenge of growing his own business. If a new restaurant is not profitable within a short period of time, however, he will quickly change direction and take up new opportunities.

After the September 11 crisis, Paul responded quickly to keep the technical support center running at a high-tech computer company. He created a tactical team, with specific individuals focusing on major customers. He enjoyed the hands-on problem solving and the challenge that the situation presented. After the immediate crisis had passed, the VP wanted to work on mapping process improvements, but Paul was reluctant to implement structured policies because he felt strongly that the support center needed the flexibility to respond to any situation.

Recalling

When starting a new project, Chris, an engineer, always says, "You have to go back to what you've done in the past. How else would you know where to start?" He refers back to previous projects and evaluates carefully what worked and what didn't work. Then he suggests an approach for process improvements. When other team members suggest an approach that has never been tried before or that seems impractical, he sometimes finds things wrong with the idea before giving it due consideration.

When Jim, the operations manager, has to select a vendor to work with his retail team, he specifically looks for someone who has a proven track record in retail. He respects the practical experience vendors possess. When he has to tackle a project that he has never undertaken before, he struggles initially and then asks one of his teammates who has worked on a similar project for advice.

Brainstorming

Claudia, a VP of HR, is constantly looking at new ways to improve the functioning of the HR department. She always keeps her eyes open for new ventures and confidently tries new methods. At every meeting there is an update on new possibilities and a discussion of ideas. Her team approaches her if they get stuck on an issue because she enjoys exploring different approaches and is often able to "think outside the box."

By talking with customers and discussing current market research with his team, Gary, the president of a retail company, can see trends in the market and hypothesize how his company could provide the goods and services required by customers. He enjoys bouncing ideas around with his team members, but he sometimes frustrates his team when he jumps from one idea to the next without considering the specific practical implementation issues. He also encourages his team to undertake scenario planning, which involves brainstorming everything that could go wrong and imagining possibilities for each situation.

Visioning

Susan was trying to finalize an agenda for a book. She reviewed input from the publisher, read various other books on the subject, and reread some of the programs she has led. She became somewhat frustrated because the theme for the book was not clear. However, the next morning she woke up with the complete picture of the book in her head, a visual to represent the concept, and a premise on which to base the book. When the publisher wanted to rearrange some content, she was reluctant to change but was unable to clearly articulate why.

When trying to solve a systems-level problem, Mike gathers as much data as he can about the root causes and symptoms. He finds it difficult when other team members try to push on to problem resolution without taking the time to allow the information to "solidify." Often the solution to a problem comes to him in the middle of the night, bearing little resemblance to the original hypotheses.

Self-Assessment

Now that we have described the four information-gathering functions and reviewed how they might be manifested in work behavior, it is time for you to decide which function you identify with most.

EXERCISE 17
Exploring Information-Gathering (Perceiving) Functions

1. Review the descriptions of all four information-gathering functions in table 4 (pp. 52–53). If you used more concrete words in exercise 14 (pp. 49–51), focus more on Experiencing and Recalling. If you used more abstract words, look first at Brainstorming and Visioning.
2. Now review your notes from exercise 15 (pp. 53–57).
3. Review your responses from exercise 16 (pp. 58–60).
4. Finally, review the examples of each of the functions at work (pp. 61–62). Which information-gathering function do you most identify with, and why? If you are not sure, rank the functions from 1 to 4, 1 being most like you, and continue through the discovery process.

(Sensing)		(Intuition)	
☐ **Experiencing**	☐ **Recalling**	☐ **Brainstorming**	☐ **Visioning**

____

____

____

____

____

5. In each box below, write down whatever helps you further understand each perceiving function; you can use the following suggestions to help you get started:
   - People you know who might use a particular perceiving function
   - A phrase or visual representation of each function that helps you identify it

Experiencing	**Recalling**
Brainstorming	**Visioning**

6. Share your results with your teammates.

Coaching Point

Each person gravitates toward different kinds of information. If we can recognize the information that we perceive first, we can better understand the strengths we might bring to the team, as well as the possible challenges we might face.

End of Exercise

Making Decisions (Judging)

Now that we have reviewed the different approaches we might use to gather information (perceiving), let's review the different approaches we might use in making decisions (judging).

Learning About Thinking and Feeling

The second two cognitive processes, Thinking and Feeling, describe how each person makes decisions or comes to conclusions. Decisions based on Thinking tend to be made objectively, logically, and analytically. If we make decisions based on Feeling, we are more interested in subjective criteria such as personal values, the people involved, and special circumstances.

> ***Foul!***
>
> It is important to let go of our usual understanding of the words *Thinking* and *Feeling*. Having a Feeling preference does not mean you are a blubbering, emotional wreck, and having a Thinking preference does not mean you are as cold as Mr. Spock! Both are rational decision-making processes, with each considering different criteria. Neither is better or worse than the other. In fact, the best decisions involve considering both sets of criteria.

Exercise 18 will help you experience the difference between Thinking and Feeling.

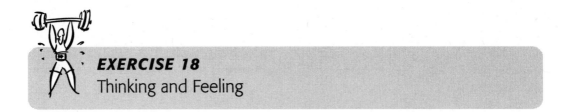

EXERCISE 18
Thinking and Feeling

1. Imagine you are in charge of forming a team for a high-profile project. Participation on the project team involves a significant raise and an increased chance of promotion. The project will require long hours and considerable travel. You are deciding between two employees who have expressed interest in the role.
2. Fill in the objective and subjective criteria you might use to determine which employee to add to the team. Objective criteria are more definitive and easier to quantify than subjective criteria.

Objective Criteria	Subjective Criteria
Example: • Years of experience	Example: • Relationship with others on the team

(For additional examples of possible objective and subjective criteria, see p. 307).

Which criteria would you weigh more heavily in making that decision?

Objective ________ Subjective________

Why?

____

____

____

3. Based on your response, check the type of process that seems most natural for you.

☐ **Objective = Thinking** ☐ **Subjective = Feeling**

Team Dynamics from the Inside Out

- *Artisans* and *Guardians* may differ: some will prefer Thinking criteria and some will prefer Feeling criteria.
- *Rationals* tend to gravitate toward Thinking criteria.
- *Idealists* tend to gravitate toward Feeling criteria.

Don't worry about matching processes with your perceived temperament now. Just choose which processes you tend to use primarily.

End of Exercise

Learning About the Decision-Making (Judging) Functions

Four functions are used in the mental activity of judging information (making decisions)—two Thinking (T) functions and two Feeling (F) functions—as shown in figure 5. They are described in detail in table 5.

FIGURE 5 **Judging Processes and Their Functions**

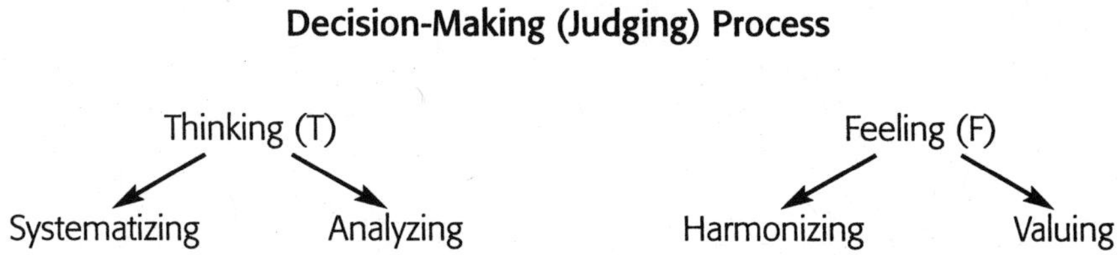

Table 5 Descriptions of Decision-Making (Judging) Functions

	Judging Functions			
	Thinking		Feeling	
Characteristics	**Systematizing**	**Analyzing**	**Harmonizing**	**Valuing**
Objective or Subjective	• Objective	• Objective	• Subjective	• Subjective
Description	• Making decisions using logical criteria to sequence and organize resources to achieve goals in the external environment • Using cause-and-effect logic	• Making decisions where information gathered is evaluated and sorted against a mental model • Analyzing data for logic	• Making decisions using subjective criteria to optimize interpersonal harmony • Determining what is appropriate behavior in a situation	• Making decisions based on a subjective value and internal belief system • Determining what is the right thing to do in a situation
Primary Users	• Some Guardians and Rationals	• Some Artisans and Rationals	• Some Guardians and Idealists	• Some Artisans and Idealists
Work Signals	• Driving for closure • Defining roles and boundaries: who is responsible for what, by when	• Being comfortable with gathering new data • Questioning ideas to clarify logic	• Pushing for closure • Showing emotions—positive and negative—on face	• Being flexible and adaptable • Appearing easy-going until values are crossed and then becoming stubborn in defending decisions/principles
Work Techniques	• Using flow charts, pros and cons lists, fishbone diagrams, etc. • Using time management skills such as prioritizing and goal setting • Creating a plan or schedule	• Evaluating ways to improve the flow of content • Creating metaphors and models • Debating a point of view	• Employing consensus decision making • Working in groups • Being sensitive to group dynamics	• Building dialogue • Bringing values into work • Exhibiting integrity in leadership
Advantages at Work	• Being organized and able to plan and prioritize work output • Being assertive and to the point	• Being able to disengage and ask questions to clarify logic in a given situation • Asking questions to improve the system	• Recognizing group dynamics and ensuring all team members are involved in decisions • Being able to build bridges between team	• Acting as the conscience of the group • Being tolerant and supportive of individual differences—working well with all types

Table 5 Descriptions of Decision-Making (Judging) Functions (cont'd)

	Judging Functions			
	Thinking		Feeling	
Characteristics	**Systematizing**	**Analyzing**	**Harmonizing**	**Valuing**
Possible Challenges	• Pushing for closure too quickly and wanting to control too many decisions • Appearing too rigid or blunt	• Being unwilling to change their mind—holding on to their models, wanting to win in debate • Having difficulty quantifying a decision that is internally based	• Showing all emotions on face and in body language, with sudden outbursts • Finding it hard to function during severe conflict	• Appearing stubborn when high moral standards, possibly unrealistic, are crossed • Losing enthusiasm for work when values are disappointed
Aims	• Accomplishing goals in a structured manner	• Improving a system or theory	• Making everyone comfortable	• Achieving alignment between external environment and internal beliefs

Important note: The descriptions in this table are defined and characterized by how they would appear as a "first" function, that is, the one used most often and most comfortably. Each function would look different as a second, third, or fourth function, that is, as a backup function. See pages 94–95 for more on first and backup functions.

EXERCISE 19
Trying On Decision-Making (Judging) Functions

TEAM EXERCISE

As a team, work through the next four activities following the three steps below.

1. Have one person read the instructions and have team members individually write down their responses.

2. Then, as a group, discuss your responses to each question. Consider carefully the differences you observe between how different team members respond to the questions.

3. Rate your ability to use each function on the following scale:

   High: "I instantly recognized those behaviors and know I do that."

   Medium: "I do this somewhat but not all the time."

   Low: "I did not understand the behaviors—I am not really like that."

Coaching Point

Remember, if you get bored with any of the following activities or don't understand what is being requested, this could be an indicator that the function is not one that you use easily!

Systematizing

List the steps you would take to plan and achieve a successful vacation. Delegate responsibilities, set deadlines, and determine resources involved. Then, organize your information into an action plan.

____

____

____

How did this exercise feel? How easy was it? How often do you use this function without being prompted? Rate your ability to use this function naturally on the scale below.

☐ *High* ☐ *Medium* ☐ *Low*

Coaching Point

If the thought of putting this much planning into a vacation was painful, rate Systematizing as low! If planning the vacation this way made you feel comfortable and you knew you would optimize your time on your trip, rate Systematizing as high!

Analyzing

Write down your job role at the top of a sheet of paper. List all the tasks you need to achieve on Post-it® Notes—one per Post-it Note. Then, divide these tasks into logical categories by grouping together the Post-it Notes with similar subjects. Make sure you have no more than six major categories. How could you reallocate your workload to be more productive? What tasks could you delegate?

____

____

____

How did this exercise feel? How easy was it? How often do you use this function without being prompted? Rate your ability to use this function naturally below.

☐ *High* ☐ *Medium* ☐ *Low*

Coaching Point

Exercise 42, "Defining Your Team's Key Result Areas," in chapter 5 will give you another opportunity to use Analyzing. Analyzers create their own mental model of how to best represent the information.

Harmonizing

Think about the energy in the room as you conduct your team meeting. How involved are team members? What conflicts, if any, exist? How interested are people in the different subjects? How do you feel during a tough discussion? How appropriately do people behave?

How did this exercise feel? How easy was it? How often do you use this function without being prompted? Rate your ability to use this function naturally below.

☐ *High* ☐ *Medium* ☐ *Low*

Coaching Point

If you find it difficult to function when there is severe conflict between two team members, rate Harmonizing as high.

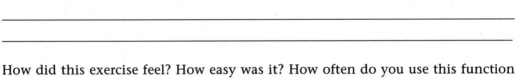

Valuing

Think about companies in the marketplace. What companies, if any, would you not do business with, and why? To what extent do you keep these values private? To what extent do you make decisions based on these values? Have you ever changed a job because the company did something that was against your value system? How tolerant of human differences do you perceive yourself to be?

____

____

____

How did this exercise feel? How easy was it? How often do you use this function without being prompted? Rate your ability to use this function naturally below.

☐ *High* ☐ *Medium* ☐ *Low*

Coaching Point

Every person has a value system that has been developed through his or her upbringing; this is not the same as Valuing. Individuals who use Valuing with ease have their own internal value system that serves as the strongest influence on their decisions.

Which judging function did you gravitate toward most?

(Thinking)		(Feeling)	
☐ **Systematizing**	☐ **Analyzing**	☐ **Harmonizing**	☐ **Valuing**

End of Exercise

Decision-Making (Judging) Functions Questionnaire

If you are still struggling to identify your best-fit judging process, use this questionnaire to help you in your further exploration. If you feel comfortable with your selection, you can move on to the next section, observing how the judging functions are manifested at work, on pages 76–77.

EXERCISE 20
Decision-Making (Judging) Functions Questionnaire

To assess the functions that you use to make decisions, give some thought to the following questions, using a scale of 1–4.

Function: Systematizing

	1	2	3	4
1. Do you sequence events and resources in the external environment to achieve an end result?	Always ○	Sometimes ○	Seldom ○	Never ○
2. Are you skilled in taking a project through a systematic, step-by-step, replicable process?	Always ○	Sometimes ○	Seldom ○	Never ○
3. Do you rely on published facts and data in the external environment to make decisions?	Always ○	Sometimes ○	Seldom ○	Never ○
4. Do you organize things by categories, colors, sizes, types, etc.?	Always ○	Sometimes ○	Seldom ○	Never ○
5. Do you make lists of pros and cons and then push for a decision?	Always ○	Sometimes ○	Seldom ○	Never ○
Total Systematizing	☐	☐	☐	☐

Function: Analyzing

	1	2	3	4
1. Do you internally consider facts and data to develop your own rationale?	Always ○	Sometimes ○	Seldom ○	Never ○
2. Do you sometimes find your logic is at odds with that of others?	Always ○	Sometimes ○	Seldom ○	Never ○
3. When you have an opinion do you stick to it, basing your arguments on logical deductions?	Always ○	Sometimes ○	Seldom ○	Never ○
4. Do you pull inward to analyze different options and approaches?	Always ○	Sometimes ○	Seldom ○	Never ○
5. Once you have made an important decision, is it hard for you to change that decision?	Always ○	Sometimes ○	Seldom ○	Never ○
Total Analyzing	☐	☐	☐	☐

Function: Harmonizing

	1	2	3	4
1. In individual and group interactions, are you aware of everyone's feelings?	Always ○	Sometimes ○	Seldom ○	Never ○
2. Do you prefer that everyone be in agreement with a decision or that the decision be made in the best interest of the group?	Always ○	Sometimes ○	Seldom ○	Never ○
3. Do you find conflict extremely stressful and try to avoid it and restore harmony where possible?	Always ○	Sometimes ○	Seldom ○	Never ○
4. Do you tend to self-disclose and talk to others about personal situations?	Always ○	Sometimes ○	Seldom ○	Never ○
5. Do people say that you show all your emotions on your face?	Always ○	Sometimes ○	Seldom ○	Never ○
Total Harmonizing	☐	☐	☐	☐

Function: Valuing

	1 Always	2 Sometimes	3 Seldom	4 Never
1. Do you act in accordance with strongly held internal opinions and beliefs?	Always ○	Sometimes ○	Seldom ○	Never ○
2. Are you hesitant or reluctant to explain those beliefs to others?	Always ○	Sometimes ○	Seldom ○	Never ○
3. Do you strive to live by your values and struggle when values conflict? When your belief system is challenged do you react strongly or make drastic decisions, e.g., leave a job?	Always ○	Sometimes ○	Seldom ○	Never ○
4. Have you been accused of making decisions devoid of logic when you knew you were doing the right thing?	Always ○	Sometimes ○	Seldom ○	Never ○
5. Do you run situations through a "How would that make me feel?" analysis when reacting?	Always ○	Sometimes ○	Seldom ○	Never ○
Total Valuing	☐	☐	☐	☐

Total your scores for each function. Your lowest total should give you some indication of your main decision-making function, but use your best judgment in this decision.

(Thinking)		(Feeling)	
Systematizing	**Analyzing**	**Harmonizing**	**Valuing**
☐	☐	☐	☐

End of Exercise

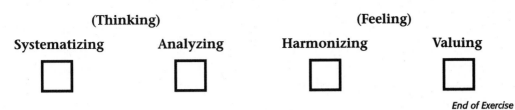

Decision-Making (Judging) Functions at Work

As the use of cognitive processes tends to be unconscious and occur rapidly, recognizing the function in action can be a challenge. The following case studies provide examples of how these functions are manifested in the working world.

Systematizing

As Jim continues his new stores' rollout, he makes quick, objective decisions about which are the correct sites and then swiftly creates an implementation plan, marshalling people and resources in an optimal manner. He has created a flow chart and master project plan to allocate responsibilities—what a document! He sees problems others might overlook and carefully critiques ideas and implementation procedures. Jim also gets impatient with others who are not as quick to make decisions. In addition, his direct communication style can sometimes offend others, and he may sometimes disregard the people considerations called for in establishing new stores.

Theresa acts as a business consultant to senior executives. When establishing the contract, she clearly defines the end goal for the assignment and then categorizes the main strategies for achieving the goal. She can give tough messages directly and is clear about boundaries and accountabilities. She follows up with her internal clients and uses a variety of models to increase organizational productivity.

Analyzing

Claudia loves to tackle difficult problems at work. She has developed a system for analyzing a situation from a number of perspectives and can always pick out the inconsistencies in an approach that others would overlook. To Claudia, her job is like working in a laboratory—she is constantly trying to observe and get to the bottom of things to improve the way the system operates.

Jerene attends a training program with her team on temperament and type but went into the program with a personality model formed from her background in psychology. Initially, she refused to accept any information that did not fit into her preconceptions and was quick to point out any possible inconsistencies in the theory. As she receives more relevant data, and upon reflecting on how the model has worked for her and others, Jerene is able to incorporate these ideas into her logical premise and develop an enriched perspective on personality that reflects both her model and the temperament and type data.

Harmonizing

Sam, an adult education instructor, is always able to make the group feel comfortable and to create a safe learning environment. He does this by welcoming people to the class, paying attention to their interests and needs, offering supportive feedback, and disclosing relevant personal information that forms a connection with the group. In addition, he is extremely sensitive to the group process and the way the group is responding at any point in time. If he feels a disconnection, Sam raises the issue with participants so he can adapt the process as required to maximize group learning.

Candace, a member of the marketing team, really likes to maintain a supportive environment. She takes on the responsibility of ensuring that everyone has fun at team get-togethers and pays special attention to new members of the team. Occasionally, when she is overloaded, her negative emotions are written on her face, but when the pressure point has passed, her warmth quickly returns. She naturally extracts personal data from team members with her warmth and empathy.

Valuing

Paul had worked for a high-tech company for many years, under a succession of different bosses. Unfortunately, when his most recent boss joined the firm, she made some cost-cutting decisions that conflicted with his internal value system, and he decided it was time to leave. Even though his ideal of the company was shattered, Paul did not give that as a reason when he handed in his notice; he felt that it was too private and related only to his personal beliefs. At the same time, his boss was surprised at his decision, because she thought he was very happy in his role and with the company.

Jay has a firm code of beliefs about ethics in technical product marketing. While he is usually very open to new ideas, when the general manager suggested another approach Jay firmly defended his method with a zeal the general manager had never seen in him before. Occasionally, when he speaks up to argue about what is fair in a team meeting, other team members are surprised at the rigidity of his approach, because they normally find him really easy to work with. After the issue has been addressed, Jay once again becomes the person his teammates know: very tolerant of differences and easygoing.

Self-Assessment

Now that we have described the four decision-making functions and reviewed how they might be manifested in work behavior, it is time for you to decide which function you identify with most.

EXERCISE 21
Exploring Decision-Making (Judging) Functions

1. Review the descriptions of all four decision-making functions in table 5 (pp. 68–69).
2. Review your notes from exercise 18 (pp. 66–67).
3. Review your responses from exercise 20 (pp. 73–75).
4. Then, read the descriptions of the decision-making functions at work, which follow the questionnaire.
5. If you think you gravitate more toward logic (Thinking), focus more on Systematizing and Analyzing. If you believe you tend to use more Feeling criteria, look first at Harmonizing and Valuing.
6. Determine which decision-making function you most identify with, and why. If you are not sure, rank the functions from 1 to 4, 1 being most like you, and continue through the discovery process.

(Thinking)		(Feeling)	
☐ **Systematizing**	☐ **Analyzing**	☐ **Harmonizing**	☐ **Valuing**

____

____

____

____

____

7. In each box below, write down whatever helps you further understand each judging function; you can use the following suggestions to help you get started.
   - People you know who might use a particular judging function
   - A phrase or visual representation of each function that helps you identify it

Systematizing	**Analyzing**
Harmonizing	**Valuing**

Coaching Point

Each person uses different criteria to make decisions. If we can recognize the criteria that we gravitate toward first, we can better understand the strengths this might bring to the team and the possible challenges we might face from not considering other options.

End of Exercise

In your everyday life, you will most likely encounter tasks that employ your stronger functions and others that challenge you to use more underdeveloped functions. However, each cognitive process brings a unique perspective to any particular task or activity.

Coaching Point

One of the biggest benefits for a team is having all functions accessible to team members. This can guarantee that all information is considered and different criteria are used in making decisions.

Time Out!

Remember that when doing any specific task, we may be using multiple functions almost concurrently. For instance, if I am planning a project, within a few seconds I may think back to a past project (Recalling), look at information at hand (Experiencing), consider how people will feel about the project (Harmonizing), and estimate how quickly we can put an action plan together (Systematizing). Rather like a ball in a pinball machine, we bounce from one function to another.

Cognitive Processes in Action

Now that we have reviewed the cognitive processes (gathering information and making decisions) and the functions associated with each, let's apply this knowledge to identifying the functions used in the following case studies. We have used the case studies from chapter 1 with more specific data about how the functions appear at work.

EXERCISE 22

Identifying Cognitive Processes and Functions in Case Studies

1. Review the profiles of the eight individuals in four jobs on pp. 82–85; you have already identified their temperaments. We have added some supplemental information about the functions each uses. (You can review the rest of the information about each case study on pp. 30–33.)
2. Now, with the rest of the team, identify which functions appear to be the best fit for each individual, and note why.

Team Dynamics from the Inside Out

Remember:

- *Artisans* tend to use Experiencing and Valuing or Analyzing
- *Guardians* tend to use Recalling and Harmonizing or Systematizing
- *Rationals* use either Brainstorming or Visioning and Systematizing or Analyzing
- *Idealists* use either Brainstorming or Visioning and Harmonizing or Valuing

Subcontract Trainers

Jennifer

When Jennifer is researching, she likes to gather information over a period of time and then "let it sit." After this gestation period she will often wake up with a way to formulate the entire model in her head.

Jennifer is great to have around whenever there is a large project to be rolled out. She immediately defines the outcome and the steps required, with responsibilities and time lines. She is extremely goal oriented. Additionally, when individuals struggle with tough decisions, she is able to assist them in creating a pros-and-cons list.

Information-Gathering Function: ______________________________

Why?

____

____

Decision-Making Function: ______________________________

Why?

____

____

Tony

One of Tony's strengths is his ability to pick up on really small changes in body language that other people might not notice. This allows him to change his approach on the spot to keep the energy up and the session fun. He is also great at "play acting" in front of the room to demonstrate certain skills.

Tony enjoys a good debate when he is teaching certain principles: he enjoys dissecting a point of view and then looking at the argument from a different perspective. He is comfortable with the short-term friction this debate might produce. He normally has his own point of view when discussing subjects!

Information-Gathering Function: ______________________________

Why?

____

____

Decision-Making Function: ______________________________

Why?

____

____

Sales/Account Managers

Karen

Karen really enjoys building new marketing strategies and exploring creative opportunities. Her ability to read between the lines at customer meetings aids the customer relationship. The only disadvantage is that she is so full of new ideas that sometimes she forgets to follow through on "old" ideas or leave functioning models as they are!

Karen also maintains a high standard of integrity when dealing with customers, ensuring that she never works with two companies if a conflict of interest might be involved. She does not talk about what is important to her, but if customers behave unethically, she will stop working with them.

Information-Gathering Function: ______________________________

Why?

____

____

Decision-Making Function: ______________________________

Why?

____

____

Sharon

Whenever Sharon begins work with a new client, she researches other clients from that industry with whom she has worked in the past to gain practical ideas for the new client. She also talks to other team members to see if they have had any experience with this customer.

Sharon is very tuned in to customers and what is important to them. She has the ability to see things from the customer's perspective. She builds strong friendships with the internal customers because they feel comfortable talking to her about work and home situations. She likes to get as many people as possible at the customer's site involved in the decision to ensure that everyone agrees with whatever approach she is suggesting.

Information-Gathering Function: ______________________________

Why?

____

____

Decision-Making Function: ______________________________

Why?

____

____

IT VP/Directors
Tim Tim excels in using past experience to plan for contingencies and avoid future recurrences of problems. His memory of the detailed causes of problems and the steps that were taken to solve them is what keeps the team from reinventing the wheel. Tim likes to have a plan in place and stick to that plan. His approach to planning is very sequential, with clearly defined steps and accountabilities at every stage. He defines specific milestones and tracks task completion against these deliverables. He is particularly adept at creating complex project plans. **Information-Gathering Function:** ________________________ **Why?** ____ ____ **Decision-Making Function:** ________________________ **Why?** ____ ____ **Adam** Adam welcomed the challenge of establishing a new group combining three separate organizations. Even though he had never created a group from scratch before, he just knew he could make a success of it. He gathered data about the groups and after reflection came up with an innovative way of structuring the department, incorporating a completely new major-account team. Adam enjoys working in a nonconfrontational culture with team members who consider people as well as the task at hand. He naturally sees potential in his people and struggles with tough decisions such as terminating employees, even if they have been given chances to improve. **Information-Gathering Function:** ________________________ **Why?** ____ ____ **Decision-Making Function:** ________________________ **Why?** ____ ____

CEOs

Alison

Alison eventually left the running of the business to someone else and forged ahead with developing a foundation. She wanted to be where the action is and gather information firsthand through experience. She enjoys traveling around the world, living with different people, and immersing herself in their culture and situation.

Alison values community in the workplace, so she set up a program to solicit employee input. Each piece of mail was answered by the board. But, when an employee said, "Get rid of this community activism; we are a shampoo shop," she answered quite bluntly that he could find another place to work if he did not support key company values.

Information-Gathering Function: ____________________________

Why?

____

____

Decision-Making Function: ____________________________

Why?

____

____

Bob

Bob enjoys the challenge of repositioning this company for growth: exploring new possibilities, considering strategic partnerships with other firms, and devising new ways to position the company's offerings. The new direction is very different from the original company's business plan.

When team members bring Bob suggestions for new products, he is adept at questioning the logic and considering how the approach could be improved or modified to increase the chances of success. He enjoys debating different approaches and can seem oblivious sometimes to the effect that this has on people in his team.

Information-Gathering Function: ____________________________

Why?

____

____

Decision-Making Function: ____________________________

Why?

____

____

3. Now look at the answers on pages 308–11 to see how you did.

Team Huddle!

Discuss the exercise using the following questions:

- How easy was it to recognize the clues for each function?
- What problems, if any, did you have in recognizing different functions?

Foul!

Remember, these are straightforward, somewhat mechanistic exercises to highlight certain observable cues. Be careful not to oversimplify this information and label others! Think how difficult it was to assess which functions you use. Also, don't make conclusions about abilities based on these case studies. For instance, even if you don't use Recalling primarily, you will still remember some past experiences. Plus, each person can access every function to a greater or lesser extent.

End of Exercise

Trying On All Eight Functions

Now that you have become familiar with the cognitive processes, let's use another exercise where you can try on all eight functions.

EXERCISE 23
Trying On All Eight Functions

TEAM EXERCISE

This exercise is best performed as a team. Team members will have the opportunity to observe a wider variety of functions reflecting their peers' preferences.

1. For each of the following scenarios, list how you would use each information-gathering and decision-making function.

Information-Gathering (Perceiving) Functions

	Perceiving Functions			
	Sensing		Intuition	
Task	Experiencing	Recalling	Brainstorming	Visioning
Putting Together a Budget	• •	• •	• •	• •
Organizing an Off-Site Event	• •	• •	• •	• •
Writing a Report	• •	• •	• •	• •
Solving a Problem	• •	• •	• •	• •

Decision-Making (Judging) Functions

	Judging Functions			
	Thinking		Feeling	
Task	Systematizing	Analyzing	Harmonizing	Valuing
Putting Together a Budget	• •	• •	• •	• •
Organizing an Off-Site Event	• •	• •	• •	• •
Writing a Report	• •	• •	• •	• •
Solving a Problem	• •	• •	• •	• •

Coaching Point

This is one of the most difficult exercises in this book! To be able to step into and articulate all eight functions is not easy! We must rely on teammates who use the other functions to help out.

2. Now, as an individual team member, answer the following questions:

- For which functions did you find it easiest to list responses? Those functions are likely to be your most easily accessed functions on the team.

☐ **Experiencing**	☐ **Recalling**	☐ **Brainstorming**	☐ **Visioning**
☐ **Systematizing**	☐ **Analyzing**	☐ **Harmonizing**	☐ **Valuing**

- For which functions did you struggle hardest to list responses?

☐ **Experiencing**	☐ **Recalling**	☐ **Brainstorming**	☐ **Visioning**
☐ **Systematizing**	☐ **Analyzing**	☐ **Harmonizing**	☐ **Valuing**

Coaching Point

For maximum team productivity, it is beneficial if

- All types of information are gathered (using Experiencing, Recalling, Brainstorming, and Visioning)
- All types of criteria for making decisions are weighed (using Systematizing, Analyzing, Harmonizing, and Valuing)

3. Compare your answers on the grids to the sample answers on pages 312–13.

End of Exercise

If we do not have all the information-gathering functions represented on our team, we may miss certain opportunities. Conversely, if we do have team members utilizing all information-gathering functions, we may sometimes seem to be at cross-purposes. In addition, if we do not consider all the different criteria when making a decision, we may not make the best possible decision. However, if all four decision-making functions are being used, but we don't understand them, the team may experience some conflict as a result.

Wrap-Up

The addition of cognitive processes moves us from the abstract patterns or themes associated with temperament into the specific actions we take on a day-to-day basis—"where the rubber meets the road." The cognitive processes each team member uses to gather information, whether using concrete Sensing (S) data (via Experiencing or Recalling) or through abstract Intuition (N) patterns and meanings (via Brainstorming or Visioning), can affect the way the team approaches any situation. Also, the cognitive processes each team member uses to make decisions, whether using logical Thinking (T) criteria (via Systematizing or Analyzing) or subjective, more intangible Feeling (F) criteria (via Harmonizing or Valuing), if understood, can raise the quality of decisions and reduce the possibility of blind spots. In the next chapter we will show how temperament and cognitive processes are integrated to create each team member's type, or working style.

SCORECARD

Before moving on to chapter 3, answer the following questions:

- ☐ Have you identified the information-gathering and decision-making functions that feel easiest for you to use?
- ☐ Did you complete the individual exercises on cognitive processes?
- ☐ Have your team members identified the functions they use most easily?
- ☐ As a team, did you complete the case studies and try on all eight functions?
- ☐ Have you reviewed all eight functions so that you have a high-level understanding of each?

3

Keys to Diagnosing Working Style

GAME PLAN

As you continue to assess your behavior and that of your team members, this chapter will help you

- Understand which functions you use and in what sequence
- Understand the purpose of the *Myers-Briggs Type Indicator*® (MBTI®) instrument
- Tie together temperament, cognitive processes, and working style
- Provide descriptions of the sixteen working styles
- Select your best-fit working style for you and your teammates
- Learn more about your teammates and the way they prefer to behave on the team

Which Functions Do You Use Most Easily?

In the first two chapters we reviewed how team members are different in terms of their driving forces (temperament) and how they perceive information and make decisions (cognitive processes). As you and your teammates completed the exercises in chapter 2, it probably became obvious that some of you were able to use certain functions more easily than others. Think about Recalling for instance: Was there one team member who amazed you with his or her in-depth recollection of details, while others were struggling to remember what they did yesterday?

The final step in understanding how members are individually wired is to confirm which functions they use more easily and which they use with more difficulty. This will provide a holistic profile of team members' working style.

EXERCISE 24
Which Functions Do You Use Most Easily?

As you recall from the exercises in chapter 2, the four cognitive processes include Sensing, Intuition, Thinking, and Feeling, each with two functions.

	Cognitive Processes			
	Sensing (S)		Intuition (N)	
Function	**Experiencing**	**Recalling**	**Brainstorming**	**Visioning**
Concrete or Abstract	• Concrete	• Concrete	• Abstract	• Abstract
Description	• Gathering concrete data in the here and now • Seeing options in the moment • Reading sight, sound, smell, taste, and body language cues immediately	• Gathering sensory data and using them to compare and contrast with past sensory experiences • Viewing past data almost like watching a videotape • Using past data to understand what is "real" in a given situation	• Inferring patterns and meanings from current information • Reading between the lines • Thinking out loud: hypothesizing and exploring possibilities	• Assimilating data unconsciously, which then comes into consciousness as a complete picture • Incubating ideas until they are clear • Coming up with "Aha!" and "shower" solutions

	Cognitive Processes			
	Thinking (T)		Feeling (F)	
Function	**Systematizing**	**Analyzing**	**Harmonizing**	**Valuing**
Objective or Subjective	• Objective	• Objective	• Subjective	• Subjective
Description	• Making decisions using logical criteria to sequence and organize resources to achieve goals in the external environment • Using cause-and-effect logic	• Making decisions where information gathered is evaluated and sorted against a mental model • Analyzing data for logic	• Making decisions using subjective criteria to optimize interpersonal harmony • Determining what is appropriate behavior in a situation	• Making decisions based on a subjective value and internal belief system • Determining what is the right thing to do in a situation

1. Study the cognitive process charts above. Which functions do you recognize most in yourself? Which did you select in the exercises in chapter 2?

2. Now compare notes with fellow team members. What differences do you observe?

End of Exercise

Defining Working Style

Working style, or MBTI type, indicates which functions an individual tends to use, and with what degree of ease they are used, resulting in typical observable behaviors from individuals sharing the same pattern of functions.

Time Out!

Why *working style* and not *type?* We prefer the term *working style* because this indicates how type might manifest itself in the team environment. It also avoids "typecasting."

The way that each team member reacts to any given situation is often the result of a complex interaction between multiple funtions. For instance, if someone were to ask you to write a report, your brain might cycle through several functions:

- How is this similar to previous reports I have written? (Recalling)
- Who can support me as I write the report? (Harmonizing)
- How could I put this information into a model? (Analyzing)
- How else could I present this information? (Brainstorming)

The "Hierarchy of Functions"

Understanding which functions each team member accesses first, second, third, and fourth—the sequence known as the "hierarchy of functions"—is the final element in understanding working style (see table 6). This hierarchy colors how we respond to certain situations.

Table 6 The Hierarchy of Functions

Function	Characteristics
First Function (Adult)	This is your most reliable, most dependable, and best-developed function. This is like your preferred hand: effortless to use, smooth, and quick. We also call this your adult function because it develops first and naturally comes to the forefront in a controlled manner. This is the function that we tend to lead with and use most effectively.
Second Function (Parent)	This function is still relatively easy to access but tends to develop a little later. It is not as consistently or reliably available as your adult function but serves to balance it. For instance, if your first function is a perceiving function (Experiencing, Recalling, Brainstorming, or Visioning), your second function will be a judging function (Systematizing, Analyzing, Harmonizing, or Valuing), and vice versa. We call it the parent function because it "looks after" the first function. For instance, a Guardian who uses Systematizing as his or her adult function to make quick and ordered decisions will rely on Recalling as a parent function to ensure that decisions are grounded by precedent.

Table 6 The Hierarchy of Functions (cont'd)

Function	Characteristics
Third Function (Child)	Your third function is generally more difficult to access and somewhat inconsistent when used. We call this your child function because it tends to manifest in less developed, more playful behavior. This means that on a good day it appears fun and helps you reenergize, but on a bad day it can appear more awkward.
Fourth Function (Balancing)	Your fourth function plays a critical role in individual development. Along with the first function it can act as the "trunk" of your personality. If you develop a skillful use of this function, it can provide balance and grounding to your behavior. If not, the function may appear distorted or "larger than life" when you try to use it. A fourth function appearing in stress mode appears more uncontrolled.
Fifth to Eighth Functions (Shadow)	While we are able to a greater or lesser extent to develop our first four functions, use of the second four functions tends to reside in our unconscious, and we are able to exert very little conscious control over them. For more information on these functions, see Linda V. Berens, *Dynamics of Personality Type* (1999).

Foul!

It is a mistake to think that someone will *never* have strong use of the functions low on their hierarchy. While we have an innate functional order, our environment and experiences inevitably affect the development of each function. The cognitive processes are dynamic. When people are put into a situation that forces them to use functions lower on their hierarchy, they will most likely become more skillful in their use. Understanding human behavior is not a precise science!

Not only do we have different preferences and levels of ease in using certain functions, but our background and upbringing can hasten or inhibit their development as we interact with the world. As a result, trying to assess which functions we use in which sequence is difficult.

The *Myers-Briggs Type Indicator*® (MBTI®) Instrument

The *Myers-Briggs Type Indicator* (MBTI) instrument was designed to try to assess which functions we use most easily and then in what sequence we use them: the hierarchy of functions. It reports preferences on four dichotomies, each consisting of two opposite poles. This results in a four-letter type code (e.g., ESTJ), which in essence acts as a license plate to broadly describe how an individual might approach the world and the typical behaviors he or she might demonstrate—we refer to this code as one's working style. However, MBTI results should always be validated through a self-selection process such as the approach taken in this fieldbook.

Foul!

Don't think that because two people share the same pattern or working style they are the same! Many other factors influence an individual's behavior and cause differences.

The Four Dichotomies

In the previous chapter we reviewed two of the dichotomies originally described by Jung and assessed by the MBTI instrument: (1) how we gather information—Sensing (concrete) or Intuition (abstract); and (2) how we make decisions—Thinking (objective) or Feeling (subjective). Now let's integrate the other two dichotomies the indicator assesses: Extraversion or Introversion and Judging or Perceiving (see figure 6).

Extraversion and Introversion

Many analysts of personality think of Extraversion and Introversion in terms of where you get your energy: from the outer world (Extraversion) or the inner world (Introversion). The common analogy is "how you charge your batteries." This definition does not take temperament into account at all. An individual is most content and energized when his or her core needs are being met. An Introverted Idealist may feel most energized when working with individuals with whom he or she shares a connection or when getting involved in an organization that works to improve social conditions. In the same way, Artisans naturally seek sensory data and, therefore, may look Extraverted even though they have a preference for Introversion.

FIGURE 6 **The Four Dichotomies**

Direction of Energy

Extraversion (E) — Introversion (I)

Information-Gathering (Perceiving) Process

Sensing (S)
- S_E Experiencing
- S_I Recalling

Intuition (N)
- N_E Brainstorming
- N_I Visioning

Decision-Making (Judging) Process

Thinking (T)
- T_E Systematizing
- T_I Analyzing

Feeling (F)
- F_E Harmonizing
- F_I Valuing

Cognitive Process Used in the External World

Judging (J) — Perceiving (P)

- *Extraversion* is when your energy naturally flows primarily outward to the external world of people and events
- *Introversion* is when your energy naturally flows primarily inward to ideas and thoughts

As a result, individuals with a preference for Extraversion tend to spend more time initiating and externally processing, whereas those with a preference for Introversion tend to spend more time in the inner world receiving and reflecting.

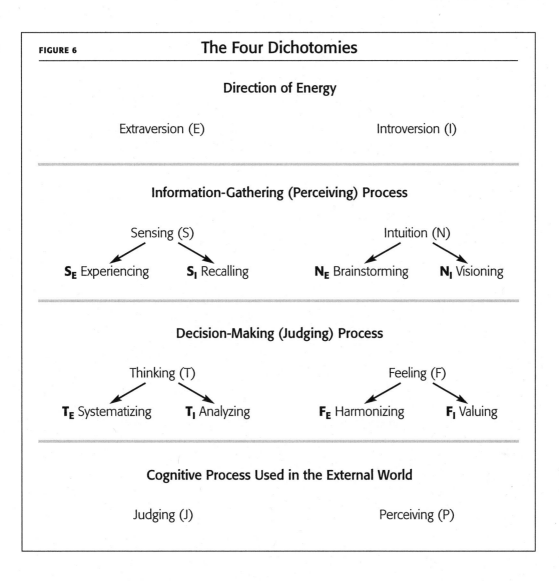

Time Out!

Each process (Sensing, Intuition, Thinking, and Feeling) can be directed externally, as denoted by a subscript E, as in S_E, or internally, as denoted by a subscript I, as in S_I. Functions that have an external orientation (Experiencing, Brainstorming, Systematizing, and Harmonizing) tend to focus more on external events. Functions that have an internal orientation (Recalling, Visioning, Analyzing, and Valuing) tend to focus more on internal interpretation.

Foul!

We have to live in both worlds! Having a preference for Extraversion does not mean that an individual never reflects and allows his or her energy to move inward. In the same way, having a preference for Introversion does not mean that an individual never comes out to interact! It is a matter of where the energy primarily flows most naturally.

EXERCISE 25
Assessing Working Style

The diagrams on the following page integrate temperament, functions, dichotomies, and working style. We will move through them step by step from top to bottom. The end result will be your working style code, which is equivalent to your MBTI type. For each temperament you will notice a partial working style code. These indicate, respectively, that Artisans tend to use Sensing and Perceiving (_S_P); Guardians, Sensing and Judging (_S_J); Rationals, Intuition and Thinking (_NT_); and Idealists, Intuition and Feeling (_NF_).

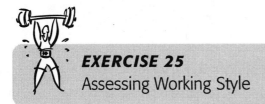

Working Style Profile Worksheet

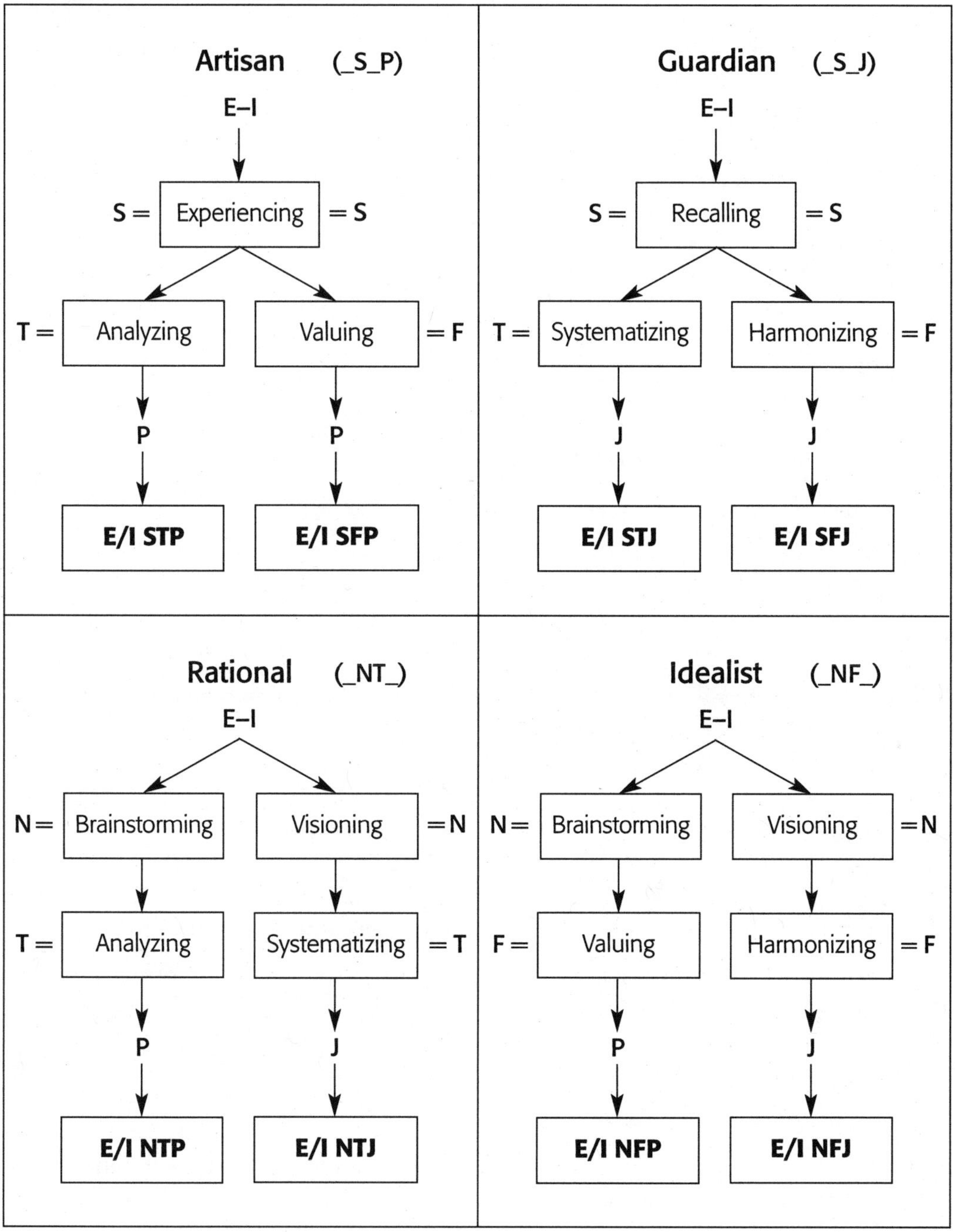

1. Temperament (Artisan, Guardian, Rational, Idealist)

   Review the information on temperament in chapter 1 and put an *X* in one of the checkboxes below to indicate your best-fit temperament. If you are vacillating between two, mark both with an *X*.

   My temperament is: ☐ **Artisan** ☐ **Guardian** ☐ **Rational** ☐ **Idealist**

   Circle the temperament you selected on the Working Style Profile Worksheet on page 99.

2. Extraversion or Introversion Preference

   Now look at the Extraversion and Introversion dichotomy, represented by *E–I* in the diagrams. Review the characteristic behaviors associated with an Extraversion or Introversion orientation in the table below.

Extraversion and Introversion Dichotomy

Individuals with an Extraversion Preference	Individuals with an Introversion Preference
Are drawn to the *external* world	Are drawn to the *internal* world
Are often drawn out to interact	Are often pulled in to reflect
Act first and then think (initiate)	Think first and then act (respond)
Process information in the external environment—talk everything over	Process information in the internal world—think everything over
May be easier to read—self-disclose readily	May be harder to read—share personal information with few, close people
May talk more than listen	May listen more than talk
May communicate with enthusiasm	May keep enthusiasm to self
May use more expressive body language	May use more reserved body language
May respond quickly with a verbal stream of consciousness	May respond after taking time to think—more deliberate speaking pattern

Put an *X* in the checkbox next to the orientation that seems most like you below.

My orientation is: ☐ **Extraversion (E)** ☐ **Introversion (I)**

Circle your selection, *E* or *I*, on the Working Style Profile Worksheet beneath the temperament you selected earlier.

3. Sensing or Intuition Preference (Perceiving/Gathering Information)

   As we saw in chapter 2, we use two main processes to gather information: Sensing (concrete) and Intuition (abstract). We also saw that each of these processes includes two functions: Experiencing/Recalling (Sensing) or Brainstorming/Visioning (Intuition). Now go back to exercise 16 (pp. 58–60) and review which of these functions you identify with most to determine which information-gathering process, Sensing or Intuition, you prefer. Indicate your preference by putting an *X* in the appropriate checkbox below. The definitions are also included in exercise 24 in this chapter.

   My information-gathering process is:

   ☐ **Sensing (S)** ☐ **Intuition (N)**

   Circle your selection—*S* or *N*—on the Working Style Profile Worksheet.

Coaching Point

As we continue through the worksheet, don't worry if the processes you select do not correspond with your temperament. We will provide more ideas to help you clarify your choices later in the chapter.

4. Thinking or Feeling Preference (Judging/Making Decisions)

   As we also saw in chapter 2, we use two main processes to make decisions: Thinking (objective) and Feeling (subjective). Each process includes two functions: Systematizing/Analyzing (Thinking) or Harmonizing/Valuing (Feeling). Now go back to exercise 20 (pp. 73–75) and review which of these functions you identify with most to determine which decision-making process, Thinking or Feeling, you prefer. Indicate your preference by putting an *X* in the appropriate checkbox below. The definitions are also included in exercise 24 in this chapter.

   My decision-making process is:

   ☐ **Thinking (T)** ☐ **Feeling (F)**

   Circle your selection—*T* or *F*—on the Working Style Profile Worksheet.

Coaching Point

Again, don't worry if the process you selected does not correspond with your temperament or information-gathering function—mark it anyway. We will provide additional guidance later in this chapter.

5. Judging or Perceiving Preference

The final dichotomy, Judging and Perceiving (J–P), was added to Jung's typology by Myers and Briggs to help explain which process individuals extravert, or use in the external world.

- Individuals with a Judging (J) preference prefer to use their judging process in the external world; Systematizing (T_E) and Harmonizing (F_E) are the external judging functions.
- Individuals with a Perceiving (P) preference prefer to use their perceiving process in the external world; Experiencing (S_E) and Brainstorming (N_E) are the external perceiving functions.

Using a function in the external world can mean that it is more visible, resulting in some of the characteristics associated with Judging and Perceiving. Individuals who have a Judging preference prefer to achieve closure, make decisions, and make plans through either Systematizing (organizing resources to achieve an end goal) or Harmonizing (making decisions to achieve group harmony). Individuals with a Judging preference tend to make a plan and stick to it.

Individuals who have a Perceiving preference prefer to remain flexible and open to possibilities and enjoy the exploration process using either Experiencing (exploring options from current concrete data) or Brainstorming (moving outward to generate possibilities and infer future patterns and meanings). Individuals with a Perceiving preference either make decisions and change them easily (Artisans) or keep their options open and postpone making decisions while they gather more data (Idealists and Rationals).

The general characteristics associated with the Judging and Perceiving preferences are listed in the following table.

Judging and Perceiving Dichotomy

Individuals with a Judging Preference	Individuals with a Perceiving Preference
Use Harmonizing or Systematizing	Use Experiencing or Brainstorming
Are most comfortable after a decision has been made and then stick to it	Are most comfortable leaving options open or quick to change if circumstances change
Set goals and work toward achieving them on time	Change goals as information becomes available
Prefer knowing what events are coming up	Like adapting to new situations
Finish the task in a structured manner and enjoy the result	Enjoy the process and complete the task in order to move on to the next project
Derive satisfaction from finishing projects	Derive satisfaction from starting projects
Take deadlines seriously: time is finite	See deadlines as elastic: time is a renewable resource
Push for closure	Like "going with the flow"
Tend to schedule time, plan, and organize	Tend to be more spontaneous

Put an *X* in the checkbox next to the preference that seems most like you below.

My preference is: ☐ **Judging (J)** ☐ **Perceiving (P)**

Circle *J* or *P* on the Working Style Profile Worksheet.

Team Dynamics from the Inside Out

- *Artisans* have a Perceiving preference—they often make a decision and then change it as new information becomes available.
- *Guardians* have a Judging preference—let's not change just for the sake of change!
- *Rationals* have either a Judging (Systematizing) or a Perceiving (Brainstorming) preference—some are very structured and drive for closure, while others prefer to stay open to new information.
- *Idealists* have either a Judging (Harmonizing) or a Perceiving (Brainstorming) preference—some organize to achieve harmony around them, while others adapt to information as it becomes available.

6. Based on your self-assessment, circle one preference of each dichotomy below and then enter the four-letter working style.

E–I S–N T–F J–P ___ ___ ___ ___

End of Exercise

Validating Working Style

If you have finished working your way down the diagram, congratulations! Read the relevant working style descriptions that follow to validate your assessment. If the description of the style you selected sounds accurate, then you have correctly identified your working style. If not, then read descriptions of other versions of the same temperament or of different styles. Later you can also try the troubleshooting guide in exercise 27 (pp. 124–30).

The working style descriptions on the following pages reflect the temperaments that access certain functions including those you selected. For instance, if you identify the Recalling and Systematizing functions, yet selected the Rational temperament, you may want to review Guardian/STJ. You may also want to review the cognitive process questionnaires in exercises 16 and 20 (pp. 58–60 and 73–75). You can also benefit from the two exercises at the end of this chapter: exercise 26, "Background Influences on Developing Functions," and exercise 27, "What Is Your Best-Fit Working Style?"

Working Style Descriptions

The following descriptions of working styles (table 7) include both information on each temperament and a brief overview of the hierarchy of functions mentioned earlier. Understanding your individual hierarchy of functions will provide you with a greater insight to your own strengths and weaknesses.

Coaching Point

Remember, these descriptions describe certain general patterns of behavior only! No one is going to find a complete match, with everything in agreement. Look for the working style that appears to be the best fit for you!

Keep reading until you think you have found the best fit. Remember, no one working style description can fit every person—use other reference sources (listed in appendix 2 and the bibliography) to find additional descriptions for validating type.

Table 7 Working Style Descriptions

Working Style	ESTP: Extraverted Tacticians *(Team Asset: Immediate Action)*
Description	**Extraverted Tacticians** are high-energy, action-oriented, quick-thinking, objective decision makers. Their focus on making things happen can make them appear impatient with slow-moving, theoretical discussions and concepts. They are direct, and their word choice focuses on getting to the point. They possess intense observation skills, can tune in to what's happening in the moment, are acutely aware of nonverbal cues, and then respond as needed. They think so rapidly that their words are often left behind, as they push on for a result or to make an impact. They constantly find new ways of doing things. Sometimes perceived as uncaring by their team members, they nonetheless protect the people who are important to them.
Temperament	**Artisan.** Tend to act in the moment, be noticed, and produce immediate, tangible results.
Direction of Energy	**Extraversion.** Energy flows outward; tend to process externally and initiate interaction.
First Function (Adult)	**Experiencing.** Are capable of rapid intake of sensory data from the external environment in the moment; possess acute awareness of specifics and realities in the world around them.
Second Function (Parent)	**Analyzing.** Make decisions using internal logical criteria and principles; analyze how and why things work.
Third Function (Child)	**Harmonizing.** Are aware of subjective criteria to optimize group interaction; may be gregarious and empathetic.
Fourth Function (Balancing)	**Visioning.** Occasionally information comes to them as a complete idea or approach; will verify with sensory data. When under stress, might mistakenly perceive doom and gloom.
Strengths on a Team	• Have optimistic, can-do attitude • Are excellent negotiators: play to win • Are realistic, hands-on, logical problem solvers • Are action-oriented implementers
Potential Challenges on a Team	• May get bored easily if concrete progress is not made • May work around rules and not get to the root cause of a problem • May act autonomously, "call their own shots"
Leadership Qualities	• Are able to think on their feet • Focus on action • Recognize opportunities quickly and get things moving—roll up their sleeves and get involved
Favored Working Environment	• Want lots of freedom and fun • Want as few rules as possible and the opportunity to take risks
Working Environment Dislikes	• Dislike hearing a lot of complaining • Dislike talking things through without seeing any action

Table 7 Working Style Descriptions (cont'd)

Working Style	ISTP: Introverted Tacticians *(Team Asset: Hands-On Analysis)*
Description	**Introverted Tacticians** live in the present and act in the moment to get to root causes and solve problems. They are the most analytical of the Artisans, enjoying theoretical constructs with practical reasoning. They can absorb large amounts of impersonal data and have a high affinity for numbers. They thrive on variety and focus on doing what needs to be done with the least amount of fuss. They will change direction readily as additional information becomes available and maneuver systems to meet their needs. They are adept with tools and are able to reason impersonally and objectively. They may alienate their teammates with their apparent manipulation, but then working in teams is a game to them.
Temperament	**Artisan.** Tend to act in the moment, be noticed, and produce immediate, tangible results.
Direction of Energy	**Introversion.** Energy flows inward; tend to process, reflect, and respond to interaction.
First Function (Adult)	**Analyzing.** Make decisions using internal logical criteria and principles; analyze how and why things work. Always approach data from an independent perspective, with their own logical point of view.
Second Function (Parent)	**Experiencing.** Capable of rapid intake of sensory data from the external environment in the moment; possess acute awareness of specifics and realities in the world around them.
Third Function (Child)	**Visioning.** Occasionally information will come to them as complete idea or approach, particularly when solving problems; will verify with sensory data.
Fourth Function (Balancing)	**Harmonizing.** Will be aware of subjective criteria to optimize group interaction. When under stress, may show emotional reactions such as anger and frustration with sharp outbursts; may be uncomfortable with displays of emotion from others.
Strengths on a Team	• Are confident, independent, and determined • Believe in economy of effort • Are concretely analytical—can dissect arguments • Are naturally adept with tools and numbers
Potential Challenges on a Team	• May be overly critical and cynical when questioning to clarify logic • May lack long-term vision and an understanding of how their behavior affects others • May appear indifferent to others' needs
Leadership Qualities	• Are great tactical troubleshooters • Expect a tolerance for ambiguity from team • Are willing to gamble for big stakes
Favored Working Environment	• Prefer working solo with the ability to fight fires at will • Like a variety of short-term projects
Working Environment Dislikes	• Dislike working with team members who display intense emotional reactions • Dislike working with individuals who are overly structured and controlling

Table 7 Working Style Descriptions (cont'd)

Working Style	ESFP: Extraverted Improvisors *(Team Assets: Fun, Spirit)*
Description	**Extraverted Improvisors** are colorful, free-spirited, and people focused. Using their acute sensory inputs, they make decisions based on what is in alignment with their internal value system. They are interested in people and new experiences, enjoy working in groups, and live in the moment. They are generous of spirit, active, talkative, and flexible. Their natural exuberance attracts others, as they get the task done with the maximum amount of fun and minimum amount of fuss. They enjoy a variety of activities, especially social or physical ones. They work best in flexible, unstructured environments. Their tendency to see the light-hearted side may make other team members want them to be more serious.
Temperament	**Artisan.** Tend to act in the moment, be noticed, and produce immediate, tangible results.
Direction of Energy	**Extraversion.** Energy flows outward; tend to process externally and initiate interaction.
First Function (Adult)	**Experiencing.** Are capable of rapid intake of sensory data from the external environment in the moment; possess acute awareness of specifics and realities in the world around them.
Second Function (Parent)	**Valuing.** Make decisions quietly but firmly based on their own internal belief system; guided by strong inner values and wish life to be in congruence with their beliefs. Tolerant of differences and adaptable until their value system is crossed; then can appear rigid.
Third Function (Child)	**Systematizing.** Will make some decisions using logical criteria to plan and organize details and events in the external environment.
Fourth Function (Balancing)	**Visioning.** Occasionally information will come to them as a complete idea or approach; will verify with sensory data. Ideas may pop into their head. When under stress, may get stuck in the moment and be unable to step back.
Strengths on a Team	• Have optimistic, can-do attitude • Are friendly, energetic, generous, and people focused • Use practical problem solving—pick up possible issues quickly • Interact easily with different team members
Potential Challenges on a Team	• May get bored easily if work appears to be impractical • May appear to be too playful and not serious about work • May try to juggle too many projects
Leadership Qualities	• Are informal, social, and easygoing, with a focus on concrete results • Seek quick results and foster collaboration • Are excellent at stimulating the team to perform and encouraging teammates
Favored Working Environment	• Look for freedom and challenges • Want the opportunity to work in a group setting
Working Environment Dislikes	• Dislike excess structure and process • Dislike working on long-term, abstract issues

Table 7 Working Style Descriptions (cont'd)

Working Style	ISFP: Introverted Improvisors *(Team Asset: Relaxed Attitude)*
Description	**Introverted Improvisors** live in the present and prize the freedom to follow their own course. They are true to people and things that are important to them. They often appear unassuming, easygoing, gentle, and soft-spoken. They will provide help in tangible ways and, with their observation skills, have a gift for expressing abstract things concretely. Their playful sense of humor may not be seen until they are comfortable with their co-workers. They will adapt well to new situations and approach life from a "don't worry, be happy" perspective. In teams, their tendency to be "laid back" in their approach can be viewed as lack of interest or direction.
Temperament	**Artisan.** Tend to act in the moment, be noticed, and produce immediate, tangible results.
Direction of Energy	**Introversion.** Energy flows inward; tend to process, reflect, and respond to interaction.
First Function (Adult)	**Valuing.** Make decisions quietly but firmly based on their own internal belief system; guided by strong inner values and wish life to be in congruence with their beliefs. Tolerant of individual differences and easygoing until those values are challenged.
Second Function (Parent)	**Experiencing.** Are capable of rapid intake of sensory data from the external environment in the moment; possess acute awareness of specifics and realities in the world around them.
Third Function (Child)	**Visioning.** Occasionally information will come to them as a complete idea or approach; will verify with sensory data. Ideas will suddenly appear to them.
Fourth Function (Balancing)	**Systematizing.** Will make some decisions using logical criteria to plan and organize details and events in the external environment. When under stress, they may obsess about details and creating organization.
Strengths on a Team	• Contribute deep loyalty to the team • Are easygoing but have the ability to provide sensible solutions to practical problems • Display a quiet sense of fun • Are humane, with the ability to persuade others in a nonconfrontational way
Potential Challenges on a Team	• May not speak up about what they want • May appear indecisive when internally evaluating fairness criteria • May withdraw from situations involving anger and tension and not address core issues
Leadership Qualities	• Create supportive, egalitarian atmosphere • Set realistic, achievable goals • Lead by doing rather than telling and adapt quickly to external changes
Favored Working Environment	• Like close, informal relationships in a physically pleasing environment • Prefer a flexible environment with few rules
Working Environment Dislikes	• Dislike interpersonal conflict • Dislike having to plan and organize activities with fixed deadlines

Table 7 Working Style Descriptions (cont'd)

Working Style	ESTJ: Extraverted Organizers *(Team Assets: Planning, Getting Results)*
Description	**Extraverted Organizers** are detail-oriented, high-energy decision makers. They strive for closure with the aim of organizing, planning, and structuring the external environment. The most driven of the Guardians, they take action to get things done in a systematic and consistent way. They take an objective approach to problem solving and can be tough when the situation demands. They enjoy activity that produces tangible results and are adept at creating systems that assign responsibilities and allocate resources. They enjoy interacting with others, especially around games and team activities. As team members, they set high standards and have a clear internal sense of "right and wrong."
Temperament	**Guardian.** Want to be part of a group or a team, fulfill responsibilities, and make a contribution.
Direction of Energy	**Extraversion.** Energy flows outward; tend to process externally and initiate interaction.
First Function (Adult)	**Systematizing.** Make decisions to achieve goals using logical criteria to plan and organize details and events in the external environment. Adept at sequencing tasks and resources with a strong push for closure; very action oriented.
Second Function (Parent)	**Recalling.** Gather information by referring back to a rich data bank of past sensory experiences, which they compare and contrast to the present. Able to bring the best of the past into the future; monitor and evaluate for realism.
Third Function (Child)	**Brainstorming.** Exhibit some external exploration of future possibilities, patterns, and meaning, building on concrete, experience-based information.
Fourth Function (Balancing)	**Valuing.** May consider their internal values and beliefs, but decisions will be subservient to logical criteria. When under stress, they rigidly adhere to "right and wrong."
Strengths on a Team	• Contribute hard work to complete activities • Are economical with resources • Have ability to set up and implement systems • See the right way to get the job done and focus on timely completion
Potential Challenges on a Team	• May dismiss ideas that they perceive to be impractical • May be too driven for closure and uncomfortable with ambiguity • May ignore team members' feelings in their push to complete the work
Leadership Qualities	• Have a confident, down-to-earth approach • Set clear, measurable targets with implementation plans • Respect systems and procedures for monitoring performance
Favored Working Environment	• Prefer an environment where they can make things happen • Like a structured role working with experienced team members
Working Environment Dislikes	• Dislike it when team members are sloppy and "break the rules" • Dislike constant change with no access to reliable data

Table 7 Working Style Descriptions (cont'd)

Working Style	ISTJ: Introverted Organizers *(Team Assets: Process, Structure)*
Description	**Introverted Organizers** are logical, practical, organized, and thorough. They rely on past experience for creating concrete action plans. They create processes and procedures to smooth workflow, eliminate redundancy, and achieve economy of effort. They are loyal and dutiful and work steadily to ensure that commitments are met on time. They tend to want time alone and may appear serious and orderly. They trust facts, are task oriented, and can manage extensive detail. They work hard at whatever they do and once they learn a skill, perform it with competence. As team members, they are dedicated and committed but may frustrate their colleagues with their sequential, one-thing-at-a-time approach combined with a reluctance to change.
Temperament	**Guardian.** Need to be part of a group or a team, fulfill responsibilities, and make a contribution.
Direction of Energy	**Introversion.** Energy flows inward; tend to process, reflect, and respond to interaction.
First Function (Adult)	**Recalling.** Gather information by referring back to a rich data bank of past sensory experiences, which they compare and contrast to the present. Able to bring the best of the past forward and audit the reality of any given situation.
Second Function (Parent)	**Systematizing.** Make decisions using logical criteria to plan and organize details and events in the external environment. Sequence events and resources to achieve goals in a timely manner.
Third Function (Child)	**Valuing.** May consider their internal values and beliefs but base decisions on logical criteria.
Fourth Function (Balancing)	**Brainstorming.** Exhibit some external exploration of future possibilities, patterns, and meaning, building on previously experienced events. When under stress, they may derive distorted patterns and meanings and foresee doom and gloom.
Strengths on a Team	• Are quiet, dedicated, and organized; have great follow-through skills • Are thorough, dependable, and trustworthy • Are no-nonsense, hard-working team members who deliver on responsibilities given clearly defined roles • Give meticulous attention to detail; aim for perfection
Potential Challenges on a Team	• May be rigid with time schedules and rules; go by the book • Instead of delegating, may get bogged down in details • May neglect the big picture and people when focused on task completion
Leadership Qualities	• Conduct thorough and thoughtful planning of team activities • Set clear targets and define clear accountabilities • Guard against waste and can make tough decisions
Favored Working Environment	• Like being teamed with hardworking, organized people who understand the importance of completing projects on time • Need periods of alone time to focus on their own deliverables
Working Environment Dislikes	• Dislike unstructured environments with minimally defined or constantly changing goals • Dislike teams that crave lots of personal interaction and "touchy-feely" activities

Table 7 Working Style Descriptions (cont'd)

Working Style	ESFJ: Extraverted Protectors *(Team Asset: Cohesiveness)*
Description	**Extraverted Protectors** are warm, personable, and outgoing. They enjoy harmonious team environments, working within that structure to ensure that organization is established and responsibilities are met. They are conscientious and loyal and value security and stability. They use information from their extensive data bank of past sensory experiences to apply in their concrete, task-focused work. They are energized by being with others and are genuinely interested in others' lives and concerns. They enjoy participating in committees and are good at organizing celebrations and preserving traditions. Sometimes they may overload themselves with responsibilities.
Temperament	**Guardian.** Need to be part of a group or a team, fulfill responsibilities, and make a contribution.
Direction of Energy	**Extraversion.** Energy flows outward; tend to process externally and initiate interaction.
First Function (Adult)	**Harmonizing.** Make decisions using subjective criteria to optimize group harmony. Sensitive to other people's wants and needs. Self-disclose to connect and may show emotions on face when stressed.
Second Function (Parent)	**Recalling.** Gather information by referring to a rich data bank of past sensory experiences, which they compare and contrast to the present. Able to audit events and data for realism.
Third Function (Child)	**Brainstorming.** Exhibit some external exploration of future possibilities, patterns, and meaning, building on concrete, experiential information.
Fourth Function (Balancing)	**Analyzing.** May compare and contrast data against an internal model, but this will be superseded by appropriateness to the group. When under stress, they can appear overly critical, questioning logic and rationale.
Strengths on a Team	• Are energetic, enthusiastic, and warm • Like helping others who want to help them in return • Are aware of, and cater to, others' needs • Are responsible and focus on building team cohesiveness
Potential Challenges on a Team	• May avoid conflict • May make decisions based on individuals' needs and appear illogical at times • May seem too talkative as they involve others in team activities
Leadership Qualities	• Use discussion to achieve consensus • Give and expect personal loyalty and hard work • Are ready with positive feedback for good work and advice if team members are facing issues
Favored Working Environment	• Prefer a culture that is organized and somewhat predictable • Like a structure where their people skills can contribute to tangible results
Working Environment Dislikes	• Dislike conflict and backbiting • Dislike hearing criticism

Table 7 Working Style Descriptions (cont'd)

Working Style	ISFJ: Introverted Protectors *(Team Assets: Support, Dependability)*
Description	**Introverted Protectors** are stable, supportive, empathetic team members who work tirelessly behind the scenes to achieve team goals. They take care of possessions and are economical with resources. From traditions and past experience they make decisions that will meet the needs of the group. When communicating, they follow a detailed, sequential thought process and tend to establish orderly procedures. They enjoy helping others, are dependable and considerate, and gravitate to roles that involve service to others. Maintaining the cohesiveness of the team and living up to their responsibilities are fundamental to the way they operate. As team members, they have to be careful that they are not taken advantage of, because they will do tasks for others in such an unassuming way that their efforts go unnoticed.
Temperament	**Guardian.** Need to be part of a group or a team, fulfill responsibilities, and make a contribution.
Direction of Energy	**Introversion.** Energy flows inward; tend to process, reflect, and respond to interaction.
First Function (Adult)	**Recalling.** Gather information by referring back to a rich data bank of past sensory experiences, which they compare and contrast to the present. Able to bring a realistic assessment to current tasks.
Second Function (Parent)	**Harmonizing.** Make decisions using subjective criteria to optimize group harmony; sensitive to, and considerate of, other people's feelings.
Third Function (Child)	**Analyzing.** May compare and contrast data against an internal model, but this will be superseded by appropriateness to the group.
Fourth Function (Balancing)	**Brainstorming.** Exhibit some external exploration of future possibilities, patterns, and meaning, building on past sensory experience. When under stress, may negatively fantasize and perceive "doom and gloom."
Strengths on a Team	• Are conscientious; will probably pick up tasks that others have dropped • Work steadily to plan and follow through on team activities • Look after others on the team within an established structure • Are strong tactical implementers who use contingency planning
Potential Challenges on a Team	• May worry too much about events • May not assert their own needs; instead may become resentful • May be uncomfortable with confrontation
Leadership Qualities	• Provide clear targets with a consideration for what others like to do • Establish a clear structure with defined roles and responsibilities • Prefer a democratic leadership style using concrete facts and data
Favored Working Environment	• Prefer a relatively stable, supportive environment • Like the opportunity to plan, prepare, and have ample private time for regeneration
Working Environment Dislikes	• Dislike highly competitive, confrontational cultures • Dislike constant change with no positive feedback

Table 7 Working Style Descriptions (cont'd)

Working Style	ENTP: Extraverted Innovators *(Team Assets: Debate, Ideas)*
Description	**Extraverted Innovators** are normally quick thinking, verbally expressive, and focused on future opportunities. They thrive on looking at concepts and possibilities from multiple angles and then arguing their own philosophy or hypothesis. They are optimistic, gregarious, and social. They enjoy debate and can be very persuasive. They naturally generate options and then are able to analyze them strategically, which makes them creative, abstract problem solvers. They are enterprising and resourceful, but they may have difficulty in the implementation of ideas. As team members they are upbeat and enthusiastic, but their need to take center stage and challenge others' viewpoints can wear down those around them.
Temperament	**Rational.** Tend to be competent and knowledgeable; seek to understand the operating principles in any system and strive to create their own destiny.
Direction of Energy	**Extraversion.** Energy flows outward; tend to process externally and initiate interaction.
First Function (Adult)	**Brainstorming.** Involved in constant external exploration of future possibilities, patterns, and meanings. Read between the lines, with the ability to look at situations from fresh, new angles; like to bounce ideas around.
Second Function (Parent)	**Analyzing.** Make decisions using internal logical criteria and principles; analyze how and why things work. Evaluate and sort against a mental model to achieve improvements. Possess a clear point of view, which they are able to defend against differing perspectives.
Third Function (Child)	**Harmonizing.** Are aware of subjective criteria to optimize group interaction; may play the role of social organizer.
Fourth Function (Balancing)	**Recalling.** May go back to past data to compare and contrast possibilities. When under stress, may get stuck on what went wrong and project that into the future.
Strengths on a Team	• Are great at providing energy and thrust to new projects • Are naturally optimistic and future focused • Rely on abstract data to infer solutions to problems—look at problems from a fresh perspective • Are self-confident and assertive, with an ability to argue both sides of an issue
Potential Challenges on a Team	• May talk too much as they externally process ideas and possibilities; could benefit from learning to think before speaking • May not be able to track details, as they overextend to explore multiple possibilities • May appear arrogant when holding center stage to present their viewpoint
Leadership Qualities	• Create logical arguments for innovative approaches • Look beyond the conventional solution and challenge team members to believe in other possibilities • Can be generous with praise, persuasive, and dismissive of unnecessary bureaucracy
Favored Working Environment	• Like bright people who are willing to try new things • Prefer experts who need little day-to-day direction
Working Environment Dislikes	• Dislike a culture with excess structure or traditional ways of operating • Dislike excessive focus on detail-specific directions

Table 7 Working Style Descriptions (cont'd)

Working Style	INTP: Introverted Innovators *(Team Asset: Logical Improvement)*
Description	**Introverted Innovators** spend their lives in a quest for logical purity and accuracy. Using abstract data from ideas and future possibilities, they analyze this information to create their argument or to improve a system. They possess an insight into complex theories and constantly search for patterns and systems to internally categorize data. They often function autonomously as they absorb themselves in mastering and perfecting their theories. They possess a unique ability to dissect complexities and comprehend conceptual subtleties. They enjoy creating theoretical solutions but then may struggle with their implementation. As team members, they may appear distanced from the "real" world and too intense, although they prove to be excellent strategists.
Temperament	**Rational.** Tend to be competent and knowledgeable; seek to understand the operating principles in any system and strive to create their own destiny.
Direction of Energy	**Introversion.** Energy flows inward; tend to process, reflect, and respond to interaction.
First Function (Adult)	**Analyzing.** Make decisions using internal logical criteria and principles; analyze how and why things work. Evaluate and sort against a mental model to improve the operation of the system. Able to dissect arguments and data to assess validity and to come up with a completely different logical perspective.
Second Function (Parent)	**Brainstorming.** Are able to explore future possibilities, patterns, and meanings and to read between the lines to see trends and form theories.
Third Function (Child)	**Recalling.** May explore past experiences with photo albums, genealogies, historical visits, etc.
Fourth Function (Balancing)	**Harmonizing.** Are aware of how people are feeling and appear "laid back" and empathetic. Under stress, may be oblivious to what is appropriate for group interaction.
Strengths on a Team	• Contribute an alternative, logical, detached perspective • Use precision in communication—exactly the right nuance for any given situation • Easily create theoretical systems to explain how and why things work • Are great researchers, as they integrate new and complex data into their unique and multifaceted models
Potential Challenges on a Team	• May not see need to meet deadlines if project can still be improved • May be skeptical and overly analytical and struggle with practical implementation • May confuse others with overly long, complex explanations
Leadership Qualities	• Expect people to take responsibility for their own actions; let team members define objectives and work toward achieving them independently • Constantly challenge the status quo; contribute quality ideas • Tend to focus on abstract systems and models in diagnosing and understanding team performance
Favored Working Environment	• Want consistent access to new, cutting-edge projects • Need freedom to explore how things work and to generate new ideas
Working Environment Dislikes	• Dislike routine tasks that require detailed, concrete application and have tight deadlines • Dislike working with nonexpert team members or dealing with content that might be viewed as redundant

Table 7 Working Style Descriptions (cont'd)

Working Style	ENTJ: Extraverted Marshallers *(Team Asset: Strategic Planning)*
Description	**Extraverted Marshallers** are direct and organized and possess a strong desire to make their inner visions a reality. They are quick-thinking, strategic, logical decision makers possessing a drive for closure. They value intelligence and competence and abhor inefficiency. They conceptualize and theorize readily and have the ability to take charge and make things happen. They exude confidence and appear energetic and driven. They are aware of intricate connections, which they can explain with a logical model. As team members, they want to ensure that the team is working efficiently to produce results and may appear uncomfortable with emotional issues.
Temperament	**Rational.** Tend to be competent and knowledgeable; seek to understand the operating principles in any system and strive to create their own destiny.
Direction of Energy	**Extraversion.** Energy flows outward; tend to process externally and initiate interaction.
First Function (Adult)	**Systematizing.** Make decisions using logical criteria to achieve goals by planning and organizing details and events in the external environment. Adept at marshalling resources to achieve goals in the most expedient manner; have a strong push for closure.
Second Function (Parent)	**Visioning.** Gather information by absorbing data, mentally stepping back, and allowing the complete picture to form.
Third Function (Child)	**Experiencing.** May observe and gather sensory data as a support for the future picture. May explore using the function in such activities as art, exercise, or hobbies.
Fourth Function (Balancing)	**Valuing.** May consider their internal values and beliefs but base decisions on logical criteria. When under stress, may be rigid in defending principles.
Strengths on a Team	• Create an organized, systematic approach to defining plans and outcomes • Are decisive, clear, direct, and assertive in their communication • Think in terms of systems and models to achieve an objective or solve a problem • Assemble resources and drive others to participate
Potential Challenges on a Team	• May be perceived as controlling as they push to achieve closure • May be direct and to the point, to the extent of being offensive • May appear cold, impersonal, and somewhat oblivious to interpersonal interaction
Leadership Qualities	• Sell long-term directions and ideas boldly to others • Thrive on building plans to achieve complex, long-term outcomes • Constantly strive to make decisions using their strong presence
Favored Working Environment	• Like committed people who deliver results and are assertive with their own needs • Prefer a culture that encourages independence and autonomy
Working Environment Dislikes	• Dislike team members who appear overly emotional or unenthusiastic • Dislike working in a cautious culture in which nontraditional decision making is discouraged

Table 7 Working Style Descriptions (cont'd)

Working Style	INTJ: Introverted Marshallers *(Team Asset: Independent Perspective)*
Description	**Introverted Marshallers** approach life with an independent, long-term vision coming from their internal world of ideas. While they develop abstract visions, they put concrete action plans in place to achieve their goals. They offer a detached, objective perspective with a propensity for original thought, as they see patterns in external events. With their ability to categorize data, they are confident in their ideas and their ability to achieve outcomes. They are determined to achieve high standards of performance. As team members, they may not reveal their inner emotions, but they can be deeply loyal to the team and can always be relied on for a neutral, independent opinion.
Temperament	**Rational.** Tend to be competent and knowledgeable; seek to understand the operating principles in any systems and strive to create their own destiny.
Direction of Energy	**Introversion.** Energy flows inward; tend to process, reflect, and respond to interaction.
First Function (Adult)	**Visioning.** Gather information by absorbing data, mentally stepping back, and allowing the complete picture to form. Often able to suggest breakthrough approaches.
Second Function (Parent)	**Systematizing.** Make decisions using logical criteria and achieve goals by planning and organizing details and events in the external environment. When their future picture is complete, they are adept at organizing resources to achieve the desired result.
Third Function (Child)	**Valuing.** May observe and gather sensory data as a support to the future picture. When an action goes against their value system, will explain in clear, logical terms.
Fourth Function (Balancing)	**Experiencing.** May consider their internal values and beliefs but base decisions on logical criteria. When under stress, may become overabsorbed in sensory data.
Strengths on a Team	• Provide an innovative, independent, and original perspective • Are conceptual long-range thinkers with an ability to relate the parts to the overall picture • Create general structures and devise strategies to achieve goals • Use cause-and-effect logic to organize and integrate ideas
Potential Challenges on a Team	• May become impatient with those who do not see their vision quickly enough • May appear rigid with ideas and insist on having their own way • May become aloof and abrupt when trying to influence team members about their future picture
Leadership Qualities	• Create a challenging framework for the future • Aid teammates through developmental coaching; can be tough when necessary • Present a strategy with a focus on excellence and performance
Favored Working Environment	• Enjoy working with a team of equally talented individuals • Value a high degree of autonomy and independence
Working Environment Dislikes	• Dislike working with individuals who need extensive positive feedback • Dislike a detail-focused, rule-based environment where there is no opportunity for independent decision making

Table 7 Working Style Descriptions (cont'd)

Working Style	ENFP: Extraverted Advocates *(Team Assets: Enthusiasm, People Focus)*
Description	**Extraverted Advocates** are energetic, spontaneous, warm-hearted individuals who constantly generate creative, ingenious options for the future. They see endless possibilities for the people around them. They love abstract concepts and are able to see beyond the obvious to the hidden meanings and patterns. Their strong inner values guide their decision making. They are empathetic, supportive, engaging, and keenly perceptive about others, and use their verbal fluency to persuade and influence those around them. As team members, they are enthusiastic and committed to the relationships that are important to them, although they sometimes frustrate their colleagues with their lack of concrete focus and their seemingly impractical ideas.
Temperament	**Idealist.** Need to have a purpose and make a meaningful contribution to the greater good; value potential, connection, and unique identity.
Direction of Energy	**Extraversion.** Energy flows outward; tend to process externally and initiate interaction.
First Function (Adult)	**Brainstorming.** Involved in constant external exploration of future possibilities, patterns, and meanings. Favor verbal discussion of possibilities and have an ability to read between the lines.
Second Function (Parent)	**Valuing.** Make decisions quietly but firmly based on their own internal belief system. Guided by strong inner values and try to live accordingly. Tolerant of differences until those values are crossed; then they can appear rigid.
Third Function (Child)	**Systematizing.** Will make some decisions using logical criteria to plan and organize details and events in the external environment. May enjoy organizing such things as dinner parties and social events.
Fourth Function (Balancing)	**Recalling.** May refer back to past data to compare and contrast. When under stress, may project negative past experiences into the future inappropriately.
Strengths on a Team	• Are quick thinking and verbally expressive in exploring new ideas • Have zest for life and enthusiasm for the cause, group, or team • Act as a catalyst or crusader for new ideas • Generate creative possibilities
Potential Challenges on a Team	• May appear scattered as they take on multiple projects • May be reluctant to close the door on opportunities and, therefore, leave too many options open • May miss detailed implementation steps and fail to follow through on ideas
Leadership Qualities	• Inspire belief in possibilities and create an open, participative environment • Believe in the value of what each individual can contribute • Share tasks with an informal, collegial approach versus a top-down directing style
Favored Working Environment	• Like it when creativity is supported • Value the human element in the workplace
Working Environment Dislikes	• Dislike rules and a formalized, logical structure for achieving results • Dislike power struggles or the implementation of plans that might be adverse to people's interests

Table 7 Working Style Descriptions (cont'd)

Working Style	INFP: Introverted Advocates *(Team Asset: Integrity)*
Description	**Introverted Advocates** are quiet pursuers of their life's quest as they strive to live according to their strongly held internal values. Not wanting to take center stage, they can appear reserved and somewhat aloof until their internal belief system is challenged, when they can react strongly in its defense. With a moral commitment to the fundamental worth of the individual, they celebrate individual differences and want a purpose beyond a paycheck. They are adaptable and enjoy opportunities to explore new ideas and see connections everywhere. They value relationships based on authenticity and true connection. However, they may frustrate their teammates with their constant push to live life according to their own internal ideals.
Temperament	**Idealist.** Need to have a purpose and make a meaningful contribution to the greater good; value potential, connection, and unique identity.
Direction of Energy	**Introversion.** Energy flows inward; tend to process, reflect, and repond to interaction.
First Function (Adult)	**Valuing.** Make decisions quietly but firmly, based on their own internal belief system. Guided by strong inner values and try to live life accordingly. Tolerant of differences until others' behavior is not in alignment with internal values.
Second Function (Parent)	**Brainstorming.** Enjoy external exploration of future possibilities, patterns, and meanings. Can read between the lines and identify themes and relationships.
Third Function (Child)	**Recalling.** Will review past experience to generate alternative ideas. May explore past experiences with photo albums, genealogies, historical visits, etc.
Fourth Function (Balancing)	**Systematizing.** Make some decisions using logical criteria to plan and organize details and events in the external environment. When values are crossed, are able to articulate a logical argument for their viewpoint. When under stress, may obsess about details and developing structure.
Strengths on a Team	• Show deep concentration when involved in a project • Are loyal to other team members if they believe in the cause • Reflect and produce intuitive insights, particularly in written form • Can act as the conscience for the team
Potential Challenges on a Team	• May find it difficult to do what they perceive to be meaningless work • May find it difficult to follow through on detailed implementation plans • May react strongly when values are crossed
Leadership Qualities	• Encourage creativity and participation • Are passionate about causes, values, and ideals • Start from a base of "how we will behave" and provide praise to motivate other members
Favored Working Environment	• Need behavior to be in alignment with articulated values and beliefs • Prefer a flexible environment where they can work in a burst of energy
Working Environment Dislikes	• Dislike impersonal, regimented environments • Dislike interacting with people all the time and tight, rigid deadlines

Table 7 Working Style Descriptions (cont'd)

Working Style	ENFJ: Extraverted Mentors *(Team Asset: Mentoring Ability)*
Description	**Extraverted Mentors** are outgoing, empathetic, expressive developers of people. They have a remarkable gift for seeing human potential and want to help others "be all that they can be." With their long-term focus, they like closure in their lives as they work to make their visions a reality. They are gifted communicators whether one-on-one, where they are able to get almost anyone to open up to them, or in front of a group, where they are able to stimulate enthusiasm. They are highly attuned to the moods and emotions of those around them and work to create a harmonious environment. As team members, they focus on meaningful communication in the team and strive to create genuine interactions with their team members. However, their focus on achieving their vision could detract from their achieving team harmony.
Temperament	**Idealist.** Need to have a purpose and make a meaningful contribution to the greater good; value potential, connection, and unique identity.
Direction of Energy	**Extraversion.** Energy flows outward; tend to process externally and initiate interaction.
First Function (Adult)	**Harmonizing.** Make decisions using subjective criteria to optimize group interaction. Sensitive to other people's wants and needs, with an ability to self-disclose to connect. When stressed, may show emotions on their face.
Second Function (Parent)	**Visioning.** Gather information by absorbing data, mentally stepping back, and allowing the complete picture to form. Trust own intuitive insights.
Third Function (Child)	**Experiencing.** May observe and gather sensory data to support the future picture. May explore sensory activities in a playful way: in exercise, art, cooking, etc.
Fourth Function (Balancing)	**Analyzing.** May compare and contrast data against an internal model, but this will be superseded by appropriateness to the group. Under stress, may question excessively and overanalyze a situation.
Strengths on a Team	• Use fluent verbal skills to unite disparate views and achieve consensus • Create a positive, safe communication climate with warmth and connection • Are adept at eliciting the ideas and thoughts of others to increase collaboration and team involvement • See potential in others; they welcome the opportunity to develop it
Potential Challenges on a Team	• May reject logical choices for decisions that will achieve group harmony • May need frequent positive feedback and be sensitive to criticism • May show emotions under stress
Leadership Qualities	• Spot talent and are generous in encouraging it • Offer a team vision that includes people behaving well toward each other • Have a warm, inclusive, and supportive style
Favored Working Environment	• Prefer a supportive culture where there are strong individual relationships • Prefer a culture that is future focused, where the importance of people is understood
Working Environment Dislikes	• Dislike open conflicts and when people seem cold • Dislike organizational politics resulting in unfair practices

Table 7 Working Style Descriptions (cont'd)

Working Style	INFJ: Introverted Mentors *(Team Asset: Future Vision)*
Description	**Introverted Mentors** are quietly insightful individuals who are constantly searching for deeper meanings and the realization of their inner visions. They understand the feelings and motivations of others and are loyal to people and institutions. As tactful, thoughtful, and concerned individuals they demonstrate interest in the development of others. They are very private people, though they quietly exert an influence over others. They use language that is full of imagery as they structure the external environment to work toward their vision of the future. In their quest to make their vision a reality they remain sensitive to their colleagues' emotional needs. However, their vision may not be tempered with reality.
Temperament	**Idealist.** Need to have a purpose and make a meaningful contribution to the greater good; value potential, connection, and unique identity.
Direction of Energy	**Introversion.** Energy flows inward; tend to process, reflect, and repond to interaction.
First Function (Adult)	**Visioning.** Gather information by absorbing data, mentally stepping back, and allowing the complete picture to form. Confident in suggesting innovative solutions.
Second Function (Parent)	**Harmonizing.** Make decisions using subjective criteria to optimize group interaction. Sensitive to team dynamics and team members' wants and needs.
Third Function (Child)	**Analyzing.** May compare and contrast data against an internal model, but consideration of people will come first.
Fourth Function (Balancing)	**Experiencing.** May observe and gather sensory data to support the future picture. When under stress may overload on sensory input.
Strengths on a Team	• Have a creative, conceptual approach • Are sensitive, compassionate, and empathetic • Are organized; have good follow-through skills • Integrate people and systems effortlessly
Potential Challenges on a Team	• May be unclear in articulating their vision • May forget to apply reason to their insights • May become single-minded in pursuit of their vision and make arbitrary decisions
Leadership Qualities	• Build consensus through patient one-on-one discussions • Are persistent in working toward their ideal outcome • Are confident in their vision; they will encourage and support others in pursuit of the goal
Favored Working Environment	• Prefer organizations that allow them to influence people in the longer term • Need a clear identity and purpose
Working Environment Dislikes	• Dislike clashes between values and actual behavior • Dislike being forced to carry out practical, detailed tasks within an impersonal culture

Troubleshooting to Get to "True Type"

Sometimes we identify strongly with a function that is not shown in our working style. Our life experiences can cause us to select certain functions and gravitate to a different working style. Factors such as education, upbringing, experiences, and family background can enable us to develop specific functions. For instance, an HR manager selected Analyzing, yet she agreed with the description of her working style ISFJ (a Guardian using Recalling and Harmonizing). Later, she disclosed that she was the youngest of five, with four older brothers, both her parents were professors, and she had completed a master's degree in biology—a perfect environment for developing her Analyzing function!

Influences on Cognitive Process Functions

After reviewing the cognitive processes and their functions in figure 7, complete exercise 26 to identify how your type development may have been influenced by your unique background.

FIGURE 7 Cognitive Processes and Their Functions

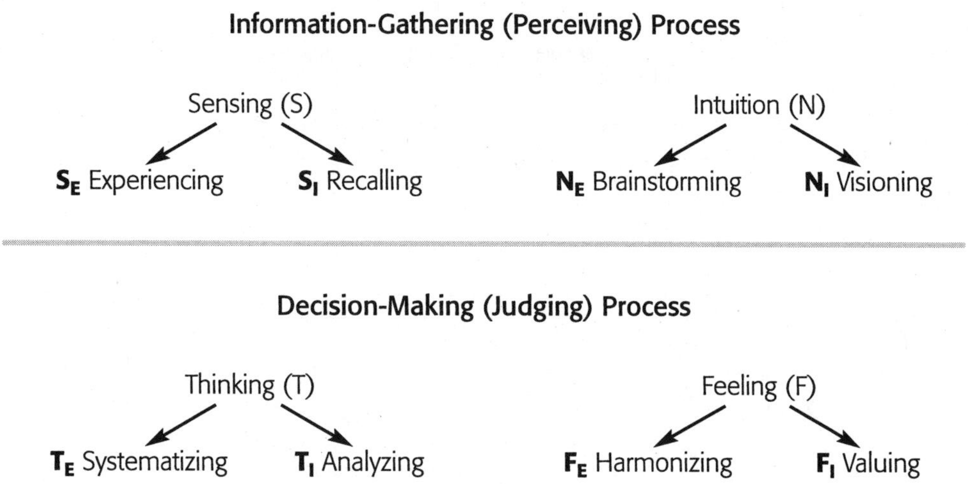

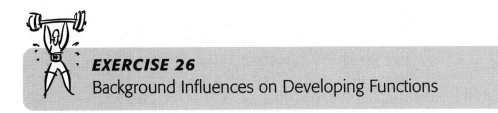

EXERCISE 26
Background Influences on Developing Functions

Review the table below. Think about your background and what might have influenced you to develop specific functions. Write down those influences in the right-hand column.

Influences on Function Development

Perceiving Function	Description	Possible Influences	Your Influences
Experiencing	• Gathering concrete data in the here and now • Seeing options in the moment • Reading sight, sound, smell, taste, and body language cues immediately	• Growing up in a family that is aware of aesthetics, design, and style • Working in a situation with the need to respond in the moment and take advantage of a current situation (e.g., sales, troubleshooting, or technical problem solving)	
Recalling	• Gathering sensory data and using them to compare and contrast with past sensory experiences • Viewing past data almost like watching a videotape	• Growing up in a family that values tradition and encourages the telling of family stories and history • Working in a situation where remembering previous projects and being consistent are key (e.g., manufacturing, quality control, or finance)	
Brainstorming	• Inferring patterns and meanings from current information • Reading between the lines • Thinking out loud: hypothesizing and exploring possibilities	• Growing up in a family that encourages talking about abstract theories and possibilities • Working in a situation where it is important to "think outside the box" and come up with new approaches (e.g., product design, process reengineering, or strategic planning)	

Influences on Function Development (cont'd)

Perceiving Function	Description	Possible Influences	Your Influences
Visioning	• Assimilating data unconsciously, which then comes into consciousness as a complete picture • Incubating ideas until they are clear • Coming up with "Aha!" and "shower" solutions	• Growing up in a family where intuition isn't questioned; being asked to "sleep on it" • Working in a situation that constantly challenges existing ways of looking at concepts or models and being rewarded for articulating completely new theories (e.g., academic work, inventing, or strategizing)	
Judging Function	**Description**	**Possible Influences**	**Your Influences**
Systematizing	• Making decisions using logical criteria to sequence and organize resources to achieve goals in the external environment • Using cause-and-effect logic	• Growing up in a family where order is required and where feedback is provided in a direct and clear way • Working in a situation that requires extensive planning and organization to achieve a goal (e.g., project management, purchasing, or procurement)	
Analyzing	• Making decisions where information gathered is evaluated and sorted against a mental model • Analyzing data for logic	• Growing up in a family where a point of view and the ability to debate and defend it logically are encouraged • Working in a situation that requires extensive analysis to improve a system or process (e.g., software design, scientific research, or law)	
Harmonizing	• Making decisions using subjective criteria to optimize interpersonal harmony • Determining what is appropriate behavior in a situation	• Growing up in a family where other people's needs and wants are considered and discussed • Working in a situation where it is necessary to put yourself in another person's shoes to achieve buy-in (e.g., marketing, sales, or any type of counseling)	

Influences on Function Development (cont'd)

Judging Function	Description	Possible Influences	Your Influences
Valuing	• Making decisions based on a subjective value and internal belief system • Determining what is the right thing to do in a situation	• Growing up in a family where individual differences are respected and supported • Working in a situation involving a cause and where values are emphasized (e.g., nonprofit work and counseling)	

What conclusions can you draw from this analysis? Which might be your preferred function? Which functions have you learned to use, that is, which are your adapted functions?

___

___

___

End of Exercise

Troubleshooting Your Working Style Selection

Even after you have reviewed the descriptions of working styles, it is possible that you may still be struggling to find your best-fit style. After all, it has taken many years to develop your personality, and it is not an easy process to determine what is your adapted style versus your best-fit style. Exercise 27 can serve as a troubleshooting guide to help clarify your working style.

EXERCISE 27
What Is Your Best-Fit Working Style?

1. List below the working styles you are evaluating.

___

___

2. Describe the sources of your confusion.

3. Think about your background. What might have influenced you to develop specific functions? What in your upbringing might have made certain temperaments more appealing to you? What were your conclusions from exercise 25 (pp. 98–103)?

4. Now use the following guide to further delineate your adapted and best-fit working styles.

Working Style Troubleshooting Guide

Temperament Distinction	Shared Function/ Similarity in Approach	Questions to Answer	Suggested Solutions
Between Artisan (_S_P) and Guardian (_S_J)	Both temperaments tend to focus on concrete sensory data. Both tend to be more literal in their communication style.	Do you like to make a plan and stick with it? Do you tend to get frustrated when people change the plan?	If yes, consider Guardian, because Guardians enjoy having a plan and resist changing it at the last minute. If no, consider Artisan, because Artisans tend to view plans as a possible choice to be adapted in the moment.
		Do you enjoy change? Are you comfortable with it?	If yes, consider Artisan, because Artisans tend to enjoy the stimulus and variety offered. You may enjoy change for the sake of change. If no, consider Guardian, because Guardians tend to prefer more stability and are uncomfortable with change for the sake of change.
		When gathering data for a new project, do you prefer to think back to what you have done previously and about what worked and what did not work?	If yes, consider Guardian, because this might be an indicator that you are using the Recalling function. If no, consider Artisan, because Artisans tend to think, "What past data?"

Working Style Troubleshooting Guide (cont'd)

Temperament Distinction	Shared Function/ Similarity in Approach	Questions to Answer	Suggested Solutions
Between Artisan (_S_P) and Guardian (_S_J)		Do you like having rules in place? Do you welcome process for the structure it provides?	If yes, consider Guardian, because Guardians inherently employ processes and abide by rules to achieve consistency. If no, consider Artisan, because Artisans like to get around rules and believe that excess structure reduces the ability to achieve results spontaneously.
Working Style Distinction	**Shared Function/ Similarity in Approach**	**Questions to Answer**	**Suggested Solutions**
Between Artisan (ISTP) and Rational (INTP)	Both use Analyzing to make decisions. Experiencing and Brainstorming can look similar in certain ways as they both are Extraverted functions that are drawn to options and possibilities from the external environment.	Do you look for concrete examples to compare with your internal analysis?	If yes, consider Artisan (ISTP), because Artisans quickly validate analysis with concrete facts and evidence. If no, consider Rational (INTP), because Rationals enjoy ideas and do not necessarily require concrete data.
		Do you move quickly from analysis to action? Does analysis mean nothing unless you can do something with it?	If yes, consider Artisan (ISTP), because Artisans tend to move quickly from analysis to implementation to achieve concrete outcomes. If no, consider Rational (INTP), because Rationals, in their drive to improve the system and attain perfection, may want to stay in the analysis phase.
		Are you able to hold multiple arguments in your head at the same time without verbalizing them? Are you reluctant to change your perspective when new data are presented?	If yes, consider Rational (INTP), because even when new data are presented, Rationals may take longer to accept a different point of view or be willing to wait longer for results. If no, consider Artisan (ISTP), because Artisans will adapt their position based on the new data available, particularly if the data support the new point of view.

Working Style Troubleshooting Guide (cont'd)

Working Style Distinction	Shared Function/ Similarity in Approach	Questions to Answer	Suggested Solutions
Between Artisan (ESTP) and Rational (ENTP)	Experiencing and Brainstorming can look similar in certain ways as they both are Extraverted functions that pick out options and possibilities from the external environment. Both use Analyzing to make decisions.	Are you tuned in to body language, and do you get easily distracted by your environment?	If yes, consider Artisan (ESTP), because Artisans use Experiencing to detect changes in the external environment and may be distracted by data. If no, consider Rational (ENTP), because Rationals tend to focus more on ideas and concepts; the external environment is not as important to them.
		Do you push for closure to get the concrete result you want?	If yes, consider Artisan (ESTP), because Artisans tend to push to achieve concrete outcomes. If no, consider Rational (ENTP), because Rationals will be more patient and flexible as they value learning while moving toward their goal.
		Do you tend to focus on the here and now? Do you trust the future to take care of itself?	If yes, consider Artisan (ESTP), because Artisans focus much more on the here and now. If no, consider Rational (ENTP), as Rationals tend to be future focused with a drive to achieve their ultimate goal.
Between Artisan (ISFP) and Idealist (INFP)	Valuing involves the need to take action in alignment with a strong internal value system. Both working styles use Valuing, but they differ in the way they gather data; ISFPs use Experiencing; INFPs use Brainstorming.	Do you easily turn your beliefs into action rather than struggle to define them?	If yes, consider Artisan (ISFP), because Artisans naturally push for concrete outcomes. If no, consider Idealist (INFP), because Idealists tend to live more in the world of ideas and possibilities.
		Do you view yourself as pragmatic—doing what it takes to get the job done?	If yes, consider Artisan (ISFP), because even the Artisans who use Valuing tend to be more pragmatic. If no, consider Idealist (INFP), because Idealists tend to struggle more with making their ultimate goals realistic.

Working Style Troubleshooting Guide (cont'd)

Working Style Distinction	Shared Function/ Similarity in Approach	Questions to Answer	Suggested Solutions
Between Artisan (ESFP) and Idealist (ENFP)	Brainstorming and Experiencing can look alike as they both are Extraverted functions that pick out options and possibilities from the external environment. Plus, they share Valuing, the need to take action in alignment with a strong internal value system.	Do you tend to focus on the here and now? Do you trust the future to take care of itself?	If yes, consider Artisan (ESFP), because of the here-and-now focus inherent in using Experiencing. If no, consider Idealist (ENFP), because Idealists tend to be more future focused as they constantly explore ideas and possibilities associated with Brainstorming.
		Do you tend to be intensely observant of the physical environment—sound, look, smell, taste?	If yes, consider Artisan (ESFP), because Artisans use Experiencing, suggesting a complete awareness of external sensory data. If no, consider Idealist (ENFP), because Idealists focus more on concepts and as a result may be relatively unaware of tangible current data.
Between Rational (ESTJ or ISTJ) and Guardian (ENTJ or INTJ)	Systematizing involves making decisions using logical data to organize and make plans in the external environnment. Who is going to do what by when? Both functions call for quick, action-oriented decision making.	Do you tend to base your decisions on history, tradition, experience, and concrete data? Do you remember past events, particularly specific data?	If yes, consider Guardian (ESTJ/ISTJ), because Guardians prefer to work with what is real and concrete, based on what they have experienced before. If no, consider Rational (ENTJ/INTJ), because Rationals prefer to create their own destiny, and that might not necessarily involve concrete data or previous experiences.
		Do you tend to have a big-picture focus associated with a future strategy? Do you often not bother with details?	If yes, consider Rational (ENTJ/INTJ), because Rationals use Visioning to see a complete picture of the desired future outcome. If no, consider Guardian (ESTJ/ISTJ), because Guardians often prefer to take concrete steps to make the vision a reality.

Working Style Troubleshooting Guide (cont'd)

Working Style Distinction	Shared Function/ Similarity in Approach	Questions to Answer	Suggested Solutions
Between Guardian (ENFJ or INFJ) and Idealist (ESFJ or ISFJ)	Both working styles use Harmonizing to make decisions. Harmonizing involves making decisions in the external environment to optimize interpersonal harmony. They differ in the way they gather information: NFJs use Visioning; SFJs use Recalling.	Do you want to make the world a better place? Do you want to live up to your potential and help others achieve theirs?	If yes, consider Idealist (ENFJ/INFJ), because Idealists are driven by a need for meaning and purpose. They seek to self-actualize and develop their potential and the potential of those around them. If no, consider Guardian (ESFJ/ISFJ), because Guardians, while interested in helping people develop, are not necessarily driven to develop their own potential.
		Do you consider yourself a hands-on, practical person?	If yes, consider Guardian (ESFJ/ISFJ), because Guardians are naturally practical and adept at implementing plans and activities. If no, consider Idealist (ENFJ /INFJ), because Idealists, while able to plan, do not necessarily enjoy the practical implementation.
Between Artisan (ESTP) and Rational (ENTJ)	While each working style uses different decision-making functions—ESTPs use Experiencing and Analyzing; ENTJs use Visioning and Systematizing—the combination of functions makes them look similar in terms of behavior. They are both quick, action-oriented, take-charge decision makers.	Do you tend to focus on action in the here and now?	If yes, consider Artisan (ESTP), because Artisans are the most action oriented. If no, consider Rational (ENTJ), because Rationals have a more future- and goal-focused approach.
		Is fun paramount to you at work?	If yes, consider Artisan (ESTP), because Artisans have an innate sense of fun at home or work. If no, consider Rational (ENTJ), because Rationals tend to take their work more seriously.

Working Style Troubleshooting Guide (cont'd)

Working Style Distinction	Shared Function/ Similarity in Approach	Questions to Answer	Suggested Solutions
Between Artisan (ISFP) and Guardian (ISFJ)	Both are supportive and caring and value the people around them: ISFPs from the perspective of their strong value system, and ISFJs from the perspective of harmony in the team.	Do you feel obliged to respond to e-mails in a formal, step-by-step fashion?	If yes, consider Guardian (ISFJ), because Guardians innately approach work in a structured, sequential manner. If no, consider Artisan (ISFP), because Artisans, though outcome focused, will be more flexible and free-flowing.
		Do you tend to assume other people's responsibilities when they do not follow through and then feel overloaded as a result?	If yes, consider Guardian (ISFJ), because Guardians are the most likely to unassumingly take on others' responsibilities and end up overloaded. If no, consider Artisan (ISFP), because Artisans tend to be more easygoing and carefree.

5. Based on the table and your other readings, which do you now think is your best-fit working style? Why?

____

____

____

End of Exercise

Wrap-Up

As we discovered in this chapter, it is possible to integrate your temperament (Artisan, Guardian, Rational, or Idealist) with the information-gathering function (Experiencing, Recalling, Brainstorming, or Visioning) and decision-making function (Systematizing, Analyzing, Harmonizing, or Valuing) you use most easily to create your four-letter working style, or type as normally described by the *Myers-Briggs Type Indicator* instrument. Your working style serves to highlight the ways in which you might behave at work, the types of strengths you inherently bring to the team, and the potential challenges you might face. By identifying the working styles on the team, you are now ready to move on to part 2 to investigate how this knowledge might influence *teamwork from the inside out.*

SCORECARD

Before moving on to part 2, make sure you answer the following questions:

- ☐ Are you naturally drawn to the inner world or the external environment? What impact might this have on your interaction with the team?
- ☐ To what extent do you feel clear about your working style? Were you able to complete the Working Style Profile Worksheet (p. 99)? Where did your teammates finish up?
- ☐ If you were unclear, to what extent were you able to resolve any confusion using the Working Style Troubleshooting Guide?

PART TWO

Building Your Dream Team

In part 1 we reviewed how team players approach work, not only from the perspective of their driving forces (their temperament), but also according to the cognitive processes and functions they access primarily to gather information and make decisions (their working style). Now that you have profiled each team player, you are ready to use this knowledge to raise team performance and build your Dream Team!

In part 2 we begin by profiling your team as a unit using the Inside Out approach—understanding the team profile in terms of temperament, cognitive processes, and working style to assess team strengths, diagnose potential team issues, and from there create a plan of attack to improve team performance. We then assess your team performance against the characteristics of high-performing teams in terms of "SCORE" as you begin working through the exercises and examples most relevant to your needs in the following chapters:

- Chapter 5: Creating a Cohesive Strategy
- Chapter 6: Establishing Clear Roles and Responsibilities
- Chapter 7: Promoting Open Communication
- Chapter 8: Enacting Rapid Response
- Chapter 9: Providing Effective Leadership in the 21st Century

Using the Inside Out approach, you will gain a new understanding of your team's hidden strengths, possible pitfalls, and motivating factors.

Coaching Point

Based on your team assessment, you may choose to work on the specific category that seems to be the most needed or where you think you will get the greatest return. You don't necessarily have to begin with chapter 5 and finish with chapter 9! Remember, building a team is a process, not an event; you can return to any of these focus areas time and time again. Good luck!

4

Where Is Your Team Now?

GAME PLAN

As we begin part 2, "Building Your Dream Team," this chapter will help you

- Create a team profile that evaluates your current team's strengths and potential challenges
- Build an action plan based on your specific team needs to raise performance and improve results
- Define the different types of teams and understand where your team fits
- Understand the benefits resulting from effective team performance
- Comprehend what it takes to make a team successful—the characteristics of high-performing teams' "SCORE"

The Benefits of Teams

In order to focus on improving team performance, let's experience firsthand the synergy that teamwork can bring and see why teams are so popular. The following exercise should provide some concrete proof for those who doubt their power. Try it out in a team meeting.

EXERCISE 28
Lost on the Moon

This exercise is to be completed in two rounds—first individually, then as a team.

Round 1: Individual Exercise

Individual team members should complete this exercise without talking to each other. Take ten minutes for this round.

Scenario

While en route to the site planned for your company's first division on the moon, your team's spaceship has just crash-landed. You are 200 miles from your destination on the lighted side, where an office has been built. The rough landing has ruined your ship and destroyed all the equipment on board, except for the 15 items on the list below. Your team's survival depends on reaching the office site, so you must choose only the most critical items to take for the 200-mile trip.

Instructions: Your task is to rank the 15 items in terms of their importance for survival. In the Individual (I) column, place the number 1 by the most important, number 2 by the second most important, and so on through number 15, the least important. A ranking must be entered next to each item.

Name: ______________________________

I	T	
_____	_____	Box of matches
_____	_____	Parachute silk
_____	_____	Two .45-caliber pistols
_____	_____	Two 100-lb. tanks of oxygen
_____	_____	Magnetic compass
_____	_____	Signal flares
_____	_____	Five gallons of water
_____	_____	50 feet of nylon rope
_____	_____	Food concentrate

I	T	
_____	_____	Stellar map of moon's constellations
_____	_____	One case dehydrated milk
_____	_____	Self-inflating life raft
_____	_____	First-aid kit with injection needles
_____	_____	Solar-powered heater
_____	_____	Solar-powered FM receiver/ transmitter

Source: NASA/Human Synergistics.

Round 2: Team Exercise

Now divide the group into teams of three to five members. For the same scenario, each team is responsible for attaining consensus on the ranking of the items. All viewpoints should be listened to, and everyone must finally agree. Take twenty minutes for this round.

Instructions: Mark your team's ranking in the Team (T) column. A ranking must be entered next to each item. **Important:** The individual rankings should not be changed as your team arrives at the team ranking.

Scoring: Individual and Team

Follow the instructions on the score sheet in appendix 1, pages 314–15, to obtain your individual and team scores. After doing the calculations, each team should create a flip-chart showing both their team and individual scores.

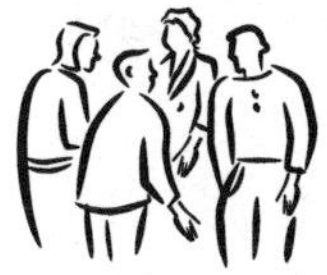

Team Huddle!

Discuss the following questions:

- What was the difference between the individual scores and the team scores?
- How easy was it to achieve consensus?
- If one team member performed better than the team, how were his or her suggestions received? To what extent was he or she listened to?
- What did you learn from the exercise?

Normally, the team score is better (lower) than the individual score, exemplifying how teams perform better than individuals. Although the team exercise takes longer, the overall benefits outweigh the time cost. Providing a team-oriented environment also positively affects individuals by supporting an atmosphere of trust, fun, and ongoing relationships.

Coaching Point

The old adage "two heads are better than one" is a key reason why teamwork is an effective way to produce results. The synergy of minds and their varied outputs usually outweigh the challenge of having to consider many perspectives.

End of Exercise

Profiling Your Team

You experienced the power of teams in the previous exercise. By profiling and analyzing your team, you will increase your results exponentially by capitalizing on your team attributes and minimizing possible challenges. So let's create a team profile from the individual knowledge of working styles as a basis for applying the Inside Out approach.

Coaching Point

Team members might first want to review the self-assessment exercises and descriptions of working styles in chapters 1–3 to validate their individual style. Having a professional facilitator lead a session on temperament and working style may prove useful. Finally, written online assessments are available that could provide additional data (see appendix 2).

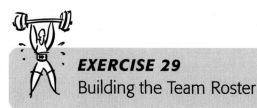

EXERCISE 29
Building the Team Roster

TEAM EXERCISE

Using the following grid as a template, create a flip-chart team roster to be filled in by the individual team members.

Team Roster

Name	Title	Temperament	Working Style	First Function	Second Function

End of Exercise

Now you are ready to compile the information and assess its implications for your team's performance.

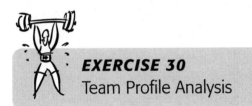

EXERCISE 30
Team Profile Analysis

This exercise has three sections requiring completion: temperament analysis, working style analysis, and function analysis.

Section 1: Temperament Analysis

1. In the grid below, summarize the following information from the team roster:
   - Total number of people with each temperament
   - Team temperament (the single most prevalent temperament within the team)
   - The team leader's temperament

Temperament Analysis Grid

Artisans	Guardians	Rationals	Idealists	Team Temperament	Team Leader's Temperament

2. Read the descriptions of the team's temperament and the team leader's temperament in table 2 (pp. 22–23).

Team Huddle!

Based on the temperaments you've determined, discuss this analysis using the following questions:

- What temperaments are not represented?
- What are the implications of one or more temperaments not being represented?
- What are some general statements you could make based on the team temperament? (See chapter 1 for additional information.)
- How is the team leader's temperament different from or similar to that of the team?
- What are the implications of that difference/similarity?

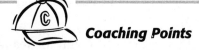

Coaching Points

- When the team has all four temperaments represented, it may take longer to make decisions due to the diversity of perspectives, but the overall quality of the decisions will be higher.
- Teams that have learned about temperament and that have all four temperaments represented will appear "richer" and more well-rounded.
- Teams with only one or two temperaments represented will make decisions quickly but may be one-sided and miss diverse viewpoints.
- Teams lacking one temperament can find advisers of the missing temperament to provide insight.
- When one temperament is not represented, it may produce communication conflicts with other teams predominantly of that temperament.

Section 2: Working Style (MBTI Type) Analysis

1. From the individual analyses in exercise 29 (p. 138) summarize below:
   - The number of people with each preference (E or I, S or N, T or F, J or P)

E: ____________	I: ____________	(Extraversion or Introversion)
S: ____________	N: ____________	(Sensing or Intuition)
T: ____________	F: ____________	(Thinking or Feeling)
J: ____________	P: ____________	(Judging or Perceiving)

   - Team working style (the four preferences with the highest number): ________
   - Team leader working style: ________

2. Read the descriptions of the team's working style and the team leader's working style in table 7 (pp. 105–20).

Team Huddle!

Discuss this information using the following questions:

- What is the balance between Extraversion and Introversion, and what implications does this have for the team?
- What is the balance between Sensing and Intuition, and what implications does this have for the team?
- What is the balance between Thinking and Feeling, and what implications does this have for the team?
- What is the balance between Judging and Perceiving, and what implications does this have for the team?
- What is the team's working style?
- What are some general statements that you could make based on the team's working style?
- What is the team leader's working style, and what implications might this have for team performance?
- How is this different from or similar to the team's working style?
- What are the implications of that difference/similarity?

Coaching Points

- Teams with individual preferences balanced evenly (E = I, S = N, T = F, J = P) will take longer to make decisions but will consider and balance more options.
- Teams with membership skewed toward one preference may miss considering the other perspectives.
- Teams missing preferences can find internal advisers to provide that perspective.
- Teams with a predominant preference for Extraversion may need to make sure members allow those with a preference for Introversion time to process.
- Teams with a predominant preference for Introversion should not rely solely on e-mail to communicate; it is important also to use face-to-face interaction to discuss issues and make decisions.

Section 3: Cognitive Process Analysis

1. Summarize the following information from the individual analyses in exercise 29 using the grid on page 138:
   - The total number of times each function appears as a first or second function
   - First function for the team (the function that is most common)
   - First function for the team leader (from the working style description)

Cognitive Process/Function Analysis Grid

Gathering Information (Perceiving)	Experiencing	Recalling	Brainstorming	Visioning
Total Individuals' First or Second Function				
Making Decisions (Judging)	Systematizing	Analyzing	Harmonizing	Valuing
Total Individuals' First or Second Function				

Team's first function: ______________________________

Team leader's first function: ______________________________

2. Read the descriptions of the cognitive processes and their functions in chapter 2.

Team Huddle!

- What is the most common function on the team, and what implications does this have for team performance?
- Which functions are present as a first or second function and which are missing? What implications does this have for team performance?
- What is the first function for the team leader? What implications does this have for team performance?
- What functions are not represented in the team at the first or second level? What impact could this have on the team's working habits?

Coaching Points

- Teams will benefit from collectively possessing all the functions in the first or second function form.
- If a particular function is not present, team members will benefit from trying to think about an issue from that function's perspective. For instance, if Harmonizing is not present, members might ask, How will people respond to this decision? What potential conflicts might arise?
- Team members need to make sure that when taking any action they consider the following information:
  - What is happening right now, and what are some options? (Experiencing)
  - What has happened in the past, and how does this compare and contrast with the current situation? (Recalling)
  - What are some other possibilities? What else is happening? (Brainstorming)
  - What is the overall vision/objective/future goal? (Visioning)
- Team members need to make sure that when taking any action they use the following criteria in making decisions:
  - What do the published facts and data suggest, and how do we sequence the activities to achieve the goal in the most logical way? (Systematizing)
  - How could we look at this decision differently? What could be done to improve the way we complete this project? (Analyzing)
  - How are people involved in the decision going to feel, and how can we ensure team buy-in? (Harmonizing)
  - To what extent is the decision in alignment with our team values? (Valuing)

End of Exercise

Now that you have analyzed the team profile, let's compare it to your individual profile.

EXERCISE 31
Comparing Your Profile with the Team Profile

The purpose of this exercise is for individual team members to gain a better understanding of the benefits and possible challenges of working in a team, based on their individual profile compared to the team profile.

1. Individually, list:

   Your temperament: ______________ The team temperament: ______________

   Your working style: ______________ The team working style: ______________

   Your first function: ______________ The team's first function: ______________

2. Using the information from chapters 1–3, consider the following questions:

   - What are the similarities between your temperament and the team temperament? What are the differences? What implications does this have for your individual performance? What about the team's performance? (chapter 1)

     ____

     ____

   - What is your working style? What is the team working style? What are the differences in the two styles? How can the team benefit from your strengths? What possible weaknesses might you need to be aware of in this team? (chapter 3)

     ____

     ____

   - What is your first function? What is the team's first function? What does this say about what you uniquely contribute to the team? What challenges might you potentially face with the team? (chapter 2)

     ____

     ____

End of Exercise

Determining the Connects and Conflicts for Your Team

The Connects and Conflicts Diagram in exercise 32 will help your team understand how individual members see things similarly or differently.

EXERCISE 32

Mapping Team Composition Using the Connects and Conflicts Diagram

TEAM EXERCISE

As a team, use the Connects and Conflicts Diagram on page 147 to profile team members in a more visual way.

1. Write the name of each team member alongside the shaded circle that represents his or her working style. As you can see, we have grouped together the Extraverted and Introverted orientations of each working style because they use the same information-gathering and decision-making functions.
2. Identify the temperament of each team member—Artisan, Guardian, Rational, or Idealist—as represented in each corner of the diagram.
3. Finally, look inside the arrows to either side of each team member's shaded circle to identify his or her primary information-gathering and decision-making functions. For example, a team member with a working style of ENTJ is a Rational, uses Visioning to gather data, and uses Systematizing to make decisions.

Connects and Conflicts Diagram

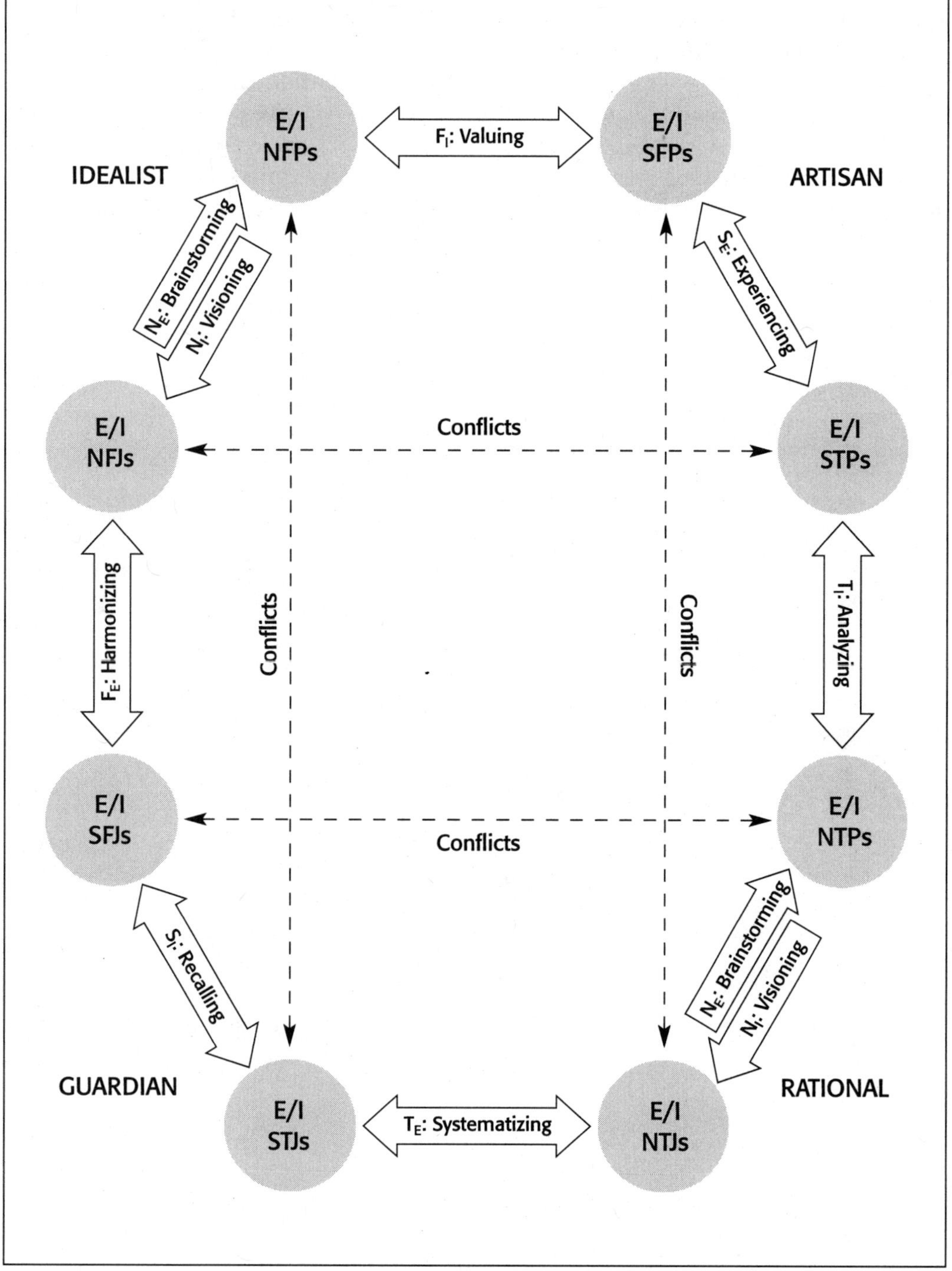

The general principle of this diagram is that the closer your working style is located to that of another team member, the more likely the two of you are to view certain situations in a similar way. For instance, if you are an NFJ next to an NFP, you are both Idealists, sharing certain core needs for purpose and meaning. In the same way, if you are an NFJ next to an SFJ, you both share Harmonizing and will naturally gravitate toward achieving consensus with teammates. Conversely, when two teammates are opposite each other, for example, STJ and NFP, there are usually two possible results: either they balance each other out with varying perspectives or they can fall into conflict if differences are not valued. Through understanding this model you can try to ensure that the former occurs.

Team Huddle!

- Are all eight "E/I" working styles represented?
- Which are dominating the diagram?
- Is there a great distance between some team members and others, that is, more than one shaded circle separation?
- If so, how is a "separated" team member perceived by the others?
- How do individuals separated by more than one shaded circle perceive one another?

Coaching Point

When a member appears "separated" from the team per the diagram, it might be surmised that he or she does not fit in. Yet, this person's perspective can be important because it may represent a point of view that the rest of the team has not considered.

End of Exercise

Now that we have a picture of your team, let's take a look at a standard definition of a team and see how yours compares.

What Is a Team?

"A team is comprised of a small number of people, with complementary skills who are committed to a common purpose, performance goals and approach for which they hold themselves mutually accountable."

—Katzenbach and Smith, THE WISDOM OF TEAMS

Let's look at the quotation above in a little more detail.

Small Number of People

The optimal number of people in a team is generally between five and nine. While more team members bring a greater diversity of perspectives and ideas, the difficulty of consensus decision making increases dramatically. Subgroups can be created, but then the entire team is at risk of losing sight of the big picture.

Complementary Skills

In establishing a team, it is critical to ensure that there is a mix of diverse, yet complementary, skills such as technical, functional, and interpersonal abilities. We discuss team member competencies in chapter 6.

Committed to a Common Purpose

Without a unified purpose, the team has no yardstick against which to measure performance. Setting a team purpose is detailed in chapter 5.

Common Performance Goals

Teams share performance goals, or objectives; if an objective is not achieved, the entire team is accountable. Commitment to these common performance objectives results in higher productivity and raised motivation levels. Performance objectives are described in chapter 6.

Common Approach

Objectives represent the "task" element of performing successfully; a common approach represents the "group process" element of working together. Neither is more important than the other, but without agreeing on how the team will interact, the chances of completing the task are pretty low! The sections on values and ground rules in chapter 5 provide applicable exercises in this area.

Mutually Accountable

Mutually accountable refers to the shared ownership and responsibility that is fundamental to real teamwork. If something goes wrong, there should not be any finger pointing but rather a group effort to fix the current situation and prevent future problems. Everyone should feel free to ask for help, just as they should feel free to offer assistance. In a team, individual and team success are one and the same.

Barriers to Teamwork

Although the definition of an effective team is clear, often teams fail to deliver on their potential. Why is this? Part of the problem usually stems from internal conflict or lack of diversity. Your team profile provided an analysis of these issues. Other performance issues stem from hidden barriers that are affecting the group process and task accomplishment. Try out the exercise below and explore the barriers that might be holding your team back and the balances that can forge effective teamwork.

EXERCISE 33
Barriers and Balances in Your Team's Performance

1. Think of three teams of which you are a member. Answer each of the following questions on a scale of 1 to 10 (1 signifying very strong, 10 meaning virtually nonexistent).

Barriers and Balances

Barriers *(elements that make teamwork difficult)*	**Team 1**	**Team 2**	**Team 3**
To what extent is the organization's culture competitive?			
To what extent is the team composed of individual contributors?			
To what extent is the team competitive?			
To what extent do politics rule the organization?			
Total Barriers			

Balances *(elements that can help forge effective teamwork)*	**Team 1**	**Team 2**	**Team 3**
To what extent are your goals clear?			
To what extent are the team rewards linked to performance goals?			
To what extent is senior management committed to teams?			
To what extent have you received training in making teams work?			
Total Balances			

2. Analyze your scores.
    - If the barrier and balance totals are approximately the same, you have a chance of making team performance work. The techniques provided here will help.
    - If the barrier total is low and the balance total is very high, you may be fighting the organization in trying to make team performance work. It may be worthwhile to address some broader organizational issues before undertaking a lot of work in this fieldbook. Furthermore, bear in mind that positive results may not appear as quickly as you want because the broader organizational context is not in alignment with what you are trying to do.
    - If the barrier total is very high and the balance total is very low, congratulations—effective teamwork is a step away!

Coaching Point

Make sure you consider the broader context when trying to improve teamwork. Factors outside of your control may influence potential team productivity.

End of Exercise

"SCORE": Characteristics of High-Performing Teams

A high-performing team demonstrates a high level of synergism—the simultaneous actions of separate entities that together have a greater effect than the sum of their individual efforts. It is possible, for example, for a team's efforts to exemplify an equation such as 2 + 2 = 5! High-performing teams require a complementary set of characteristics known collectively as "SCORE"—cohesive strategy, clear roles and responsibilities, open communication, rapid response, and effective leadership—as outlined in table 8.

Table 8 "SCORE": Characteristics of High-Performing Teams

Characteristics	Descriptions
S: Cohesive Strategy	High-performing teams with a cohesive strategy will demonstrate why they are in existence by articulating a strong, uniting purpose that is common to all team members. They will describe how they work together by defining team values and ground rules. Finally, they will be clear about what they do by defining key result areas.
C: Clear Roles and Responsibilities	Successful teams determine overall team competencies and then clearly define individual member roles and responsibilities. High-performing teams realistically examine each individual's responsibilities in terms of personality, interest, and ability, resulting in an accurate understanding of each member's accountability and contribution to the team.
O: Open Communication	Communication is the key component in facilitating successful team performance; its lack limits team success. Effective communication relies on the proper use of communication channels such as e-mail and voicemail. In addition, a cohesive culture is attained when interpersonal interactions flow smoothly and individual differences are also respected and leveraged to enhance overall team functioning.
R: Rapid Response	A high-performing team responds quickly, as necessary, to changes in the environment, using creativity and "outside the box" thinking. When faced with a problem, these teams brainstorm possible solutions and create innovative resolutions.
E: Effective Leadership	An effective team leader is able to adjust his or her style as necessary depending on the task at hand and the skill level of each team member performing that task. The team leader also plays a critical role in raising morale by providing positive feedback and coaching team members to improve performance. Finally, the team leader takes an active role in guiding the team through each stage of team development by using team-building activities and celebrating successes.

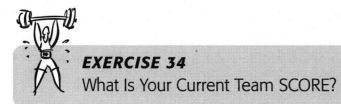

Coaching Point

In high-performing teams, leadership shifts during the stages of team development based on team needs. Unlike organizational leadership, which remains somewhat constant, team leadership can shift from very directing, when the team is being formed, to more delegating, when the team is functioning effectively. See chapter 9 for more information.

These five SCORE characteristics—cohesive strategy, clear roles and responsibilities, open communication, rapid response, and effective leadership—are described in the remaining chapters of the book. When you have assessed your team's current performance level and needs, you will be ready to move on to building your Dream Team in whatever SCORE category you choose to begin.

EXERCISE 34
What Is Your Current Team SCORE?

Review the descriptions of the five SCORE characteristics of high-performing teams and consider where your team stands in regard to these factors. What elements need to be enhanced? What aspects will be the most difficult to incorporate? How easy will it be for your team to achieve the maximum SCORE?

1. Individual SCORE

Based on your team's current status, rate each of the SCORE characteristics on a scale of 1 to 10 (1 signifying the highest performance, 10 indicating the lowest).

S: Cohesive Strategy

Consider the following questions to assess the cohesiveness and effectiveness of your strategy:

- What is your team purpose?
- How committed are the team members to the team purpose?
- To what extent is the team purpose aligned with the company's organizational vision and mission?
- How clear are your team values?
- To what extent do these values guide behavior?

- Do you have ground rules, and, if so, to what extent are they effective in governing team interaction?
- To what extent are the team's responsibilities clear to all team members?

____

____

Your rating, from 1 to 10 (1 for very cohesive and effective, 10 for not cohesive or effective): ________________

C: Clear Roles and Responsibilities

Consider the following questions to assess the clarity of your roles and responsibilities:

- To what extent were you able to select team members based on team requirements?
- To what extent are team members working on tasks that they enjoy?
- To what extent do team members meet contractual obligations with each other?
- To what extent are team members' responsibilities clearly defined?
- To what extent is there clear accountability for specific tasks?
- To what extent is team members' performance guided by their objectives?

____

____

Your rating, from 1 to 10 (1 for very clear, 10 for not clear): ________________

O: Open Communication

Consider the following questions to assess how open your communication is within your team:

- How effective is communication within your team?
- To what extent are team members open and honest about their feelings and work responsibilities?
- To what extent are communication channels being used correctly (voicemail, e-mail, meetings, etc.)?
- If there are conflicts, how effectively are they managed within the team?
- To what extent are all team members respectful of personality and other interpersonal differences?
- To what extent do team members listen to diverse points of view and value different perspectives?

____

____

Your rating, from 1 to 10 (1 for very open, 10 for not open): ________________

R: Rapid Response

Consider the following questions to assess your ability to respond quickly to changes:

- How quickly does your team respond to changes in the environment?
- To what extent do team members consider unconventional or less traditional solutions when faced with challenges?
- How easy is it for team members to change and adapt to new solutions when new data are presented?
- To what extent do all team members apply creative problem solving?

____

____

Your rating, from 1 to 10 (1 for very rapidly, 10 for very slowly): __________

E: Effective Leadership

Consider the following questions to assess the effectiveness of your team leader:

- To what extent does the team leader vary his or her style depending on the skill level of the team member and the task involved?
- How often does the team leader provide individuals with positive feedback as well as constructive criticism?
- How often does the team leader provide team members with specific guidance for raising team performance?
- To what extent has the team leader introduced exercises/events to help smooth the team development process?
- To what extent is the team leader's role transparent (i.e., not obvious) when the team is performing well?

____

____

Your rating, from 1 to 10 (1 for very effective, 10 for not effective): __________

Your Individual SCORE Ratings: S: _____ C: _____ O: _____ R: _____ E: _____

2. Team SCORE

Now, as a team, combine the ratings of all team members to create an average rating for each specific SCORE characteristic, using the grid on page 156.

- Discuss each characteristic in turn and identify why individuals rated them the way they did and what could be done to improve each rating.

- Discuss any marked differences in ratings; for instance, if one member rated "Open Communication" a 9 and another member rated it a 2, discuss the reasons for the disparity.

____

____

____

____

____

____

Team SCORE Assessment Grid

Characteristic	Combined Ratings	Number of Participants	Average Rating	Points to Note
Cohesive Strategy				
Clear Roles and Responsibilities				
Open Communication				
Rapid Response				
Effective Leadership				

Coaching Point

Each of the SCORE characteristics of high-performing teams will be specifically addressed in the following chapters to help you improve your team's weak spots and raise your team SCORE. Once you have diagnosed your team's trouble areas, you may head directly to the relevant chapter to get to work. For instance, if you rated "Open Communication" as low-performing, you may want to go directly to chapter 7. Alternatively, you can continue sequentially through the book, gathering information to improve your team's status in each of these imperative areas.

End of Exercise

Wrap-Up

In this chapter, you initially identified the benefits of teamwork. To gain the maximum output from your team, you profiled your team in terms of temperament, cognitive processes, and working style. By defining what constitutes a team and examining the types of barriers that might inhibit team productivity, you set the broader context for raising team performance. Finally, you assessed your team's performance in each of the SCORE characteristics of high-performing teams to decide which area you will focus on first in beginning to build your Dream Team.

SCORECARD

Before moving on to chapter 5 or other chapters, ask yourself the following questions:

- ☐ Did you create and analyze your team profile?
- ☐ Have you identified possible barriers to team performance?
- ☐ Have you assessed your team SCORE and decided which SCORE category you will move on to next?

5

Creating a Cohesive Strategy

GAME PLAN

The first characteristic that will help you build your Dream Team is creating a Cohesive Strategy (the S in SCORE). This chapter will help you

- Identify how well your team strategy is aligned with your organization's vision
- Assess the effectiveness of your current team purpose
- Build your team purpose in a nontraditional way to raise buy-in
- Define your team's mission statement
- Evaluate the degree to which your team is working according to the values of its members
- Establish ground rules to guide team interaction
- Construct an accurate list of team projects and tasks
- Categorize activities into key result areas
- Observe how each working style and temperament approach contributes to creating a team strategy

The Components of Team Strategy

Team strategy is defined as the overall planning and direction of team activity that allows the team to focus on meaningful and acceptable results, integrating

- Team purpose ("Why are we here?")
- Mission statement, key result areas, and objectives ("What are we trying to achieve?")
- Team values and ground rules ("How do we want to work together?")

One of the greatest indicators of team success is an effective, well-articulated, cohesive strategy. In this chapter we examine methods and approaches that teams can use to establish a clear strategy, one that is in alignment with the company's direction and business goals, beginning with the Strategic Planning Pyramid (figure 8).

The Strategic Planning Pyramid is used to show how each step is a building block for achieving the overall purpose, where no one factor stands alone. A high-performing team will have a strong, uniting purpose that is common to all team members and clearly articulated so that it is meaningful to the entire team. The team purpose must be integrated with the organization's vision and mission to be valid. While the purpose provides the overall inspiration, high-performing teams also

FIGURE 8 Strategic Planning Pyramid

verbalize their core values and clarify specifics about how team members wish to work together following team ground rules, enabling a smooth group process. Responsibilities are also clearly stated in the team's key result areas, allowing members to focus on their core tasks.

Coaching Point

While some of the exercises in this section may not seem directly linked to team deliverables, completing them will produce long-term benefits for the team. These exercises are often used in the team's forming stage. However, they are equally useful when a team is already in place, as they help reevaluate direction, resulting in a sharper team focus.

Team Dynamics from the Inside Out

Each temperament approaches building a strategy with a different focus:

- *Artisans* specialize in tactical strategy—the ability to set a short-term direction depending on the current situation—and can help ensure that the team strategy is realistic. They may resist less-tangible exercises such as defining team purpose because they do not see their immediate application.
- *Guardians* approach strategy sequentially and methodically and value the contribution that a cohesive direction makes to team peformance. They also appreciate the structure that ground rules and key result areas provide. They may be hesitant to embark on a totally new direction if they have had no prior experience in it and will question approaches and exercises that they perceive as unrealistic.
- *Rationals* develop strategy from the abstract, long-term, big-picture perspective. They enjoy the mental exercise of defining future outcomes. They may focus less on the more people-related elements of building strategy such as defining team values and ground rules.
- *Idealists* are driven to create a cohesive strategy by their need for meaning and purpose. They will naturally gravitate toward establishing a team purpose and defining values as a way of creating a collaborative culture. They may appear unrealistic and ungrounded when considering detailed tactical implementation.

For more information about the different temperaments, review chapter 1 in this fieldbook or chapter 5 of the book *Turning Team Performance Inside Out*.

Linking Company Vision with Strategy

The organization or division that sponsors a team heavily influences the team's performance and purpose. The organization's vision provides the platform on which the team's performance is staged. Trying to establish a team strategy without evaluating the company's vision can result in an unrealistic or unaligned purpose. In addition, defining a team purpose without considering the organizational environment is likewise ill-fated.

The Company Vision Statement

The company vision statement is a clear image of a desired future state including purpose and opportunity. It is intended to be inspirational and to act as a general direction for the organization and its teams. It should guide daily decision making in the organization and capture the essence of what the organization needs to do to succeed.

The core of Williams-Sonoma, a specialty retailer focusing on home products, for example, is expressed in its vision statement, as follows:

> *"We are in the business of enhancing the quality of life at home. This means helping people derive greater pleasure and social enjoyment from their home environment through high-quality, well-designed and innovative products and services."*

When teams in each of the company's divisions were defining their strategy, this vision statement acted as their yardstick. For instance, the company teams responsible for Pottery Barn, Hold Everything, Gardeners Eden, and Chambers products all contributed to enhanced quality of life at home as laid out in the vision statement.

Team Dynamics from the Inside Out

Remember, when perceiving data:

- For those team members who prefer to gather information abstractly (through the two Intuition functions—Brainstorming and Visioning), developing a vision statement is usually a relevant activity because of the future focus and discussion of what could be (not what is or was).
- For those team members who prefer to gather information concretely (through the two Sensing functions—Recalling and Experiencing), a focus on an abstract vision can sometimes appear not to relate to the actual tasks of "getting the job done."

For more information about the different cognitive processes and functions we use to gather information and make decisions, review chapter 2 in this fieldbook or chapter 5 in *Turning Team Performance Inside Out.*

The following exercise will help you assess how well your team purpose is aligned with your organization's vision.

EXERCISE 35
Team Purpose Alignment with Organization's Vision

TEAM EXERCISE

In this team exercise, each team member should complete the following steps:

1. Write down the company vision and team purpose *from memory* in the boxes below. Then note how the two connect/align in the box on page 164.

Company Vision	Team Purpose

How do the company vision and team purpose connect/align?

____

____

____

2. Compare your answers in step 1 with those of other team members. To what extent are the statements similar? How much do individuals in the team know or care about the company vision?

____

____

Team Huddle!

As you consider the company vision, discuss the following questions:

- Is the company vision in alignment with your team's stated purpose?
- To what extent is the company vision aligned with the team's direction?
- If the two are not aligned, what can you do about it?
- If they are partially aligned, what can you do to increase the alignment between your team's purpose and the overall company direction?

Coaching Point

Remember, if the company vision and your team purpose are not in alignment, the chances of your team succeeding are greatly diminished. You may need to revisit your team's purpose and direction.

End of Exercise

As discussed earlier, creating a clear strategy encompasses not only building a sense of purpose into team activities, but also beginning to establish the way team members are going to work together and determining their actual work responsibilities. Only then can the more tactical elements of team performance be addressed. Let's begin building a strategy, following the sequence in the Strategic Planning Pyramid (figure 8), using a series of exercises and examples to help complete each stage.

Team Purpose

When we ask a team if they have a purpose, the response is often, "Of course we do!" However, while the value of a team purpose is self-evident, experience with many organizations has shown that often the team purpose is not known by all, is unclear, or is too wordy to be useful in guiding team direction. Below is an exercise to give you a quick insight into the effectiveness of your current team purpose.

EXERCISE 36
Assessing Your Team Purpose

1. Fill in the information about your team purpose and answer "yes" or "no" to the questions below.

Our team purpose is:

____

____

____

Yes	No	
☐	☐	Did you participate in defining your team purpose?
☐	☐	Can all members of your team articulate your team purpose?
☐	☐	Do you agree with the team purpose?
☐	☐	Does the team purpose energize you?
☐	☐	Do you think the team purpose is realistic?
☐	☐	Do you think the team purpose reflects all the work of your team?
☐	☐	Do you refer to the team purpose on a regular basis?
☐	☐	Is the team purpose visible to the whole team?
☐	☐	Did you remember your team purpose without referring to a written copy?

2. Now share your answers with other team members to discover how clearly understood the team purpose truly is.

Team Huddle!

Discuss the following questions as a team:

- How easy was it to remember your team purpose?
- To what extent did you answer all the questions with a "yes"?
- To what extent was there agreement within the team about your team purpose?

All too often, the team purpose is so long that individuals cannot remember it without referring to a copy. The exercise questions are designed to raise awareness about the overall effectiveness of the team purpose as perceived by each team member. If you answered "no" to more than four questions in step 1, it might indicate that the team purpose is not owned by the team or even accurate. If that is the case, it is important to review your team purpose using the exercises included later in this chapter.

Coaching Point

To be effective, your team purpose needs to be clear, ideally not much more than nine words long, and owned by all team members.

End of Exercise

Defining Team Purpose

Time Out!

A man was passing a work site and saw three bricklayers. He approached the first bricklayer and asked, "What are you doing?" The man answered, "Making a living." He asked the second man the same question, and he answered, "Laying bricks." He asked the third worker the same question, and the man responded, "Building a cathedral." A strong team purpose enables team members to feel as though they are building a cathedral, not just laying bricks or making a living.

A team purpose performs the same functions for the team as the company vision statement does for the company. It sets the tone and aspirations for the team, helping to align goals, provide focus, and formulate strategy, and is an overall announcement of why the team exists. It provides an inspiration and motivation for performance, whereas conventional tools such as goals, rewards, and recognition provide measurement, guidance, and reinforcement.

Building Team Purpose

Questions that could be used to help build the team purpose include the following:

- Why are we here?
- What is our overall direction?
- What do we want to look like?
- What is our ultimate theme?
- What is the reason this team was brought into existence?

The team purpose needs to be applicable and desirable to everyone on the team, otherwise individuals will not support it. In addition, the team purpose must put the bar high enough to inspire performance while not appearing unrealistic. The following is an example of a team purpose for an internal training group at Oracle Corporation.

> *"To stimulate and facilitate Oracle's learning culture as its sustainable competitive advantage."*

The team created this statement through a series of exercises like the one below. As a result, everyone on the team bought into the overall direction. In addition, team members evaluated possible programs that could be developed and rejected those that could not be seen to add value to the organization.

Most teams shape their purpose in response to a demand or opportunity put in their path, usually by management. The Xerox scientists who invented personal computing developed their purpose after the company's chairman called for the creation of an "architecture of information." Teams develop direction, momentum, and commitment when they invest time in creating the team purpose. One or more broad aspirations or values often emerge that motivate team members and are fundamentally responsible for their extra effort.

Too often, trying to build a team purpose becomes a tedious wordsmithing exercise. Exercise 37 will help you build your team purpose in a more free-thinking, flexible way.

EXERCISE 37
Defining Your Team Purpose in an Unconventional Way!

TEAM EXERCISE

Follow the five steps below to create a more "right brain" team purpose.

1. Purchase or construct a number of cardboard boxes approximately 9 inches by 9 inches by 9 inches. One box can be used for up to five people; if your team has nine members, for example, you will need two boxes, one for each subteam. Fill each box with a selection of "goodies" such as:
   - Balloons
   - Glue/tape
   - Tinsel/string
   - Crayons
   - Toy figures
   - Frisbees, yo-yos, slinkies, etc.
   - Labels/paper
   - Balls
   - Scissors
   - Stickers
2. With these props, ask each subteam to create a three-dimensional presentation that symbolizes the purpose of your team. The presentation needs to include a visual representation and an actual statement of purpose.
3. Ask each subteam to present its ideas to the whole group—it's OK to have fun with this exercise!

4. After each subteam has presented, ask the following questions to hone in on a team purpose:
   - What were the common themes in each presentation?
   - What were the surprises that arose from the exercise?
   - What words were in all presentations?
5. Integrate these ideas to create a team purpose. Make sure it answers the questions for building a team purpose on page 167. Also, try to keep the statement to approximately nine words to ensure that it is easy to remember.

Team Dynamics from the Inside Out

Remember:

- *Artisans* will enjoy the freedom and creativity that this exercise stimulates.
- *Guardians* may initially view this exercise as frivolous but will value its ability to cement team dynamics and build focus.
- *Rationals* will enjoy the conceptual aspect of this exercise; they will also want to debate the merits of different suggestions.
- *Idealists* are driven by purpose and may place high importance on this exercise.

For more information about temperament, review chapter 1 in this fieldbook or chapter 5 in *Turning Team Performance Inside Out.*

Time Out!

This exercise not only is a fun team-building experience, but also results in a more effective team purpose. It challenges team members to think creatively to express the meaning of the team. The exercise also combines two different creative-thinking approaches—cerebral and hands-on (Brainstorming and Experiencing)—to achieve the best result.

End of Exercise

Team Mission Statement

While the team purpose provides the overall direction for the team, the team mission statement provides more specific concrete information about what the team is actually responsible for, who does what, and when. The team mission statement answers the following questions:

- Who is the customer?
- What customer needs is your team attempting to fill?
- How will you meet these needs, including technologies, tasks, and approaches?

An effective team mission statement must be

- Clear and understandable to all members of the team
- Brief enough for people to remember
- Specific about the business the team conducts
- Based on, and reflective of, the overall purpose of the team
- Indicative of the particular competence of the unit
- Broad enough to allow flexibility in implementation, but not so broad as to permit lack of focus
- Able to serve as a template by which decisions are made
- Reflective of the values, beliefs, philosophies, and culture of the organization
- Inclusive of a commitment to the economic objectives of the organization

Oracle's internal education group had the following mission statement:

Our mission is to support Oracle's business requirements by

- Focusing on, and listening to, our customers
- Delivering the education, training, and development employees need when, where, and how they need it
- Enabling and influencing a continuous learning environment

We are in the business of

- Providing a conduit from what people need to know to do their work to the resources that are available to fulfill that need
- Being a broker that provides a filter and a focus for information, education, training, and development services
- Adding value by understanding the business and helping our customers to apply appropriate solutions

Coaching Point

As you can see, that team's mission statement was specific about

- What the team was responsible for (delivering education, training, and development)
- How the services were going to be chosen (by listening to its customers)
- What the outcome would be (a continuous learning environment)
- How the services were to be delivered (by acting as a broker)

Remember, concrete deliverables to support the team mission statement are set by the team.

Now that you have reviewed the key elements in a team mission statement, let's use an exercise to define yours.

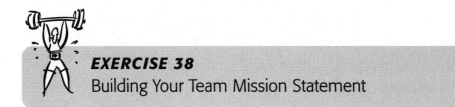

EXERCISE 38
Building Your Team Mission Statement

TEAM EXERCISE

1. Individually, complete the following worksheet to help build a team mission statement.

Team name: ______________________________

Who are your customers?

____

____

____

What do your customers need?

____

____

____

How will you meet these needs?

Tasks:

____

____

Approaches:

____

____

Technologies:

____

____

Proposed mission statement:

____

____

____

2. Now combine ideas from all the team members to create your team mission statement. Pick out the key themes and integrate them. Then, use a flip-chart to consider multiple statement versions until a single mission statement is supported by the entire team.

Ideas:

____

____

____

____

____

____

Team mission statement:

____

____

____

End of Exercise

Team Values and Ground Rules

The team purpose and mission statement give direction in terms of what the team is there to achieve, the "task" element in achieving team results. It is equally important for teams to establish a code of conduct. This involves defining team values and ground rules as a way of establishing the way team members are committed to treating each other. These values and ground rules provide the basis for the "group process" element in team performance.

Team Values

Team values are the established ways of behaving that team members regard as desirable. Building an understanding of team values is critical to establishing the culture of the team and acts as a starting point for developing team ground rules.

Team Dynamics from the Inside Out

Remember, when we talk about team values, this is very different from the decision-making function Valuing that we examined in chapter 2.

- Team values guide group behavior.
- The function Valuing (F: one of the Feeling functions) reflects how decisions are made by individuals using internal value and belief systems to ensure that alignment is achieved between the external environment and what is viewed internally as important.
- Two specific temperaments use Valuing: Artisans (SFPs), who approach the world with a sense of fun and focus on people, and Idealists (NFPs), whose search for meaning is guided through this process.

As values play such a critical role in influencing how team members treat each other, let's look at how effective your team values are. Examples of team values could include respect, honesty, customer focus, humor, and so on. For an expanded list, see *Turning Team Performance Out,* page 119.

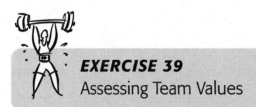

EXERCISE 39
Assessing Team Values

1. List team values in the box below.

Our team values are:

2. Assess the demonstration of your team values as follows:
   - For each value, rate how well you believe it is currently demonstrated on a scale of 1 to 10 (where 1 is high and 10 is low) on the grid below. A sample value, "respect," is provided as an example.
   - Describe what team members need to do more of to strengthen this value.
   - Describe what team members need to do less of to strengthen this value.

Value	Rating (1–10)	Need More...	Need Less...
Respect	6	Listening	Talking over each other

Source: Leslie Bendaly, *Games Teams Play* (McGraw-Hill Ryerson, 1996).

3. Share with other team members your assessment of each value.
4. Develop agreement with your teammates about which values are consistently demonstrated among team members and which need more attention.

Coaching Point

For each value that requires attention, develop a team list of actions that need to be taken or behaviors that need to be developed. Then ask individual team members to commit to taking the actions, or developing the behaviors, that have been agreed to, using the following worksheet.

Value	Action
I agree to . . .	
Signature	

End of Exercise

Ground Rules

Ground rules are the principles to which the team agrees in order to build a cohesive culture and put its values into practice. Ground rules are often difficult to adhere to when completing day-to-day tasks. For instance, when designing a new product in a virtual team, the ground rules are initially obvious and often unspoken: keep other team members informed, listen, share ideas, avoid "turf wars," and so on. However, when time pressures increase and deliverables are due, team members may move into a competitive and/or challenging mode. As a result, the ground rules go out the window. But, articulating these ground rules when there is relatively less stress puts some formal commitments in place for when the heat is turned on. Then it is the responsibility of either the team leader or another team member to pull the team back and review these principles for interaction.

Team Dynamics from the Inside Out

Remember:

- *Artisans* may view complex ground rules as tedious and redundant; emphasize to them the benefits that ground rules bring to the team in terms of making work easier.
- *Guardians* will normally observe and respect ground rules as a way of ensuring consistency and demonstrating respect for other teammates.
- *Rationals* will support the process when they understand that ground rules facilitate the smoother operation of the team system.
- *Idealists,* as the other collaborative temperament (along with Guardians), will welcome the ground rules, as they will help to reduce conflict and ensure that team members are treated fairly.

For more information on temperament, read chapter 1 in this fieldbook or chapter 5 in *Turning Team Performance Inside Out.*

EXERCISE 40
Establishing Team Ground Rules

TEAM EXERCISE

This team exercise for establishing ground rules is to be completed by all members.

1. Review the following list of questions/suggestions and consider your responses.

Ground Rules

Category	Questions/Suggestions
Holding Meetings	• How often should meetings be held? • What is the structure for the meetings? • Who facilitates the meetings? • Who attends meetings? • What are the attendance requirements? • To what extent are videoconferencing and teleconferencing to be used? • Who is responsible for follow-up notes being distributed?

Ground Rules (cont'd)

Category	Questions/Suggestions
Conduct During Meetings	• Start on time • Listen • Avoid interruptions • Refrain from coming and going except for an emergency • Maintain confidentiality • Talk one at a time • "Go for the ball, not the player"—talk about the person's behavior if it did not meet expectations but do not attack the individual's character • Have an agenda • Keep on topic
Communicating with Each Other Away From Meetings	• For what types of information will e-mail be used? • For what types of information will voicemail be used? • How promptly will communications be returned? • How often do we need to communicate? • Can we agree to constructive confrontation (no finger pointing)? • What are appropriate behaviors that are in alignment with our values? • How will we deal with gossip and political posturing?
Solving Problems	• What type of problem-solving process do we follow?
Team Leader Role	• What functions do we wish the team leader to perform?
Team Responsibilities/ Performance	• How will we measure success? • How will we monitor performance? • How will we deal with perceived failures? • How will we reward and recognize achievements? • To whom do we report our output? • How should we format reports going out to the organization? • How frequently should we report to the organization?
Team Roles	• How will we determine team roles? • How will we replace team members if they leave? • How often will we reevaluate team roles?

2. Now discuss the questions and review the suggestions as a group. Agree on which are the most critical ground rules to ensure that your team achieves the optimal SCORE.
3. Consider what other ground rules might be needed for your team. List all your ground rules below.

Our ground rules are:

4. Describe how you will ensure as a team that you adhere to your ground rules.

____

____

____

End of Exercise

Team Key Result Areas

The final elements in setting an effective, well-articulated, and cohesive strategy include conducting a Strengths, Weaknesses, Opportunities, and Threats (SWOT) analysis, as described in *Turning Team Performance Inside Out,* and building "key result areas" to categorize the team's work responsibilities. Key result areas reflect the most important areas of the team's responsibilities, the areas in which results must be achieved. This is where the team needs to concentrate its time and resources to accomplish its goals. Establishing key result areas is a valuable technique that links the overall direction and responsibilities of the team with project goals and milestones.

What We Do and What We Don't Do

An excellent method for developing key result areas is to start two lists: "What We Do" and "What We Don't Do." This procedure will immediately begin to filter tasks and projects onto or off the list of items to be considered in forming key result areas. The team may also choose to include some of the "What We Don't Do" items in the key result areas as new projects to work on in the future. Table 9 provides examples of such lists for a technical support group.

Table 9 Example "What We Do" and "What We Don't Do" Lists (for a Technical Support Team)

What We Do	What We Don't Do
Install patches	Train staff in customer service skills
Troubleshoot bugs	Provide consulting solutions
Perform preventative maintenance	Design the products
Manage call volume	Market the products
Manage cases	Provide presales support
Train staff on products	Provide postsales support
Monitor support revenues	
Suggest value-added services	

After those lists were completed the technical support group determined that two projects needed to be moved into the "What We Do" column:

- While the team was not responsible for overall product design, it was responsible for interfacing with the engineering group from a support perspective regarding product reliability, availability, and supportability; this needed to be included in the team responsibilities.
- The team needed to begin a more formalized service skills training because the profile of the company's typical customer had changed from a technical expert to a midlevel manager, requiring more interpersonal skills and less product jargon.

EXERCISE 41
What We Do and What We Don't Do

TEAM EXERCISE

In this team exercise, team members are to complete the following steps.

1. Individually, list the projects that you think the team does and does not do on Post-it® Notes. Write one specific task or activity on each Post-it Note. Place each on the form below as appropriate.

What We Do	What We Don't Do

2. Combine all the Post-it Notes containing the things the team does and does not do and eliminate duplications. Group the Post-it Notes into those two categories and create a flip-chart in the format shown below.

Combined List

What We Do	What We Don't Do

Team Huddle!

Review each item on your "What We Do" list and discuss the following:

- Should we be doing this?
- Does this task relate to our team purpose?
- Does this project contribute to our achieving our mission?
- Do we want to continue doing this?
- Anything else? (make sure this is asked at least twice)

Review each item on your "What We Don't Do" list and discuss the following:

- Should we be doing this?
- Could this task relate to our team purpose?
- Could this project contribute to our achieving our mission?
- Do we want to start doing this?

3. Add any additional tasks or projects to the list of things the team does. How could you eliminate those tasks you want to stop doing?

____

____

____

Coaching Point

In today's fast-paced environment, consciously deciding what not to do is critical for high-performing teams so that time and energy are focused on the projects that will produce the best results.

End of Exercise

Guidelines for Defining Key Result Areas

Key result areas do *not* describe the type of results to be achieved, but rather categorize work into headings. This grouping procedure is a valuable tool for teams as it complements the way the human brain naturally works (see below).

Time Out!

Did you know that ...?

- The *subconscious* brain works 24 hours a day and has, as far as we know, unlimited capacity.
- The *conscious* brain works only when we are awake and can concentrate on only one thought at a time; as a result, when we have a multitude of tasks to complete we may feel overloaded.
- The *preconscious* brain reduces this perceived overload because it can keep an overview or outline of 7 plus or minus 2 categories—that is, 5 to 9 categories.

Having defined what we do and what we don't do, we now need to group the tasks under five to nine headings to be able to build an overview of the team responsibilities: the key result areas. This process benefits the team by using the preconscious brain and giving team members a feeling of control, thereby reducing stress. Guidelines for establishing key result areas to help build an effective overview are listed in table 10.

Table 10 Guidelines for Defining Key Result Areas

Make Titles Brief	Use one to four words for your key result area titles. *Example:* "Financial Management"
Make Titles Descriptive	Key result areas should describe areas within which team results are to be achieved; they should not state specific aims or performance standards. *Example:* "Customer Satisfaction" would be a key result area, not "Increase Customer Satisfaction Scores by 20%."
Be Complete	Key result areas should cover all aspects of the team's responsibilities—all the team does and ought to do needs to be included somewhere in a key result area. *Example:* The complete list of "What We Do" from the previous exercise should appear somewhere among your key result areas.
Be Clear	Key result areas should be immediately understandable to all team members. *Example:* "Problem Identification" might be too vague: What problems?
Avoid Overlapping	When two key result areas are just different aspects of the same subject, they should be combined whenever possible. *Example:* "Marketing Communications" and "Advertising" could be combined as "Marketing Management."
Stay Within Scope	The team's key result areas should not extend beyond the team's level of authority or sphere of responsibility. *Example:* Avoid titles such as "Company Strategy"—unless you are a member of the executive team, you are unlikely to have any direct influence on the company's strategy.

The technical support team described earlier identified seven key result areas where they needed to focus their energy to be successful, as listed in table 11. To the right of each key result area is the reason for its inclusion.

Table 11 Example Key Result Areas (for a Technical Support Team)

Financial Management	First and foremost, the team has to achieve its revenue projections, meet budget requirements, and control its costs.
Customer Satisfaction	A critical metric for the group is customer satisfaction, and this key result area includes such projects as customer satisfaction surveys, major-account management, and customer councils.
Problem Resolution	The obvious role of a technical support team is to solve customer issues in a timely way, including case management and reactive and proactive support.
People Management	This key result area includes hiring, training, and motivating team members. Based on the example in table 9 (p. 180), a new project in this area will be customer service skills training.
Process Reengineering	Assessing current processes and procedures and recommending improvements is a vital key result area that had been overlooked as the team focused on day-to-day problem solving. Defining this as a key result area helped to ensure that resources and energy remain focused on this activity. Liaising with engineering on product design will also be included.
Tools	This key result area was a new project for the team; use of tools can drastically raise support center productivity.
Internal Communication	The way that companies work together internally has an important influence on external customer service levels.

Coaching Point

Defining key result areas will help you capture not only the reactive tasks and projects for which the team is responsible, but also the other proactive projects that are critical to raising overall team performance levels.

Now that we have reviewed the principles involved in defining key result areas, it is time to define your team's key result areas.

EXERCISE 42
Defining Your Team's Key Result Areas

TEAM EXERCISE

Refer back to exercise 41 and follow the steps below to agree, as a team, on your key result areas.

1. Gather your Post-it Notes from the "What We Do" column in exercise 41.
2. Start grouping the Post-it Notes together if they seem to relate to similar things, until you have five to nine categories. For instance, "Generating Invoices" and "Collecting Receivables" would be placed next to each other.

Team Dynamics from the Inside Out

Remember:

- Defining key result areas in this way uses the decision-making process Analyzing; team members for whom Analyzing is not easy may struggle with this exercise.
- Any team members with a working style of STP or NTP should be a great aid in completing this project.
- Guardians and Rationals appreciate the use of key result areas because they like the structure that this approach provides.

For more information on Analyzing, review chapter 2 in this fieldbook. For more information on working style, review chapters 3 and 5 in *Turning Team Performance Inside Out.*

3. As a team, agree on a key result area title that would describe each group.
4. Enter the key result area titles on the form below.

Key Result Area Form

Key Result Area	Description

Team Dynamics from the Inside Out

Defining key result areas focuses on the big picture (abstract), which then links to the details (concrete); this is contrary to the way approximately 80 percent of the population operates. Using Post-it Notes helps to make the exercise more concrete and should make grouping the tasks into key result areas somewhat easier.

End of Exercise

In later chapters, we will move from the high-level overview of the team's responsibilities to a more tactical breakdown in terms of who does what, and when.

Wrap-Up

Establishing a cohesive strategy is critical to your team's success. Working through the exercises in this chapter can provide a new team with motivation and be morale boosting for a preexisting team. As we worked through the steps outlined in the Strategic Planning Pyramid, we also enhanced the relevance of the techniques by providing tips and information on the influence that temperament and working style can have on this process. Being aware of these different viewpoints can increase the effectiveness of the strategy-setting process as team performance is influenced from the inside out.

SCORECARD

Before moving on to chapter 6 or other chapters, ask yourself the following questions:

- ☐ How well is your team strategy aligned with your organization's vision? What could you do to improve this calibration?
- ☐ How effective is your team purpose, and did you create a team purpose that your entire team can commit to?
- ☐ Have you defined your team mission statement with your team members?
- ☐ Have you also described your team's culture in terms of its values and ground rules?
- ☐ Have you established key result areas for your team by looking at what you do and don't do as a team and then categorizing the output?

6

Establishing Clear Roles and Responsibilities

GAME PLAN

The second characteristic of a high-performing team is establishing Clear Roles and Responsibilities (the C in SCORE) for team members. As you continue to build your Dream Team, this chapter will help you

- Define the core requirements for team members
- Assess the competencies of the current team
- Define key result areas for each person on the team
- Clarify responsibilities for each team member
- Establish realistic, yet challenging, objectives for work output

Linking Strategy to Roles and Responsibilities

In chapter 5, we established a cohesive strategy for our team. Now it is necessary to link the team acivities with individual team members' projects, deliverables, and responsibilities. As you know, if someone is not held accountable, it is unlikely that tasks will get completed in a timely manner. The link between strategy and roles and responsibilities is shown in figure 9.

FIGURE 9 Cohesive Strategy Linked to Clear Roles and Responsibilities

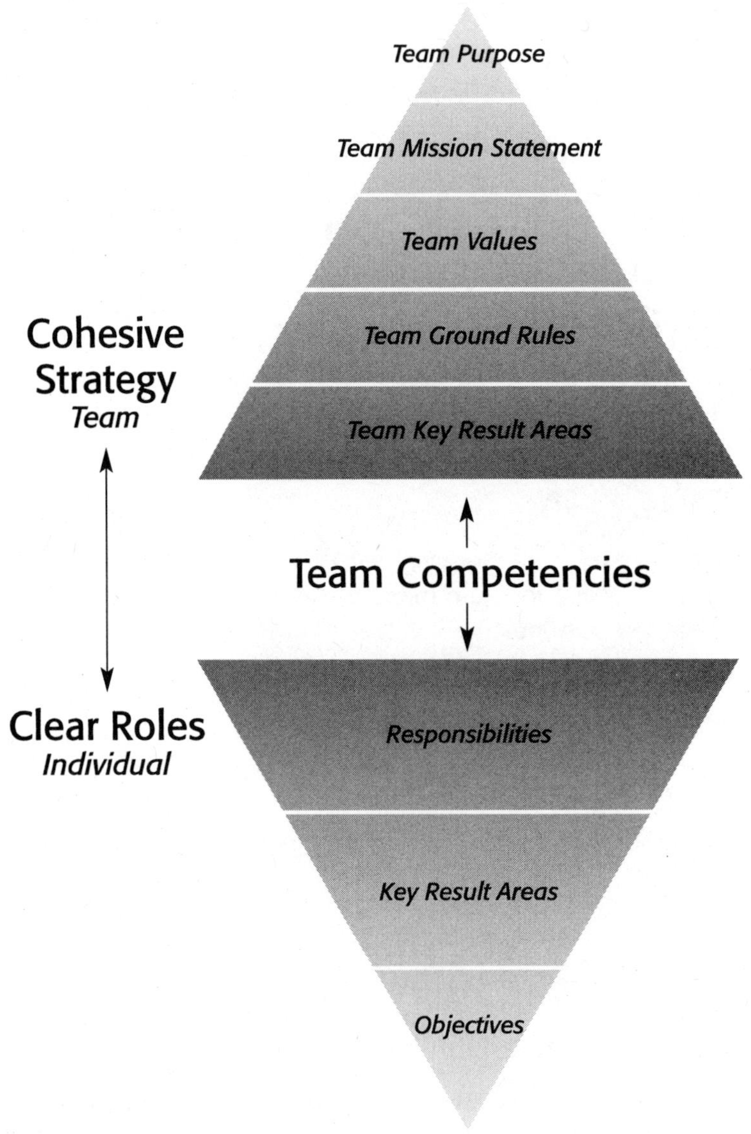

Now that we know what the team wants to achieve (see exercise 42, pp. 186–87) we need to assess what skills, knowledge, and attributes we need on our team to fulfill these overall responsibilities (the team requirements). This involves defining and assessing our team competencies. From this point we need to define the overall accountabilities for each team member (his or her key result areas), specify responsibilities (using a new tool, "RASCI"), and set objectives to establish required deliverables.

Defining Team Requirements

Deciding on individual responsibilities requires building an overview of the comprehensive functions of the team and from there determining the particular knowledge, skills, talents, and abilities that need to be represented by team members.

> ***Foul!***
>
> Don't make the mistake of putting too much emphasis on the technical skills and knowledge team members must possess to do their specific tasks. The less-tangible attributes such as leadership and motivation can greatly influence the team process and productivity.

No one person will fulfill all the requirements of any given team. Those with the desired technical skills may lack communication skills, those with excellent influencing skills may have difficulty in management functions, and so on. The team needs a balance of skills *and* competencies to manage team projects effectively.

> ***Coaching Point***
>
> Remember, it is a common preference to want team members on the team who are "just like us," rather than those with the skills and competencies required for the position. Then we end up with more people who can't do the job!

Table 12 is a sample team shopping list.

Table 12 Examples of Team Requirements and Competencies

Requirements	Competencies
Technical/ Professional Knowledge and Skills	• Technical/professional knowledge required to achieve the team objectives, particularly any specialized information • Technical/professional skills and experience in a particular functional area—such as programming languages, statistical process control, etc. • Proficiency in machine operation and/or software applications
Communication Skills	• Oral communication: the ability to effectively communicate verbally in individual or group situations • Written communication: the ability to express ideas clearly in written form • Listening: the ability to understand and use information from oral communication
Motivation	• Job motivation: the extent to which activities and responsibilities in a job result in personal satisfaction • Initiative: proactive attempts to influence events and achieve objectives
Interpersonal Influence	• Personal leadership: using appropriate interpersonal styles and methods to guide individuals or groups toward task accomplishment • Team orientation: working with people on a team to build high morale and group commitment to objectives • Persuasiveness: using appropriate interpersonal styles to gain agreement on, or acceptance of, an idea, plan, activity, or project; ability to put people at ease and be liked and trusted and to build rapport
Personality Traits	• Persistence: adhering to a course of action, belief, or purpose until the desired objective is achieved or is no longer realistically attainable • Independence: ability to take action based on personal convictions rather than deferring to the opinions of others • Responsiveness: reacting quickly to suggestions, influences, appeals, and requests

Table 12 Examples of Team Requirements and Competencies (cont'd)

Requirements	Competencies
Management Skills	• Planning and organizing: establishing a course of action for yourself and/or others to accomplish a specific objective; planning proper assignments of personnel and/or appropriate allocation of resources • Control: establishing procedures to monitor and/or regulate processes, tasks, or activities of employees; taking action to monitor the results of delegated assignments or projects
Problem-Solving and Decision-Making Skills	• Analysis: relating and comparing data from different sources, identifying issues, securing relevant information, and identifying connections • Creativity: generating ideas and developing unique solutions to problems • Resourcefulness: acting effectively and imaginatively in difficult situations; finding ways to get desired information, resources, and/or results • Judgment: developing alternative courses of action and making decisions that are based on objective and subjective criteria

Now that we have reviewed some general competencies, let's consider your team requirements in more depth.

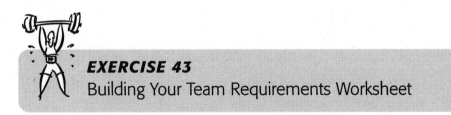

EXERCISE 43
Building Your Team Requirements Worksheet

Referring to the team's key result areas you identified in chapter 5 (exercise 42) and the competencies list in table 12, or your own competency profile, list the critical abilities, knowledge, and personality traits you believe are required for your team to achieve the desired results.

Team name: ______________________________

Major responsibilities (from key result areas on p. 187):

____

____

____

Team requirements:

Technical/professional knowledge and skills

Communication skills

Motivation

Interpersonal influence

Personality traits

Management skills

Problem-solving and decision-making skills

End of Exercise

Now let's combine the individual information into a team list.

EXERCISE 44
Creating a Team Competencies List

TEAM EXERCISE

As a team, combine the individual worksheets from all team members to create a composite team competencies list.

Team name: ____

Major responsibilities (from key result areas on p. 187):

____

____

____

Team requirements:

Technical/professional knowledge and skills

____

____

____

Communication skills

____

____

____

Motivation

____

____

____

Interpersonal influence

____

____

____

Personality traits

____

____

____

Management skills

____

____

____

Problem-solving and decision-making skills

____

____

____

Team Huddle!

Discuss the results using the following questions:

- To what extent was there agreement between team members around technical/professional knowledge and skills required?
- To what extent was there agreement between team members around those requirements—communication skills, motivation, interpersonal influence, personality traits, management skills, problem-solving and decision-making skills?
- What were the easiest categories to determine?
- What were the most difficult to determine?
- Which are the most important for your team, and why?

End of Exercise

Now let's evaluate the extent to which your actual team competencies match the team requirements.

EXERCISE 45
Evaluating Your Team Competencies

Now that you have identified the competencies that your team requires, think about each team member and his or her particular strengths. Fill in one team member's name at the top of each column. Write an *S* in the boxes that represent his or her strengths.

Evaluation of Team Strengths

	Team Members' Names							
Requirements								
Technical/Profes-sional Knowl-edge and Skills								
Communication Skills								
Motivation								
Interpersonal Influence								
Personality Traits								
Management Skills								
Problem-Solving and Decision-Making Skills								
Other (specify)								

Team Huddle!

Discuss the results using the following questions:

- To what extent is there a match between competencies you believe are required and team members' strengths?
- What competency is the team's greatest strength? What implications does this have for team performance?
- Which competencies are not represented or are in short supply on the team? What implications does this have for team performance? How can you compensate for this relative absence?

Coaching Point

Sometimes it can be beneficial to recruit a team member who lacks the key functional skills yet possesses the interpersonal and influencing skills to add diversity and a fresh perspective to the team.

End of Exercise

Having evaluated the extent to which your team competencies match team requirements, review what influence temperament might have on individual competencies.

EXERCISE 46
Team Temperaments and Competencies

TEAM EXERCISE

It's desirable to have a balance of different temperaments on your team to avoid becoming one-dimensional. As a team, complete the following steps.

1. Group team members by individual temperament. How does your team balance out?
2. Ask each temperament group to assess what it believes are the two strengths it contributes to each competency.

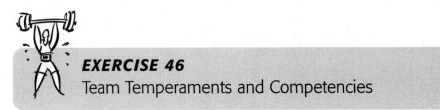

3. Have each group list its ideas and present its results to the other temperament groups.
4. Map the complete team results onto the grid below.

Team Temperaments and Competencies

	Temperament			
Requirements	Artisans	Guardians	Rationals	Idealists
Technical/Professional Knowledge and Skills				
Communication Skills				
Motivation				
Interpersonal Influence				
Personality Traits				
Management Skills				
Problem-Solving and Decision-Making Skills				
Other (specify)				

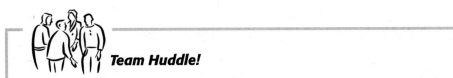

Team Huddle!

Discuss the results using the following questions:

- What seems to be the greatest contribution of each temperament to the various competencies?
- What appears to be the greatest potential challenge facing each temperament with regard to these competencies?
- What implications do these results have for team performance?
- How can you capitalize on each temperament's strengths and minimize possible weaknesses?

Coaching Point

Each temperament contributes certain innate abilities to the team competencies. Considering both temperament and functional skills in allocating roles and responsibilities can provide the best of both worlds in terms of team performance.

Each temperament brings inherent abilities to particular competencies. Following is a sample of the types of skills each temperament might contribute in a given category.

Sample Team Temperaments and Competencies

Competencies	Temperaments			
	Artisans	**Guardians**	**Rationals**	**Idealists**
Technical/Professional Knowledge and Skills	Are dexterous with tools	Possess concrete, hands-on competence	Have abstract competence in their field of expertise	Show abstract, conceptual ability
Communication Skills	Use direct, succinct communication	Use sequential, detailed communication	Use precise language in both oral and written form	Are verbally fluent, with active listening skills
Motivation	Take initiative and make things happen	Have a strong team orientation	Use thorough, logical debating skills and reasoning	Adjust style and build rapport with others
Interpersonal Influence	Make an impact; see concrete results	Make a contribution; live up to responsibilities	Display autonomy and independence; improve systems	Make a difference; have a purpose
Personality Traits	Are independent and responsive	Are persistent, with excellent follow-through skills	Are independent in considering courses of action	When working toward a purpose are persistent and committed
Management Skills	Are action oriented, quick to produce a plan of attack	Are great at contingency planning and establishing processes	Are objective focused and instructional	Will set high-level objectives and support others in reaching them
Problem-Solving and Decision-Making Skills	Make quick decisions in the moment	Like closure and will seek team involvement	Display logical critical thinking and analysis skills with an openness to new approaches	Use creative solutions to problems and are open to new ideas

Foul!

Do not make the judgment that a team member will be unsuitable or incompetent in a specific area just because he or she has a certain temperament. Temperament can influence a person's talent for, and enjoyment of, certain activities, but any person can be productive and find value in any role.

End of Exercise

Defining Roles and Responsibilities

Too often the strategy of the team is not linked to the tasks and activities that individuals take on in their day-to-day work. Now that we know what our team requirements are and we have assessed individual competencies, we can allocate responsibilities to individual team members.

The "RASCI" Process

The RASCI process is a simple but powerful tool for mapping all important team accountabilities for activities, decisions, and projects. Organization charts and job descriptions tend to be limiting definitions of organization structure. In most new work, and in much existing work, there is an enormous amount of waste resulting from poor or unclear definitions of responsibilities and accountabilities. This waste shows up as redundancy, mistakes, conflict, frustration, and higher stress. RASCI charts represent a much more powerful and flexible approach to role definition that will help unsnarl or avoid accountability confusion. RASCI defines the following roles:

R: **Responsibility.** Person on the team taking full responsibility for a specific task—the prime mover.

A: **Approval.** Person whose approval is required for inputs such as money, staff, capital equipment, etc.

S: **Support.** Person supporting the prime mover in making it happen and being accountable for agreed-on actions or resources.

C: **Consultation.** Person consulted by the prime mover before final plans or decisions are taken and having the opportunity to influence plans and decisions.

I: **Informing.** Person to be informed of final plans or decisions without previous involvement.

Team Dynamics from the Inside Out

Remember, when it comes to roles and responsibilities:

- *Artisans* welcome flexibility in the structure: too detailed a role definition may be viewed as restrictive.
- *Guardians* welcome the more formalized definition of roles and responsibilities, which provide them with clear accountabilities.
- *Rationals* enjoy the intellectual process of categorizing job tasks as a way of organizing the team operating system.
- *Idealists* enjoy the abstract approach to understanding individual accountabilities as a way of creating a positive team environment.

For more specific information on temperaments and what they contribute to different roles, see chapter 1 in this fieldbook and chapter 6 in *Turning Team Performance Inside Out.*

Table 13 is a completed sample RASCI chart for four team tasks only. An actual RASCI chart would include many more tasks. As you can see, specific tasks are listed in the left-hand column, and team members are allocated RASCI roles as described on page 202.

Table 13 Sample RASCI Chart (for an Account Management Team)

Tasks	Account Manager	Branch Service Manager	Systems Engineer	Call Center Engineer	Account Support Engineer	Sales and Service Rep	Field Engineer	Support Operations Rep
Sell Upgrades	R	C	S	I	S	C	S	A
Conduct Quarterly Reviews	C	R	S	S	S	S	S	
Solve Hardware Issues	I	S	S	S	R	I	S	
Provide Feedback to Engineering	I	S	R	I	S	I	I	

Note: A blank signifies no involvement necessary in the task.

Now that you have reviewed the RASCI process, let's try the approach for your team.

EXERCISE 47
Using the RASCI Process

TEAM EXERCISE

In this team exercise, we'll try to identify specifically who in your team is responsible for what. Follow the steps below to clear up any confusion about accountabilities!

1. In the left-hand column in the table below list the most important tasks undertaken by the team; if you completed exercises 41 and 42 in chapter 5, you can use that information as a starting point.
2. Now list the team members' names across the top: one per column.
   - In each row list the role that you think you and other team members play in the team using RASCI as described previously: one letter per box.

Remember, it is OK for individuals to have a blank box for tasks in which they are not involved.

RASCI Chart Template

Tasks	Team Members' Names							

Team Huddle!

Discuss the following questions:

- How many rows had multiple Rs? How will this affect accountability? How can you clarify responsibility? Who is responsible for each task? Who is the prime mover?
- What other tasks should be added? Are there any tasks that were listed that are not included in your key result areas and should be?
- What is each person's role for each task?
- What overlap is there between tasks and key result areas?
- Are there any key result areas that do not have tasks associated with them? Are those key result areas really relevant for your team?

Coaching Point

This RASCI exercise provides a valuable opportunity to allocate responsibilities to team members, reduce duplication of effort, and clarify accountability overlaps or omissions.

End of Exercise

Defining Team Member Key Result Areas

Now that we have determined responsibilities for team members using RASCI, we wish to build a picture of each team member's overall responsibilities, which will also include other tasks and activities in which the team member is involved and projects to which he or she contributes. We do this by defining the key result areas for each individual on the team. If team members are to accomplish the team objectives, they need to clearly visualize their deliverables and spend time on the right things, their key result areas. High-performing team members focus their time and resources on these functions.

EXERCISE 48
Defining Your Key Result Areas

1. To define your key result areas, answer the following questions:
   - Based on the RASCI analysis, what are you specifically responsible for on the team?
   - What specific knowledge do you need to add value to team performance?
   - What results are you expected to achieve?
   - Where can you make a contribution to team objectives?
   - Where do you spend your time?
   - What tasks do you complete on a daily/weekly basis that contribute to team output?
   - In which areas can you work to create specific results for your team?

Examples of Possible Individual Key Result Areas

• Financial Management	• Sales/Business Development	• Marketing
• Team Development	• Customer Service	• Communication
• Process Improvement	• Operations Effectiveness	• Projects
• Manufacturing	• Quality Improvement	• Purchasing
• Vendor Management	• Research and Development	• Reporting

2. List in the following grid what you perceive to be your key result areas. Remember, key result areas are designated by nouns. They do not indicate the type of results to be achieved, as in what, when, how, or how much, so they should not include verbs. You should list no more than ten key result areas—these are to be the *critical* areas only.

Individual Key Result Areas

1.	6.
2.	7.
3.	8.
4.	9.
5.	10.

End of Exercise

Now that you have determined your individual key result areas, it is important to share this information with the rest of your team.

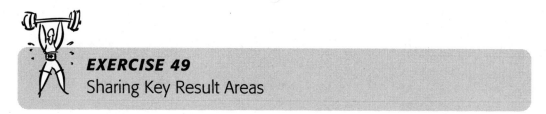

EXERCISE 49
Sharing Key Result Areas

TEAM EXERCISE

In this team exercise, each member presents his or her ideas to other members and answers questions to clarify what would be contained in each key result area.

Team Huddle!

Viewing all the team members' key result areas, ask the following questions:

- What overlap, if any, exists between team members' key result areas? If there is an overlap, how will you avoid duplication of effort and/or conflict over resources?
- Looking at the team's key result areas on page 187, are there any that are not supported by an individual team member's key result area? If so, how can you transform team members' key result areas to cover this absence?
- Are there significant key result areas for individuals that are not reflected in the team's key result areas? Is there a need to update the team's key result areas?

Coaching Point

- Aligning individual members' and the team's key result areas often takes multiple attempts and constant revisiting. Don't be discouraged!
- If the key result areas are not aligned, the team will tend to spin its wheels.
- If the key result areas are symbiotic with each other, overall team performance will be enhanced and individual effectiveness raised.

End of Exercise

Defining Objectives: What Needs to Be Accomplished?

Having defined key result areas, the next step is to create tangible objectives to define and measure work output. The objectives represent the actual outcomes expected within each of the key result areas.

Objectives

Objectives are tangible, measurable results that you can see, not merely roles or activities. According to Alan Lakein, in *How to Get Control of Your Time and Life* (1996), effective objectives need to be "SMART" objectives as defined on the following page.

S: Specific	Does the objective hone in on a particular performance component?
M: Measurable	What are the quantity, quality, cost, and revenue specifications? How will you know when you've reached the objective?
A: Aligned	Is the objective aligned with the organization's vision/mission and the team purpose/mission?
R: Results Focused	Does the objective lead to a result?
T: Time Based	Does the objective have a specific due date?

Example Objectives (for a Consultant)

Incorrect

"To contact five prospects by December 31."

This is a task; it does not tell us what the result should be or why we are doing it.

Correct

"To obtain one client by contacting five prospects for consulting services, with revenue of $15,000 by December 31."

You can see that this is an effective objective because it is

- Specific: One client
- Measurable: Revenue of $15,000
- Aligned: Obtain a client to generate revenue!
- Results Focused: Obtain a client (result), rather than just contact five prospects (task)
- Time Based: By December 31

Subobjectives

Within each major objective there will be short-term "subobjectives." These are usually less than three months in duration and can often be part of another larger objective. For instance, in the example above, another short-term objective could be to contact thirty prospective clients to qualify interest by March 31 of the following year.

Coaching Point

Sometimes it is hard to be specific when writing down objectives. For instance, when considering improving communication, it's hard to quantify an increase. In this case, tasks can be used as the measurement device, e.g., number of meetings, speed in returning calls, amount of customer feedback, and reduction in conflict.

Objectives Versus Tasks

It is quite common to confuse tasks and objectives. Be sure that you can recognize the difference, as reaching an objective has a higher payoff than merely completing a task.

Coaching Point

To differentiate between a task and an objective, ask the following questions:

- What are we trying to achieve?
- What is the benefit?
- Why are we doing this?

If you cannot answer these questions, you may be looking at a task, not an objective.

Table 14 will help illustrate the differences between the two. Make sure you use results-focused words in your objective statements such as *ensure, increase, reduce, obtain, achieve, attain, raise,* and so on.

Table 14 Tasks Versus Objectives

Task	Objective
Participate in Budget Process	Attain $3K project budget for all critical components completed and approved by end of this quarter
Fix the Machine	Ensure that machine is fixed and running with less than .5% downtime by end of this shift
Conduct a Customer Satisfaction Survey	Achieve 95% customer satisfaction in first four categories as measured by the year-end customer satisfaction survey
Write an Operations Manual	Improve operational effectiveness by 10% as measured by the manufacturing productivity report
Conduct a Team-Building Program	Raise team morale by 10% from last year as assessed by the annual internal climate survey

Writing Objectives

Now that we have reviewed the principles, let's write some objectives for our team key result areas.

EXERCISE 50
Writing Your Objectives

1. Write one objective per key result area. For each objective ask the following:
   - Is the objective SMART—Specific, Measurable, Aligned, Results Focused, and Time Based? What are the results to be achieved?
   - Why am I trying to achieve this objective?
   - What are the benefits?

Objectives Form

Date:	
Overall Objective:	
Key Result Area	Objective(s)

2. Now, to refine these objectives:
   - Work with a buddy to refine the objectives you have written.
   - Present your objectives to the other members and discuss them as a group.

Coaching Point

Writing effective objectives is a complex skill. There will often be multiple objectives within each key result area.

Team Dynamics from the Inside Out

Remember:

- *Artisans* thrive on accomplishing short-term, concrete objectives.
- *Guardians* thrive on accomplishing objectives in a structured, sequential manner.
- *Rationals* generally focus on designing strategies to accomplish long-term objectives. Rationals who use Brainstorming and Analyzing (NTPs) may tend to explore more possibilities, resulting in less focus. Rationals who use Visioning and Systematizing (NTJs) will be very structured and driven to achieve the objectives.
- *Idealists* thrive on aligning their objectives with team purpose to give work meaning. Idealists who use Brainstorming and Valuing (NFPs) may resist the call for closure around some objectives, as they tend to be more explorative in nature. Idealists who use Visioning and Harmonizing (NFJs) will tend to push for closure to achieve the objective.

Time Out!

Once objectives have been defined, tasks can then be itemized to make progress toward each objective.

End of Exercise

Wrap-Up

In this chapter we established the critical competencies required for our team in achieving its objectives. Then we reviewed the importance of linking team members' activities to overall team objectives by clarifying key accountabilities using the RASCI process to eliminate confusion, reduce conflicts, and save time that would otherwise be wasted spinning wheels. Finally, to build a complete picture of team member responsibilities, we defined key result areas and objectives for each team member and shared these results within the team.

SCORECARD

Before moving on to chapter 7 or other chapters, ask yourself the following questions:

- ☐ What did you learn when you evaluated team members' abilities against the competencies you had selected? What was the influence of temperament on these critical competencies?
- ☐ To what extent were you able to clarify accountabilities as a team using the RASCI process?
- ☐ How easy was it to create individual key result areas? To what extent did these align with the team's key result areas you had defined in the previous chapter?
- ☐ How easy was it to build realistic yet challenging objectives? What did you learn about trying to write objectives for each key result area? To what extent were your objectives cooperative?

7

Promoting Open Communication

GAME PLAN

The third step in building your Dream Team is to promote Open Communication (the O in SCORE) between team members. This chapter will help you

- Define and improve the channels you use to communicate
- Experience the challenges inherent in one- and two-way verbal communication
- Practice using communication skills to raise trust
- Understand the strengths and challenges of your working style when communicating
- Recognize the signals of different temperaments and working styles
- Adapt your working style to that of others by learning to speak the four languages of temperament
- Raise the levels of collaboration between you and other team members

Why Is Communication Always an Issue?

When most teams are asked to rate the area in which they need improvement, the first thing they are likely to cite is the need to improve communication between team members. Why?

Time Out!

Did you know that 70% of our normal waking hours are spent in communication? Of that time we spend:

- 9% writing
- 16% reading
- 30% talking
- 45% listening

Source: Ralph G. Nichols and Leonard Stevens, *Are You Listening?* (1957).

Establishing a positive communication climate represents a complex combination of means and methods. Means include evaluating and using communication channels effectively. Methods include understanding differences and applying a range of simple and complex skills to adapt to working styles. In this chapter, we provide exercises and examples to help raise communication effectiveness in both areas.

Communication Channels

Whether the team is real or virtual, there are numerous communication channels available through which to send and receive messages, as shown in the following exercise.

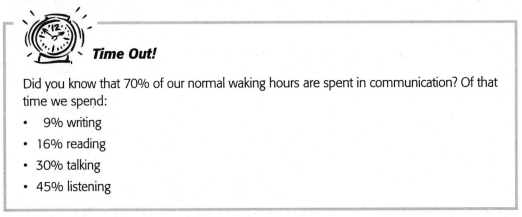

EXERCISE 51
Communication Channels

1. Complete the following grid based on how well you believe each communication channel is currently being used in your team. Rate each channel on a scale of 1 to 10 (1 being great, 10 being poor).

Communication Channels—Individual Rating

Communication Channel	Rating: 1–10 (1 = Great 10 = Poor)	Reasons for Your Rating	Suggestions for Improvement
E-mail			
Voicemail			
Informal "Hallway" Meetings			
Formal Meetings			
Off-Site Events			
Strategic Planning Sessions			
One-on-One Meetings			

2. Now as a team, review and total the ratings from each team member and enter that total in the second column on the form on page 218. Then create an average rating by dividing each total by the number of members. Finally, discuss the results and make suggestions for improvement.

Communication Channels—Team Rating

Communication Channel	Total of Individual Ratings	Average Rating: 1–10 (1 = Great 10 = Poor)	Common Reasons	Suggested Actions
E-mail				
Voicemail				
Informal "Hallway" Meetings				
Formal Meetings				
Off-Site Events				
Strategic Planning Sessions				
One-on-One Meetings				

Team Huddle!

Discuss each communication channel using the following questions:

- What were the differences in the ratings of each channel? Which did you mark as high and which as low?
- What were the reasons given for the different ratings?
- What could be done to improve the effectiveness of each channel?
- What were the similarities in ratings?
- What are two specific actions you could take as a team to improve the effectiveness of each channel?
- Who will do what by when for each of these actions? How will you follow up on these commitments?
- What correlation, if any, did you observe between team members' temperaments and the communication channels they rated highest?
- What correlation, if any, did you observe between the communication channels team members use and their preference for Extraversion or Introversion?
- What implications could this information have on team performance?

Coaching Points

Optimal Use of Communication Channels

E-mail is great for: • Effecting multiple distribution of the same information • Giving instructions • Creating a commitment trail • Communicating specific facts and data • Summarizing follow-up commitments	E-mail is not so good for: • Initiating relationships • Communicating about feelings • Debating issues that need real-time interaction • Discussing urgent issues
Real-time interaction is great for: • Initiating relationships • Communicating feelings • Dealing with issues that need person-to-person interaction • Discussing urgent issues • Building trust	Real-time interaction is not so good for: • Disseminating facts and data (with no discussion) • Giving instructions • Tracking specific facts and data

End of Exercise

Communication in Action

Now that we have reviewed the means we use to communicate, let's look at the methods of communication, which include a range of simple and complex communication skills. To set the scene, let's experience the communication process in action!

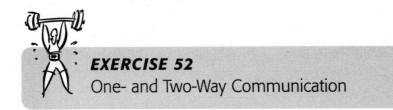

EXERCISE 52
One- and Two-Way Communication

TEAM EXERCISE

This exercise is for individual team members to complete with one another.

Round 1:

1. Pair up with another team member.
2. Choose one person to describe diagram 1 on page 316, and another person to draw it from the other's description.

> ***Foul!***
>
> The person describing the diagram must not show it to his or her partner!

- **Describer:**
  - Sit back-to-back with your partner, making sure he or she is not able to see the diagram.
  - You have three minutes to describe the diagram to your partner so that he or she can draw it. You must use one-way communication only: you can speak, but your partner can't ask questions and you can't check for understanding.
  - At the end of three minutes, turn around and compare the diagrams. How similar are they? What was missed? What was difficult about this exercise?

> ***Coaching Point***
>
> For most people, trying to communicate without receiving feedback is very difficult, and the results often leave a lot to be desired. Yet, often in our high-pressure work world, we do not solicit feedback because of time issues, resulting in communication breakdowns and lost opportunities.

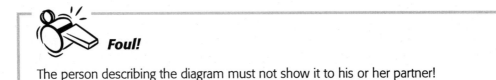

Round 2:

1. Now, switch roles: if you drew last time, you will describe this time, and vice versa.
2. The person who is describing should locate diagram 2 on page 317.

- **Describer:**
  - Sit back-to-back with your partner, making sure he or she is not able to see the diagram.
  - This time you have *five* minutes to describe the diagram to your partner so that he or she can draw it. Plus, you can both use *two-way* verbal communication: you can ask questions, and your partner can answer and then ask you questions to confirm understanding.
  - At the end of five minutes, turn around and compare diagrams. Discuss what was missed. How did you do this time?

Team Huddle!

Discuss the exercise using the following questions:

- What was easier: the first round or the second round?
- Could you see "temperament in action" when talking to your partner?
- Why do you think team members might tend to use one-way communication?
- How can you ensure that they use either one-way or two-way communication based on the needs of the message, not on time constraints?

For most groups, the second round of the exercise produces a better result due to a combination of two factors:

- Two-way communication is more effective
- Learning could be applied from round 1

Coaching Points

- One-way communication takes less time but produces less-effective results; if the message is not understood, it takes two-way communication to clarify it.
- Two-way communication produces better results but is more time consuming.

Team Dynamics from the Inside Out

- Often those team members with abstract information-gathering process functions (*Rationals* and *Idealists,* with Brainstorming or Visioning) will begin with the big-picture overview and move on to details. For instance, they might say, "The diagram is of five rectangles, all the same size, connecting with each other."
- *Artisans* and *Guardians,* who use primarily concrete information-gathering process functions (for Artisans, Experiencing, and for Guardians, Recalling), tend to start with the details and move on to the big picture. For instance, they might say, "Draw the first rectangle in the center. Then draw another rectangle touching it to the right...."
- *Artisans* may begin with the box they consider easiest to position first.
- *Guardians* may begin with the box with the number 1 in it due to their preference for sequential thinking.

For more details, see chapter 1 in this fieldbook and chapter 7 in *Turning Team Performance Inside Out.*

End of Exercise

Building Two-Way Communication

Now that we have experienced the importance of two-way communication, let's review the skills we can use to build a dialogue:

- Asking open-ended questions
- Asking closed questions
- Listening actively
- Paraphrasing

Before we use these communication skills in a couple of exercises, let's review each technique individually.

Asking Open-Ended Questions

Open-ended questions cannot be answered with "yes" or "no" and serve to open up communication between the sender and receiver. Open-ended questions begin with words such as the following:

- Tell me about...
- Describe...
- Explain...
- What...?
- Why...?
- How...?
- When...?
- Where...?
- Who...?

Make sure you allow time for a response when asking questions: four to ten seconds is OK.

> ***Foul!***
>
> Remember, silence is golden. If you answer your own question, it will imply that you don't expect an answer!

Asking Closed Questions

Closed questions can be answered with "yes" or "no" and serve to gather specific facts. They are used to close down a part of the conversation and to verify data. Closed questions begin with words such as the following:

- Do/does...?
- Is/was...?
- Have/had/has...?
- Will/would...?
- Can/could...?

EXERCISE 53
Closed and Open-Ended Questions

1. Change the following closed questions to open-ended questions.

Closed	Open-Ended
Do you watch TV?	Example: What do you like to do for fun?
Do you like to eat fish?	
Did you solve the problem?	
Can I help you?	
Was this subject interesting?	
Have you finished your project?	

2. See page 318 for possible answers.

Coaching Points

- Most of us are more comfortable asking closed questions: they are quicker and more efficient for gathering data; the risk is that more complete information might be missed.
- Open-ended questions can help raise the level of communication within the team and surface opinions and issues that otherwise could accumulate and cause future conflict.

End of Exercise

Listening Actively

Good listening is one of the most complex communication skills. Yet at school, while most of us have spent over ten years being taught how to read and write, little or no instruction is given on how to speak or listen.

Foul!

"Being seen and not heard" is not the same as being taught how to listen! It is taken for granted that hearing is the same as listening, when in reality listening is much more than sensing noise!

Time Out!

Did you know that our brain can "hear" or process information at over 250 words a minute, yet we speak at only approximately 125 words per minute? As a result, over half the time we are ahead of the speaker and bored to tears!

EXERCISE 54
Active Listening

TEAM EXERCISE

For this team exercise, pick one team member to read the following four questions (one time only) to the rest of the team. Ask each team member to write down his or her answers individually in the space provided. No talking!

1. Some months have 31 days. How many have 28?
2. If there are three apples and you take away two, how many do you have?
3. Why can't a man living in the USA be buried in Canada?
4. How far can a dog run into the woods?

1. ______________________ 3. ______________________

2. ______________________ 4. ______________________

See the answers on page 318.

Team Huddle!

Discuss what happened to your listening using the following questions:

- To what extent did assumptions interfere with your listening? How do assumptions affect your listening on the team?
- What other factors affected your ability to listen?
- How could you improve your listening with other team members?
- What correlation, if any, did you observe between team members' listening abilities and their working style?

Coaching Points

- Pay attention to other people. It sounds obvious, but it isn't easy. Stop your mind from wandering or formulating your response.
- Process the information they give you as they are speaking; try to view the data from their perspective.
- Be patient if their communication style or pacing is different from yours.
- Paraphrase what they have said, restating their ideas in your own words.
- Don't dismiss speakers because of their appearance; listen to what they have to say.

End of Exercise

Paraphrasing

Paraphrasing—rephrasing in your own words another person's statement—is a listening skill that can be used to clarify the meaning of that statement. The benefits include:

- Validating the sender
- Clarifying any misunderstandings
- Managing the interaction
- Reducing the mistakes that occur when assumptions are made
- Building trust

Foul!

Paraphrasing is not the same as parroting!

Paraphrasing involves distilling the information the sender has given you into its essence in terms of content and overall meaning. It does not involve your providing an opinion or linking the information gathered to what you want to talk about.

EXERCISE 55
Discussing an Interest

TEAM EXERCISE

Now that we have reviewed the steps for building two-way communication, let's use a brief team exercise to use all these skills in a fun way!

1. Each team member selects a partner: one person in each pair chooses to be the interviewer; the other person will then be the interviewee.
2. Each interviewee selects a topic from those listed below and relays it to his or her interviewer:

- Hobby
- Vacation

- Major accomplishment
- Favorite job

3. Interviewers have *two minutes* to ask *only* open-ended questions (at least five to ten) and listen actively to gather information on the topic selected. For this exercise the interviewees are required to provide the *shortest possible answers* to ensure that their partner has to work hard at questioning. In addition, interviewees should answer "no" if they hear a closed question!
4. All participants must start at the same time, and the interviews may last two minutes only. At the end of the two minutes, interviewers must paraphrase everything they have learned back to their partner in thirty seconds.
5. The interviewees then give feedback on how well their interviewer asked open-ended questions, listened actively, paraphrased, and probed for specifics.

Team Huddle!

Talk about the exercise using the following questions:

- How easy was it to ask only open-ended questions?
- How often did closed questions creep in?
- How accurate was the paraphrasing?
- How did the person being interviewed feel during the exercise?
- How can you ensure that you ask enough open-ended questions to stop assumptions?
- To what extent did you see examples of temperament or working style in this exercise?

Coaching Points

- Listening actively requires that we leave our own opinions aside in the short term to achieve greater overall communication effectiveness.
- Paraphrasing is a skill that most of us use occasionally; more frequent use could smooth out the communication process.

End of Exercise

Building Trust in the Team

Now that we have reviewed skills and techniques for building two-way communication, let's review how communication develops as trust builds. In *Turning Team Performance Inside Out* we described the various levels of communication within the team, using the Communication Pyramid as shown in figure 10.

FIGURE 10 **The Communication Pyramid**

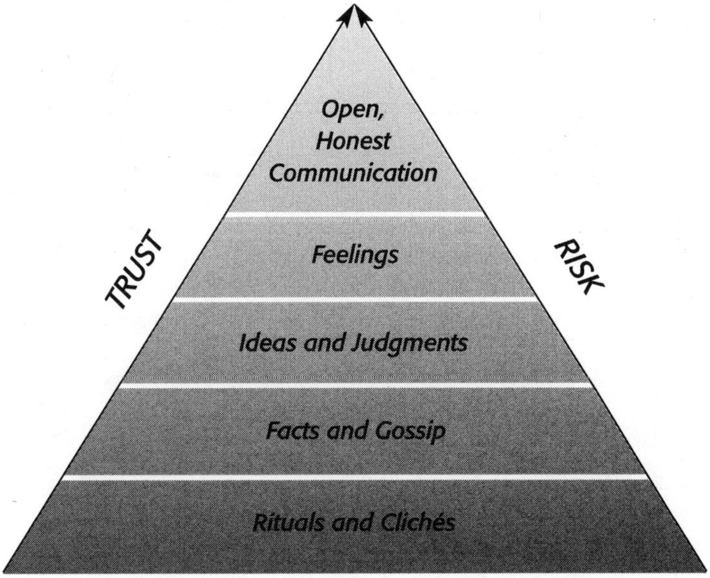

As you can see, as trust increases, more risks are taken and communication becomes more open. In the same way, the greater the risks taken, the higher the level of trust and the more open the communication. Let's introduce an exercise to raise the level of trust in your team. Exercise 56 improves overall team communication by surfacing some of the issues that might be hidden and would benefit from discussion.

EXERCISE 56
What We Talk About

TEAM EXERCISE

For this team exercise, each team member should receive a copy of this worksheet and answer the three questions anonymously.

- What do you talk about in the team?

1. ______________________________
2. ______________________________
3. ______________________________
4. ______________________________
5. ______________________________

- What would you like to talk about but don't?

1. ______________________________
2. ______________________________
3. ______________________________
4. ______________________________
5. ______________________________

- What would you never talk about?

1. ______________________________
2. ______________________________
3. ______________________________
4. ______________________________
5. ______________________________

Collect the worksheets and ask a neutral third party to transcribe the combined results.

Team Huddle!

Discuss the results by asking the following questions:

- What subjects arose as answers in all three questions from different individuals?
- What subjects do you agree you should never talk about as a team?
- What subjects do you agree you should talk about as a team? How can you ensure that these discussions take place?
- What are the reasons that individuals give for wanting to talk about something and yet not doing so?
- What ground rules/values can you implement/revisit to ensure that team members raise the issues that are important to them?
- What influence did temperament and working style have in these discussions?

Coaching Points

- If team members want to discuss certain subjects but don't, this can mean that the subjects may arise in less acceptable ways such as gossip and innuendo.
- The higher the trust, the greater the likelihood that "real" issues will be discussed and addressed in the team forum and that open, honest communication is achieved in the team.

End of Exercise

Trust and Open Communication

Studies of teams have isolated three levels of trust:

- Deterrence-based trust: team members fear they will be punished if they don't do what they say they will do
- Knowledge-based trust: this level of trust develops over time as team members become comfortable with each other and feel confident in their ability to deliver on their promises
- Identification-based trust: this level of trust is built on empathy and shared values, where the team members put themselves in each other's shoes and feel a complete ownership of team results

As identification-based trust is important for team cohesiveness, try the exercise below to get to know your team members better and to practice, for a short time, walking in their shoes.

EXERCISE 57
The Role Nouns Exercise

TEAM EXERCISE

In this team exercise, individual team members should complete the following steps:

1. Write down five to ten nouns that reflect the various roles you play in your life. Remember, a noun is a person, place, or thing. Use work-related nouns such as *team member, manager, organizer, problem solver,* and *tactician;* home-related nouns such as *friend, mother, father, brother,* and *sister;* or nouns that are hobbies such as *gardener, exerciser, woodworker,* and *car mechanic.*

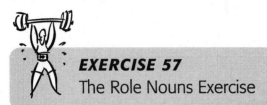

Foul!

Don't pick *objects* such as car, bike, or house! Pick *roles* you play!

- ______________________________
- ______________________________
- ______________________________
- ______________________________
- ______________________________

2. Pair up with another team member, preferably someone you do not know very well, and exchange lists.
3. Pick who will interview first. The purpose of the interview is to gather more information about each of the role nouns on that person's list so that you can explain them in more depth. Interviews are to last three minutes and occur concurrently.

The following guidelines will be helpful:

- Ask open-ended questions.
- Write down notes to help you remember information that your partner tells you.
- Make sure you clarify any information that is not clear.

4. After that interview switch roles: the interviewer becomes the interviewee, and vice versa. Conduct the interview as you did before.
5. This part is critical! You are now to introduce yourself to the group as though you were your partner, using the information gathered and following this format:
   - Begin with "My name is..." (your partner's name, not yours!).
   - Explain your partner's role nouns using the information you have gathered; be sure to stay in the first person: "I," "me," "my," and so on.
   - Conclude with "My name is...."
   - Do not say "he" or "she" during your introduction of yourself as your partner.

Team Huddle!

Discuss the exercise using the following questions:

- How easy was it to speak about your partner in the first person only?
- Of the role nouns you heard from the team members, which surprised you?
- What were some commonly used nouns?
- How did you see temperament and working style demonstrated in this exercise?
- How did this exercise build team trust?

Coaching Point

Use this exercise at any stage of team development to build trust. It is particularly effective in the team-forming stage.

Team Dynamics from the Inside Out

- Team members with a Feeling preference (Harmonizing or Valuing) tend to ask more relationship-based questions.
- Team members with a Thinking preference (Systematizing or Analyzing) tend to ask more fact-based questions.

To review details on the functions, see chapter 2.

End of Exercise

Your Working Style in Communication

The complexity of the communication within the team is increased by the influence of team members' temperament and working style on any type of interaction.

Coaching Point

Each temperament brings very different strengths and challenges to team communication. By understanding some of these differences, we can begin to value their unique contributions.

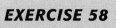

EXERCISE 58
Temperament and Communication

TEAM EXERCISE

Group team members into temperament groups—Artisans, Guardians, Rationals, and Idealists (revisit chapter 1 if you are not sure of these designations)—which should then complete the following steps:

1. List answers to the following two questions and be prepared to present your ideas to the other groups. Take about ten minutes for this exercise.

- What do you perceive to be your temperament's strengths when communicating with other team members?

- What do you perceive to be your temperament's possible challenges when communicating with other team members?

2. Present your lists to the rest of the team.

Team Huddle!

Discuss the results using the following questions:

- What did you observe from listening to each temperament group present?
- What were the differences in strengths that you observed?
- What were the differences in the challenges that were discussed?
- What are the contributions of each temperament group to open communication within the team?

Team Dynamics from the Inside Out

The following are sample comments about communication.

Temperament and Communication

Temperament	Strengths	Possible Challenges
Artisans	• Use brief, concise communication • Tell great stories and give colorful examples to clarify communication • Say what's going on as they see it	• May miss some of the steps, as they think more quickly than they can speak • May sometimes offend others with their casual/informal communication style
Guardians	• Are great at giving structured/sequential instructions • Present an organized message • Will include examples and all the details	• May have trouble processing rapid or nonsequential information • May provide too much detail
Rationals	• Use precise language—will find exactly the right word for a situation • Use critical questioning to help improve ideas • Provide an objective, independent viewpoint	• May appear overly critical • May appear arrogant
Idealists	• Are empathetic and able to build bridges between disparate viewpoints • Tend to naturally adapt their communication style to others' • Express optimism about people and their potential	• May jump from topic to topic without obvious connection • May use general statements and hyperbole—may be imprecise

End of Exercise

Now let's look at how we can adapt our style to communicate more effectively with others.

EXERCISE 59
Improving Communication

TEAM EXERCISE

Group team members into temperament groups—Artisans, Guardians, Rationals, and Idealists—which should then complete the following steps:

1. Discuss ideas for improving communication with the other three temperament groups, excluding your own temperament. (For instance, Rationals would discuss improving communication with Artisans, Guardians, and Idealists.) We assume members would know how to communicate with those of their own temperament!

Foul!

- Make sure you discuss what *you* can do to change behavior, not what the other groups need to do to communicate with you—remember, the only person's behavior you can directly influence is your own!
- Don't write down pat answers such as "Be nice to Idealists!" Each temperament group will have a chance to agree with or dispute the ideas.

2. Answer the following questions after filling in the temperaments other than your own:

- What specifically can you do to improve communication with members having the ____________ temperament?

____

____

____

____

____

- What specifically can you do to improve communication with members having the ____________ temperament?

____

____

____

____

- What specifically can you do to improve communication with members having the ____________ temperament?

____

____

____

____

3. Present your ideas to the other groups as follows:

- Artisans to Guardians, then Rationals to Guardians, then Idealists to Guardians
- Artisans to Rationals, then Guardians to Rationals, then Idealists to Rationals
- Artisans to Idealists, then Guardians to Idealists, then Rationals to Idealists
- Finally, Guardians to Artisans, then Rationals to Artisans, then Idealists to Artisans

This will result in focused attention on each temperament group in turn. Each group will have an opportunity to try to change ideas that they do not agree with and add other ideas that would smooth the communication process from their perspective. For instance, Guardians might say, "I agree that it is helpful for me if you communicate more sequentially. I would also prefer to hear detailed examples that explain your idea."

Team Huddle!

Discuss the exercise using the following questions:

- How easy was it to think about adjusting your style to facilitate more effective communication?
- Which temperament groups did you find it easiest to adapt to?
- Which temperament groups did you struggle with?
- What challenges do you observe between each temperament group?
- How easy will it be in day-to-day interaction to actually adapt your style as we have discussed?

For high-quality, diverse team communication, all four temperaments need to be represented. However, the greater the diversity, the greater the opportunity for misunderstanding and team conflict. See the chart below for some quick tips on how to avoid communication troubles!

Temperament and Communication

Temperaments	Connections	Potential Conflicts
Guardians and Artisans	• Both tend to focus on concrete information • Both tend to use more specific, literal language	• Artisans like flexibility; Guardians prefer structure and process • Artisans use more casual communication; Guardians may prefer more formal communication
Rationals and Artisans	• Both tend to talk pragmatically—doing what it takes to achieve the end result • The combination of Rational language (big picture) and Artisan language (hands-on) can be complementary	• Artisans use fewer words and colloquialisms, which could be at odds with Rationals' more elaborate, though precise, language • Artisans prefer to discuss the here and now; Rationals tend to focus on the future
Idealists and Artisans	• Both can learn by playing and incorporate fun and humor into communication • Both are adept at influencing others: Idealists through empathy, Artisans through understanding what's in it for the other person	• Artisans' here-and-now, get-to-the-point communication style might be at odds with the future-focused, explorative, Idealist language • Idealists' talk about developing potential and improving quality of life might frustrate Artisans with their *carpe diem* style
Guardians and Rationals	• Both tend to structure their information: Guardians sequentially, Rationals via headings, categories, or models • Both like to talk about the end result	• Rationals' focus on improving the whole system can be at odds with Guardians' need to protect the status quo • Rationals' talk of possibilities can conflict with Guardians' reliance on proven past data

Temperament and Communication (cont'd)

Temperaments	Connections	Potential Conflicts
Guardians and Idealists	• Both tend to build rapport and talk about the people involved on the team • Both like to coach and counsel others	• Idealists' tendencies toward generalizations and future possibilities may appear "out there" to Guardians, who tend to talk about past experience • Idealists' conversations can jump about as they integrate concepts; this can appear unstructured and random to Guardians
Rationals and Idealists	• Both temperaments connect on future-focused abstract information • Each brings a complementary perspective—Idealists as applied to people and Rationals as applied to systems	• Idealists' generalizations might be irritating to Rationals, who prefer precise language and referenceable sources of data • Rationals' tendency to use critical questioning to clarify logic could be perceived by Idealists as criticizing

End of Exercise

Now that we have reviewed conceptually how we can adapt to each temperament and the potential connects and conflicts between temperament groups, let's take the process of adapting to different temperaments one step further. Speaking another temperament's language presents a difficult challenge. However, learning to do so can be an important team skill for influencing other team members and achieving open communication.

EXERCISE 60
Speaking Four Languages

TEAM EXERCISE

For this team exercise in communicating with different temperaments, members should divide into mini-teams of no more than four members each. Each mini-team should follow the steps below.

1. Choose *one* of the following assignments.

   a. You are presenting a status report on your current team project to senior management. What features would you highlight, and what words would you use to appeal to all four temperaments on the senior management team?

   b. You are in a sales meeting with a prospect. What points about your organization would appeal to each temperament? What specifically could you say to get the business?

   c. You are giving feedback to a ___________ temperament. What behaviors would you like to highlight to personalize your feedback to each temperament? What would you say?

2. Then, discuss how to present that assignment in a way that would appeal to each temperament. Think specifically about word choice, delivery approach, and what would interest each temperament—that is, speak all four temperament languages.

3. Present your ideas to the rest of the group for discussion. All team members should be given the opportunity to try to change ideas they do not agree with and add other ideas that would smooth the communication process from their temperament's perspective. For instance, an Artisan might say, "I agree with words such as *fun* and *excitement* in your ad, but I would prefer to hear fewer words overall."

Our Assignment: ___________

To appeal to Artisans:

____

____

____

To appeal to Guardians:

____

____

____

To appeal to Rationals:

____

____

____

To appeal to Idealists:

____

____

____

Source: Linda V. Berens, Linda K. Ernst, Judith E. Robb, and Melissa A. Smith, *Temperament and Type Dynamics: The Facilitator's Guide* (1995).

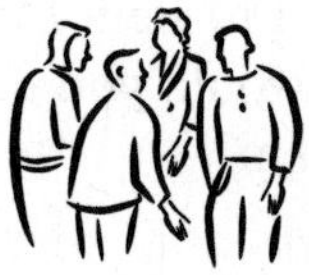

Team Huddle!

Discuss the exercise using the following questions:

- How easy was it to come up with the words and style each temperament would prefer?
- How can we practice speaking the four languages within our team?
- How easy will it be in day-to-day interaction to actually adapt our style as we have discussed?

Coaching Point

Each temperament will inherently value its own style of communication. With practice, team members will become more adept at adjusting their style. This process is rather like stretching: the more you do it, the greater the range of flexibility you develop.

End of Exercise

Wrap-Up

The process of building positive communication within the team is one of the greatest influences on team productivity. Because of the complexity of the communication process, the multitude of communication challenges available to us, and the influence that our temperament and working style may have on our language, team members must invest time and effort in this area constantly. The payoff is increased trust and reduced potential conflicts.

SCORECARD

Before moving on to chapter 8 or other chapters, answer the following questions:

- ☐ How effective are your communication channels? What could you do to improve each channel?
- ☐ What did you learn about one- and two-way communication? How can you build a more effective dialogue using open-ended and closed questions, listening actively, and paraphrasing?
- ☐ In exercise 56, what subjects did you decide, as a team, to talk about? What subjects did you decide not to talk about? How will this increase the level of open and honest communication in the team?
- ☐ To what extent did the role nouns exercise (exercise 57) raise the trust level within the team? What did you learn about each team member from that exercise?
- ☐ What did you learn about the strengths and challenges of your temperament when communicating?
- ☐ How can you increase your ability to communicate with the other temperaments and speak four languages?

8

Enacting Rapid Response

GAME PLAN

The fourth step in building your Dream Team is to enact Rapid Response (the R in SCORE). This chapter will help you

- Understand the increasing complexity of today's business world
- Recognize the critical skills and techniques required to "REACT" quickly
- Reduce resistance to introducing new ideas
- Experience the difference between making a change and undergoing a transition
- Define creativity and practice techniques to help team members think outside the box

What's Changing?

To set the scene, let's complete an exercise to raise our awareness of the changes that are taking place in the current business climate.

EXERCISE 61
Changes in the Work World

Answer the following questions about changes in the work world:

- What are some of the most significant changes that have affected your business life in the past two years?

____

____

- In the past ten years?

____

____

- In the past twenty years?

____

____

- In the past hundred years?

____

____

- What do you perceive is happening to the rate of change?

____

____

- What implications does this rate of change have for team performance?

____

____

Team Huddle!

Discuss change as a team, using the following questions:

- What do you perceive is happening to the rate of change?
- What implications does this rate of change have for team performance?
- How does this rate of change affect the individuals in the team?

End of Exercise

As you and your team have surely recognized, the rate of change is increasing exponentially. Therefore, much of what used to work does not work anymore, and there is a need to shift our thinking and become more flexible.

Time Out!

Did you know that...?

- On average, individuals now have eight careers in their working life
- In 1990, the process of creating an automobile took 6 years from concept to production; by 1997, the process took only 2 years
- In 1984, the average product development cycle lasted 3 years; in 1990, it dropped to 18 months, and in 1997, it was 6 months and still falling
- Most of Hewlett-Packard's revenues come from products that did not exist 24 months ago
- It used to take 7–14 years for half of a worker's skills to become outdated; today, it takes only 3 years

To be successful against this background of constant change, teams have to become more flexible, learn to deal with multiple changes at the same time, minimize resistance to change, and learn to look at situations differently. In this chapter we introduce a series of techniques to help team members "REACT" more quickly and positively to external changes such as those listed above to achieve team goals. These techniques are as follows:

R: Recognize the Changes Affecting Your Team

E: Embrace Change

A: Approach Change Without Bias

C: Create New Possibilities

T: Take Next Steps

Recognize the Changes Affecting Your Team

Now that we have identified some of the changes taking place in the broader organizational context, let's be more specific and discuss the changes facing your team.

EXERCISE 62
Changes Affecting Your Team

1. As you think about your current team, answer the following questions:

- What are some of the changes that have affected your team in the past three to six months? (These could include the introduction of a new process, new technology, new system, new team member, new manager, and so on.)

- What changes do you foresee affecting your team in the next three to six months?

2. Combine your list of changes with the lists of the other team members. Now, as a group, pick one of the changes that was the most commonly cited and enter it below. The team will be using this change to try out the techniques introduced later in this chapter.

Team Huddle!

Discuss the changes listed by all the team members using the following questions:

- To what extent did you agree with the changes that each individual listed?
- Which team members were more aware of the changes? Which team members were less aware of the changes?
- How did each individual's awareness of, and sensitivity to, change relate to his or her temperament and working style?

End of Exercise

As you have seen, some team members are much more aware of, and sensitive to, smaller changes, whereas other team members may recognize only major changes. Recognizing changes and our initial sensitivity to them is the first step in responding more rapidly.

Foul!

Just because a person recognizes change and initially reacts negatively does not mean that he or she is unable to adapt in the right situation!

Team Dynamics from the Inside Out

Each information-gathering function brings different advantages to recognizing change:

- *Experiencing* will help in recognizing small changes regarding what's going on and in pointing them out to others.
- *Recalling* will help in recognizing changes and in comparing and contrasting what is happening now with what happened in the past.
- *Brainstorming* will help in reading between the lines and making broader inferences when faced with change.
- *Visioning* will help by using the initial change stimulus and linking it to a broader future outcome.

Embrace Change

When we do recognize change, we often tend to resist it, preferring what is comfortable and what we are used to. This is because there is a difference between an external change and the internal behavioral change, or transition, that needs to accompany it. Think back to chapter 2, when we tried writing with our "weaker" hand!

Change Versus Transition

Change is a fact of life in any organization, whether it comes banging at the door or insidiously creeps in through the cracks. It is constant and can take place in any number of areas including leadership, team direction, team membership, company policy, and company ownership. These types of shifts are situational and take place in the external world. It is easy to discuss such changes objectively and to understand them intellectually because they are outside us.

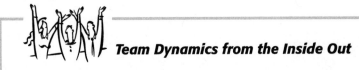

Time Out!

Did you know that the most common response to change is resistance? The problem with resisting all types of change is that it can generate negative energy. If we can instead view change positively, we will be able to capitalize on the energy associated with change.

However, when we try to change our behavior or mind-set to adjust to the external change, we often react very differently. Transition is the psychological process we go through to change our behavior to come to terms with a new situation.

EXERCISE 63
Making a Change and Experiencing a Transition

To experience the difference between change and transition, try this brief exercise:

- Fold your arms across your body; note which arm is uppermost, your left or right arm (there is no correlation between left- and right-handedness and the way you fold your arms).
- Now fold your arms the other way with the other arm on the top.

How does it feel? The idea of folding your arms the other way is easy. This change is external. The reality of having your arms folded the other way is probably uncomfortable, awkward, even difficult. This represents the internal transition that we experience when adjusting to an external change.

Coaching Point

Knowing the difference between change and transition can help clarify some of the discomfort that change produces and enable the team to remain productive in transitional times.

End of Exercise

Reducing Resistance to Change

While recognizing the difficulties inherent in making a transition, let's examine a practical technique for managing the initial resistance to change and stimulating a positive response.

In their book *If It Ain't Broke... Break It!,* Robert J. Kriegel and Louis Patler use the terms *firehosing* and *firestoking* to capture the essence of resisting or welcoming change. *Firehosing* is defined as "a method for prematurely dismissing (or even undermining) new, daring, or different ideas/suggestions/proposals."

Examples of firehosing:

- "That would never work here!"
- "We tried that before and..."
- "It's not in the budget!"
- "The group will never support that!"

Time Out!

A major U.S. bank bought all its managers squirt guns (aka water pistols) so that if they heard a firehosing statement, they could squirt the perpetrator!

Firestoking is defined as "a method for building on ideas by asking questions, providing supportive body language, and involving others."

Examples of firestoking:

- "That's an interesting idea; tell me more..."
- "We haven't tried that before."
- "Let me reflect on that for a moment."
- "How might that work in this situation?"

Let's look at firehosing and firestoking in our team environment.

EXERCISE 64
Firehosing and Firestoking

1. List below the five firehosing phrases you hear most in your day-to-day work.

- ______________________________
- ______________________________
- ______________________________
- ______________________________
- ______________________________

2. Now discuss with your teammates possible firestoking phrases in response to each firehosing phrase and list them below.

- ______________________________
- ______________________________
- ______________________________
- ______________________________
- ______________________________

Source: Break-It! Thinking™. © Louis Patler and Steve Cohen.

Team Huddle!

Discuss the following questions to summarize this exercise:

- Which was easier to use: firehosing or firestoking?
- What could happen to new ideas and your team culture if you always used firehosing before firestoking?
- How can you ensure that you give ideas a chance to develop before giving them the test of reason?
- What ground rules could you institute to make firehosing an unacceptable behavior in this team?

End of Exercise

Firehosing Through History

What would have happened if people had listened to the following and been discouraged?

- "Who wants to hear actors talk?"—H. M. Warner, 1927
- "The concept is interesting, but in order to earn better than a C, the ideas must be feasible."—Yale professor giving Fred Smith a C on his proposal for a reliable overnight delivery service (Federal Express)
- "We don't like their sound—and anyway, guitar music is on the way out."—Decca Records rejecting The Beatles in 1962
- "I'm just glad it will be Clark Gable falling on his face and not me."—Gary Cooper, on his decision not to take the role of Rhett Butler in *Gone with the Wind*
- "The telephone has too many shortcomings to be seriously considered as a means of communication. The device is inherently of no value to us."—Western Union, 1876

Team Dynamics from the Inside Out

In table 15 are firehosing phrases (the external statements) you might hear each temperament use along with the internal question that might be the reason behind the resistance.

Table 15 Firehosing Phrases by Temperament

Temperament	External Statements	Internal Question
Artisans	• It's too rigid • It's going to slow things down • It's a hassle	Process reduces flexibility—Why do we need it?
Guardians	• It's not proven • It's not broken • The person does not have enough experience	How will it disrupt team and work productivity?

Table 15 Firehosing Phrases by Temperament (cont'd)

Temperament	External Statements	Internal Question
Rationals	• Is it well thought out? • It would be better if… • It's not logical	How much will my control be affected?
Idealists	• Is it a meaningful change or just a feather in someone's cap? • It is not fair • People won't like it	What is the real purpose behind the change?

Coaching Points

- For most teams, firehosing is an inherent part of the team culture, thereby reducing creativity.
- If teams could create a culture in which new ideas were welcomed, the team as a whole would respond more quickly to the environment.
- Making the commitment to reduce firehosing will immediately raise the level of energy in the team and the quality of ideas generated.

Often, when this technique is introduced, the first response is, "So now we are going to boost every idea, no matter how stupid it is!" (Is that firehosing the firestoking technique by any chance?) Rather, the important premise is to allow the idea to grow before giving it the test of reason. Like a seed, an idea needs to be protected and nurtured before it is exposed to the elements.

Approach Change Without Bias

Often, when we approach change within our company, we block it with outdated values and beliefs about procedures and obsolete habits embedded in the way we work. We call these embedded values, beliefs, and habits sacred cows. Examples of sacred cows include the following:

- Work is restricted to eight hours a day, five days a week.
- When you join a company, you have a job for life.
- You should be loyal to a company.
- Meetings are a useful way to make decisions.
- Laying off individuals saves money.
- Working longer increases productivity.

According to Robert J. Kriegel in *Sacred Cows Make the Best Burgers* (1997), when we try to introduce new ways of working, organizational sacred cows often block innovations and improvements. He lists twenty sacred cows that, in fact, march through the hallways of most organizations! To approach change without bias, we need to clean out our "organizational closet" so that new possibilities can thrive. Let's think about what sacred cows might be inhibiting your openness to change.

EXERCISE 65
Your Sacred Cows

TEAM EXERCISE

1. As a group, identify which sacred cows are inhibiting your response to the changes you identified earlier in exercise 62.

- ______________________________
- ______________________________
- ______________________________
- ______________________________
- ______________________________

2. Question these sacred cows carefully. Are they still relevant? How could you reduce or eliminate these sacred cows? With what could you replace them?

- ______________________________
- ______________________________
- ______________________________
- ______________________________
- ______________________________

Source: Break-It! Thinking™. © Louis Patler and Steve Cohen.

Team Huddle!

As a team, discuss the following questions:

- How easy was it to identify your sacred cows?
- How easy was it to think of ways to reduce or eliminate your sacred cows?
- What happened to your energy as you discussed the sacred cows?
- Why do you think this change of energy happened?
- What could you do to reduce your sacred cows?

End of Exercise

When we begin to identify sacred cows, it becomes obvious how at home they are in our organizational infrastructure. Make sure you evaluate them carefully; getting rid of one sacred cow can speed up results in the team very quickly!

Team Dynamics from the Inside Out

Remember:

- *Artisans* naturally respond to changes in the environment and enjoy the flexibility that these shifts can provide. Their challenge can lie in not viewing *every* process as a sacred cow.
- *Guardians* can be slow to initiate change when recognizing sacred cows, particularly if it is viewed as change for change's sake. However, when Guardians see the need and are involved in the shift, they are great at implementing adjustments.
- *Rationals,* with their future focus and drive to improve systems, often question the validity of sacred cows. Their challenge lies in controlling their desire to reinvent and continuously improve, whether there is a sacred cow to address or not!
- *Idealists,* with their inner drive to grow and develop, often recognize change as another step in life's journey. While they often try to learn from change and generate possibilities, their challenge can lie in understanding the logistical need for some sacred cows.

Create New Possibilities

Creativity is defined as creating new possibilities that can be put into action. While conceptually it makes sense to approach change without bias, as we demonstrated when discussing transitions, behavior takes a while to follow! However, by practicing specific techniques, we can facilitate the opening up of opportunities. Let's look at some of these options now.

Generating Possibilities

Brainstorming is a commonly used technique for exploring options that are not immediately obvious. We call this approach "generating possibilities" to avoid confusion with the function Brainstorming. Following are some ways to generate possibilities:

- Record ideas clearly and quickly in front of the group
- Generate as many ideas as possible
- Do not evaluate or discuss ideas
- Do not criticize ideas
- Ensure that all team members are participating equally and fairly
- Allow for quiet thinking time
- Combine and build on ideas

Team Dynamics from the Inside Out

Remember, there are two cognitive process functions that naturally support this technique:

- *Experiencing* (generating options from the current context)
- *Brainstorming* (seeing abstract possibilities and patterns in the future)

For more specific information, review chapter 2 in this fieldbook and chapter 8 in *Turning Team Performance Inside Out.*

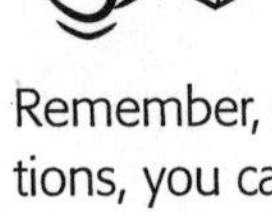

Foul!

Remember, even if neither Brainstorming nor Experiencing is one of your preferred functions, you can potentially access every function with practice!

Let's try an exercise now that can help in creating options.

EXERCISE 66
The T-Shirt Exercise

TEAM EXERCISE

This team exercise will show the process of generating possibilities in action and can act as a great energizer. Team members should divide into temperament groups, which should then complete the following steps:

1. Come up with a T-shirt logo, slogan, and theme song that represent your temperament group, taking no more than ten minutes!

2. Then, present your logo, slogan, and theme song to the other groups.

Source: Adapted from an exercise by D. D. Warrick in John Newstrom and Edward Scannell, *Still More Games Trainers Play* (1991).

Team Huddle!

Discuss the exercise using the following questions:

- How easy was it to come up with the logo, slogan, and theme song for your temperament group?
- What type of energy was generated as you approached the exercise?
- How is this energy different from the energy that is generated when you are approaching a team/business problem?
- How could you harness some of this exercise energy when working with team/business problems?

Because this exercise allows freedom of expression (there are no "vested interests" involved), use this type of activity before a serious team problem-solving session. It will help to free up thought processes and create a positive environment for creating new ideas.

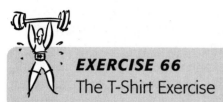

Team Dynamics from the Inside Out

Because this exercise utilizes concrete and abstract data, it allows team members access to all four information-gathering functions. For instance:

- *Experiencing:* What are some options? What colors can we use?
- *Recalling:* What songs can I remember? What types of logos and slogans have I seen in the past?
- *Brainstorming:* What are some possibilities? What else can we think of?
- *Visioning:* What is the overall theme? What is the complete image we want to present?

For more specific information, review chapter 2 in this fieldbook and chapter 8 in *Turning Team Performance Inside Out.*

End of Exercise

Reframing Data

To create new possibilities, team members also have to be able to step back and approach a subject from multiple perspectives and reframe data. Below is an exercise to demonstrate that process in action.

EXERCISE 67
Creativity Quiz

TEAM EXERCISE

As a group, take ten minutes to complete the creativity quiz below. The goal is to fill in the words that fit with the numbers, based on the capital letter clues. As you try to complete the exercise, consider:

- Religion
- Sports
- Math
- History
- Board games
- Culture
- Nursery rhymes
- Transportation
- Metaphors

This exercise forces you to look at a situation from a variety of perspectives and associate options with each. You'll find the answers to this exercise on page 319.

Example: 24 H in a D = 24 hours in a day

7	W of the AW = ________
1001	AN = ________
12	S of the Z = ________
54	C in the D with the J = ________
88	PK = ________
13	S on the AF = ________
18	H on a GC = ________
32	DF at which WF = ________
90	D in a RA = ________
200	D for PG in M = ________
9	P in the SS = ________
8	S on a SS = ________
3	BM (SHTR) = ________
4	Q in a G = ________
1	W on a U = ________
5	D in a ZC = ________
57	HV = ________
11	P on a FT = ________
1,000	W that a P is W = ________
64	S on a CB = ________
40	D and N of the GF = ________
29	D in F in a LY = ________

Source: Unknown.

Team Huddle!

Discuss the exercise using the following questions:

- How easy was this exercise?
- What happened at first?
- What happened when one or two people started to gather ideas?
- What was the best way to solve the problems?
- How many people got discouraged and said, "I just can't do this type of problem"?
- What link did you observe, if any, between individual team members' ability to explore different options and their temperament and working style?

Initially, when trying to generate new possibilities, many people experience a mental block, inhibiting creativity. This problem provides even more reason for firestoking and not firehosing! Remember, creativity does not involve a mystical ability, but rather a series of techniques that can liberate each of us.

Coaching Point

The best approach for encouraging creativity on a subject is often first taking some time to reflect (especially for those with a preference for Introversion). Then, the whole team can get together and throw out ideas, resulting in a "progressive build" to the correct answer (brainstorming helps reduce blocks!). Categorizing possible solutions might refine the creative process. Finally, allowing time after the session for additional thought will also ensure that further developments from those with a preference for Introversion will be included.

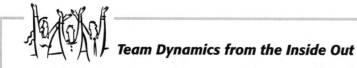

Team Dynamics from the Inside Out

Each temperament is creative in its own way!

- *Artisans* are creative as they tune into what is going on around them and take advantage of the opportunities that arise in the moment.
- *Guardians* are creative as they take what they have learned from the past and give it a different spin.
- *Rationals* are creative as they approach the world with an intense interest in innovation and evaluate new ways to achieve the future goal.
- *Idealists* are creative as they look for new ways of bringing out the best in people and enjoy exploring ideas and possibilities.

End of Exercise

For more information on creativity, see Marci Segal, *Creativity and Personality Type* (2001).

Take Next Steps

The final "REACT" step involves making a decision using differing criteria to decide between possibilities. Let's look in more detail at the decision-making process functions we might use.

Decision Making

Decision making is a vital aspect of responding rapidly to the environment. Intentions that aren't decided upon are highly unlikely to be actualized! Decision making can be a factor in the following SCORE elements:

- Open Communication: we must consider others when making decisions
- Clear Roles and Responsibilities: we must decide who does what
- Effective Leadership: leaders facilitate decisions

We will discuss decision making in this section because responding to changes with a time constraint is often the most critical decision-making application.

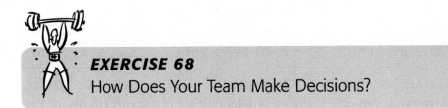

EXERCISE 68
How Does Your Team Make Decisions?

Think about the most recent decisions that have been made in your team.

- What were the five most recent decisions made by the team?

____

____

____

____

____

- Who made these decisions?

____

____

- To what extent did all individuals in the team participate in the decision-making process?

____

____

- To what extent did team members compromise in making decisions?

____

____

- What were the outcomes of these decisions?

____

____

End of Exercise

Decision-Making Approaches

There are several different types of decision-making approaches, most of which revolve around the concepts of win-win or win-lose.

- **Win-win (consensus) decision making:** The win-win philosophy predicates that while a resolution might not be the ideal result for every person on the team, it is a decision with which everyone can agree. It often involves looking for a third alternative.
- **Win-lose (nonconsensus) decision making:** A win-lose decision means that one or more team members are not happy with the conclusion, while others get their needs met.

While the ultimate goal is for team members to be committed to the team direction, it is unrealistic to expect a win-win agreement in every decision the team makes.

Consensus Decision Making

Consensus decision making occurs when a decision is reached on which everyone in the team can agree. It occurs only after there has been full participation by all team members, with active discussion of the advantages and disadvantages of the issue. Consensus decision making is the most effective approach to achieving win-win solutions and normally results in a high-quality result. When a team arrives at a consensus, there is a greater commitment to the course of action and implementation of ideas.

Foul!

Consensus decision-making techniques do not include beating the people in the other party into consensus or wearing them down!

Compromise is not the same as consensus decision making. When there is a compromise, it means that one or more of the team members have given up on their perspective and will likely view the decision as at least a partial loss for them. Consensus decision making is usually more time consuming and can require high-level skills to facilitate full agreement. To facilitate consensus decision making, you can follow these guidelines:

- Combine and summarize similar ideas
- Narrow down a long list by discussing top choices

- Eliminate unlikely choices
- Discuss pros and cons of top choices, using logic and facts to support ideas
- Allow disagreements to be discussed until they are resolved
- Check that everyone is participating—don't allow verbal people to dominate
- Eliminate other choices based on the discussions
- Summarize and review final lists
- Make the decision
- Ensure that the team agrees with the decision

Nonconsensus Decision Making

Other ways of making decisions produce win-lose results but may be justified when a speedy response is needed or when not all team members need to be involved. Different types of nonconsensus decision making include the following:

- **Majority vote:** In a majority vote, team members vote on different options, and the choice that receives the most votes wins. While this process can speed up decision making, certain individuals may end up feeling alienated from the group and, as a result, express less of a commitment to team performance.
- **Minority vote:** In a minority vote, only a few members of the team are responsible for making a decision. This type of decision making often occurs when there are subcommittees responsible for specific activities. For example, associations will normally have program subcommittees, membership subcommittees, and mandatory subcommittees. The subcommittee members have more knowledge about, and buy-in to, the subject area, so they are theoretically the most qualified voters on issues pertaining to their specialization. In this case the minority vote can speed up the decision-making process while not alienating team members. However, if a few people make the decision, even though it relates to the entire team, there is a risk that the members will lack the commitment needed to implement the approved measure.
- **Authority vote:** In an authority vote, one person alone makes the decision. This approach is often taken either when there is an expert in a particular area or when the team leader is using a more directive leadership style. This decision brings the advantage of extreme expediency, but it may result in an inadequate consideration of differing viewpoints and a poor overall result.

Team Dynamics from the Inside Out

Remember, the Judging cognitive process brings certain attributes to decision making:

- *Systematizing* considers logical criteria in the external world such as facts, data, and statistics. Team members who use Systematizing with ease will be able to clearly discuss pros and cons to arrive at an objective decision.
- *Analyzing* brings the ability to evaluate data using internal objective criteria. Team members who use Analyzing with ease approach decision making with their own logical point of view, asking "Why?" to clarify the reasons for a different approach.
- *Harmonizing* brings the ability to make a decision so that everyone involved is comfortable. Team members who use Harmonizing with ease will naturally gravitate to consensus decision making and may struggle when all team members are not in agreement.
- *Valuing* brings the ability to make a decision so that the end result is fair to all. Team members who use Valuing will appear easygoing until a decision seems either unethical or at odds with their internal belief system. At that point, they may become stubborn and unyielding.

To review these functions, see chapter 2 in this fieldbook or chapter 2 in *Turning Team Performance Inside Out.*

EXERCISE 69
Team Decisions

TEAM EXERCISE

Follow the steps in this exercise as a group.

1. Make a list of some of the decisions facing your team.

2. Select several of these decisions and write them in the left-hand column of the blank chart that follows. Evaluate to what extent it is possible or necessary to achieve a win-win (consensus) solution for each issue. If it is not absolutely necessary to reach consensus, identify what type of decision-making approach would be most appropriate for this task.

Decision to Be Made	Consensus or Nonconsensus (Majority, Minority, or Authority Vote)?

Logic might dictate that consensus decision making is always the best approach. However, when teams are under a tight time constraint, consensus decision making may not be the most viable option.

Coaching Point

Involving team members in evaluating the best type of decision-making approach for each scenario will help ensure that commitment to nonconsensus decisions will be higher. If team members can agree on which decision-making approach to use with each type of decision, team response will be speedier while still involving team members in the process.

End of Exercise

Trying On "REACT"

Now that we have reviewed each step of REACT in turn, let's finish this section with an exercise that ties all the techniques together.

EXERCISE 70
Trying On REACT

Refer back to exercise 62 (pp. 248–49), when you identified one specific change facing your team. With this change in mind, practice using the techniques we have introduced to help you REACT more quickly to the environment:

- **R: Recognize the Changes Affecting Your Team**

What is the change? ______________________________

- **E: Embrace Change**

What are three firehosing statements you have heard pertaining to this change?

1. ______________________________
2. ______________________________
3. ______________________________

What are three firestoking statements that you could use when talking about this change?

1. ______________________________
2. ______________________________
3. ______________________________

- **A: Approach Change Without Bias**

What are three sacred cows that might be restricting the ability of the team to make a change?

1. ______________________________
2. ______________________________
3. ______________________________

How could you reduce or eliminate these sacred cows?

1. ______________________________
2. ______________________________
3. ______________________________

- **C: Create New Possibilities**

How can you generate possibilities or reframe the data to approach this change in a different manner?

____

____

- **T: Take Next Steps**

What decision-making approach will you use? Who will do what, by when?

____

____

End of Exercise

Wrap-Up

As we have discussed, teams face an increased rate of change in today's business world. Using the REACT techniques against the backdrop of temperament and working style can help teams respond rapidly and thrive in tumultuous times.

SCORECARD

Before moving on to chapter 9 or other chapters, answer the following questions:

- ☐ What did you learn about the general rate of change in our business climate as a whole? What specific changes did you identify that were associated with your team?
- ☐ How did you respond to the difference between change and transition when you tried folding your arms a different way? To what extent do you experience the challenge in making transitions when faced with the changes? What did you learn about your own and fellow team members' response to change?
- ☐ How often do you observe firehosing taking place in your team? In the organization as a whole? How can you reduce the negative effects of firehosing?
- ☐ To what extent are there sacred cows in your team environment? How could you reduce or eliminate these sacred cows?
- ☐ How did you enjoy the T-shirt exercise? How much easier was it to be creative when faced with a non-business-related brainstorming activity? How could you capture this energy when trying to find unlikely solutions to team problems?
- ☐ When completing the creativity quiz on pages 260–61, what did you learn about how you can enhance your ability to reframe data to find creative solutions?
- ☐ What did you learn about how the team makes decisions? To what extent do you use consensus decision making?
- ☐ How useful were the REACT techniques when applied to the change you identified earlier in the chapter? What actions did you decide on to help you respond more quickly to the environmental changes?

9

Providing Effective Leadership in the 21st Century

GAME PLAN

The fifth and final step in building your Dream Team is providing the team with Effective Leadership (the E in SCORE). This chapter will be of particular use to team leaders, although other members of the team can benefit as well. It will help you

- Identify how you can improve your team leadership effectiveness
- Apply different leadership styles in different situations
- Build an action plan to improve the quality and quantity of the feedback you provide to team members
- Practice coaching in different scenarios
- Introduce relevant exercises to build a high-performing team at each stage of team development
- Review the influence of working style on team leadership activities

Please note: Unless stated otherwise, each exercise is for team leaders.

Why Team Leadership Is Different

One of the greatest influences on team productivity is the effectiveness and adaptability of the team leader. To begin the thought process on what attributes characterize an effective leader, let's start with a warm-up exercise.

EXERCISE 71
Differentiating Between a Team Leader and a Boss

1. On the grid below have your team members individually list things that come to mind when they hear the term *team leader* versus *boss.*

Team Leader Versus Boss

The Team Leader	The Boss

2. Analyze the tone of each list.
3. Compare those lists with the ones in the table below, which was assembled from previous research.

Team Leader Versus Boss

The Team Leader	The Boss
Coaches people	Drives people
Depends on goodwill	Depends on authority
Inspires enthusiasm	Inspires fear
Fixes the breakdowns	Fixes the blame for breakdowns
Says, "We"	Says, "I"
Says, "Let's go!"	Says, "Go!"

Source: Adapted from H. Gordon Selfridge, Selfridge's Department Store, London.

End of Exercise

In the collaborative environment of teams, there is very little place for a boss. Despite the importance of having a team leader, the leader of a task force, project team, or virtual team often has no direct authority over team members. Therefore, the traditional role of the manager or leader as the boss is inappropriate and ineffective. Even if team leaders have authority over the group (as in a functional team such as sales), for the most part it is better for them to use the coaching approach outlined later in the chapter.

Coaching Point

When members feel like they are "coached" rather than "bossed," they develop a sense of ownership, morale increases, and overall team productivity rises.

What Does a Team Leader Do?

In his book *Action Centered Leadership* (1979), John Adair outlined three responsibilities for leaders—achieve the objective, develop the people, and build the team—figure 11 on the following page shows an adaptation of those categories, whose components can be remembered by the mnemonic "LEADER" and are described below.

1. Achieve the Objective

- L: Lead When Necessary. Team leaders lead when the team gets stuck, but they allow other members to direct activity depending on the type of project the team is undertaking. We will review the different leadership styles later in the chapter.
- E: Evaluate and Intervene As Needed. Part of the responsibility of a leader is to manage the overall responsibilities of the team by organizing logistics, lobbying for resources, communicating to the organization about the team's activities, and removing obstacles from the team's path. These tasks can sometimes appear superfluous, but without them the team would be unable to perform at its best.

2. Develop the People

- A: Appreciate Team Members. Providing feedback is a valuable tool for raising team morale and improving team cohesiveness. This appreciation includes both developmental and positive feedback.
- D: Develop Individuals by Coaching. Coaching involves guiding each individual team member by creating a dialogue about what that person needs to learn in order to raise his or her current performance level.

3. Build the Team

- E: Engage the Team. Using team-building techniques and exercises at different stages of team development can motivate and inspire team performance.
- R: Reinforce Results. A critical element in building the team is providing rewards and recognition for exemplary performance.

Based on the above criteria, let's take a look at how you currently rate your leadership effectiveness.

FIGURE 11 Team Leadership Responsibilities

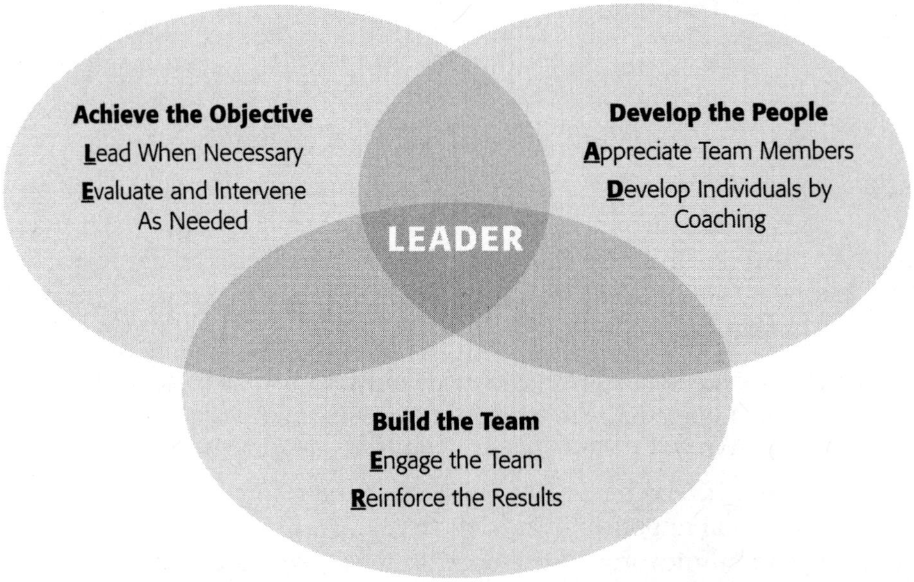

EXERCISE 72
How Effective a Leader Are You?

1. As you think about the three areas of team leadership responsibilities outlined on the preceding pages, review the questions in the table below. Rate your leadership effectiveness in each of the categories on a scale of 1 to 10 (1 for extremely effective, 10 for not effective).

How Effective a Leader Are You?

LEADER Responsibilities	Evaluation Rating: 1–10 (1 = Extremely Effective 10 = Not Effective)
Lead When Necessary • Staying flexible in your leadership style • Adapting your style based on the needs of the situation	
Evaluate and Intervene As Needed • Stepping back frequently to monitor team performance • Intervening to protect the team and its resources	
Appreciate Team Members • Providing positive feedback • Balancing developmental and positive feedback	
Develop Individuals by Coaching • Coaching members of the team • Creating dialogue using open-ended questions	
Engage the Team • Introducing team-building techniques to the team • Being aware of the group dynamics and the stages in team development	
Reinforce Results • Celebrating successes • Stopping to recognize results	

2. Compare your ratings in each category. Which area do you think is the greatest challenge for you? What will you do to improve in this area?

Which area is your greatest strength? What can you do to build on this area?

Coaching Point

Based on your responses, focus on the individual LEADER sections of this chapter that are the most relevant to you.

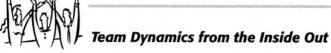

Team Dynamics from the Inside Out

Remember:

- *Artisans* tend to excel at achieving the objective—doing what it takes to get the job done. They also build the team by providing a fun, action-oriented environment. When developing people, Valuing Artisans (SFPs) appreciate team member differences and support individual development. Analyzing Artisans (STPs) develop team members through direct, honest feedback.
- *Guardians* tend to excel at building the team in a structured way and at achieving the objective by organizing and planning work output. They also tend to coach team members, enabling each person to improve performance.
- *Rationals* excel at focusing on long-term strategy and direction to achieve the objective. When they understand the importance of people in the long-term effectiveness of the system, they invest the time in building the team and developing the people.
- *Idealists* excel at developing the potential of the people on their team. They enjoy achieving results through these people and make efforts to ensure a cohesive, harmonious team.

For more information, see chapter 3 in this fieldbook and chapter 9 in *Turning Team Performance Inside Out.*

End of Exercise

Now let's review each of the leadership responsibility categories in more depth.

Achieve the Objective

As shown earlier in figure 11, the responsibility of achieving the objective involves two main tasks: lead when necessary and evaluate and intervene as needed.

Lead When Necessary (LEADER)

As we discussed in *Turning Team Performance Inside Out,* in addition to temperament and working style—which will affect the way we tend to lead—there are four leadership styles we can use depending on the specific task a team member is completing or the specific situation the team is facing. As leaders, sometimes we need to lead from the front, but at other times we can step back and let the team perform. The model to explain these different styles is known as Situational Leadership™; it was first described by Paul Hersey and Ken Blanchard in their book *Management of Organizational Behavior* (2000). The model presents two main types of behaviors: directive behavior and supportive behavior (see figure 12).

> Directive behavior involves clearly telling people what to do, how to do it, when to do it and closely monitoring their performance.... Supportive behavior involves listening to people, providing support and encouragement for their efforts, and then facilitating their involvement in problem solving and decision making.
> —Ken Blanchard, Drea Zigarmi, and Patricia Zigarmi, *Leadership and the One Minute Manager* (1985)

FIGURE 12 Situational Leadership Model

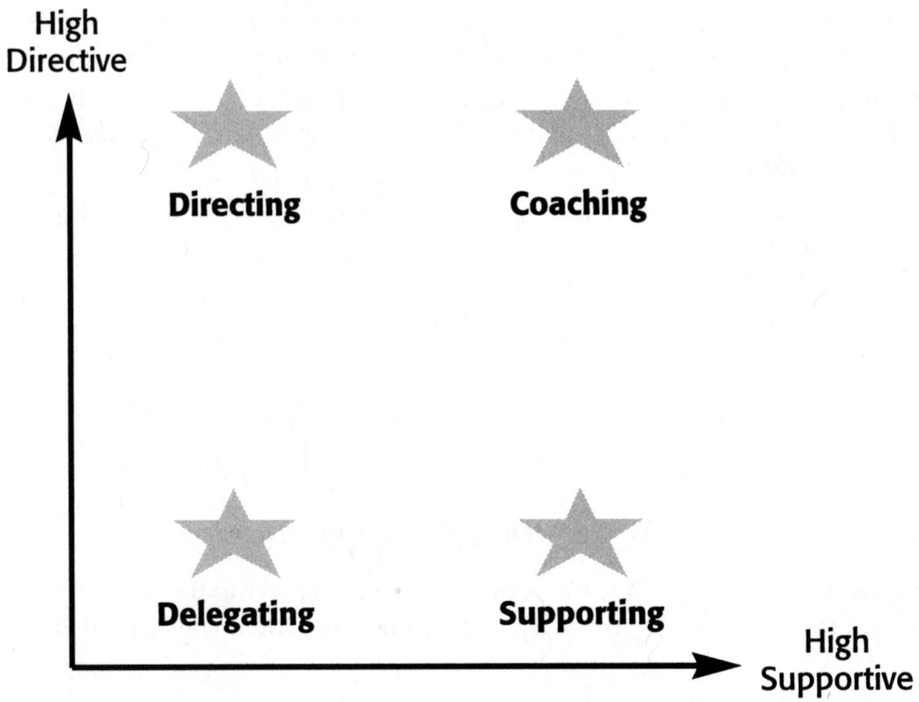

Source: Ken Blanchard, Blanchard Training and Development.

Leadership Styles

According to Hersey and Blanchard's Situational Leadership model, there are four distinct styles of leading—directing, coaching, supporting, and delegating.

- *Directing* involves giving subordinates lots of direction but little support. Leaders tell their subordinates what to do, when to do it, and how to complete the task at hand. This style is often used when team members are new to the position or task.
- *Coaching* involves giving subordinates lots of support and direction. Leaders provide a similar amount of direction as when directing but approach it in a more facilitated way; team members are more involved in the decision-making process. This style is often used when team members are building their skills within a certain context.
- *Supporting* involves giving subordinates lots of support but little direction. When using the supporting style, leaders step back and allow team members to decide the task direction, providing support where needed. This style is often used with experienced team members who are honing their skills.
- *Delegating* involves giving subordinates little direction or support. By definition it entails a much more hands-off approach on the part of the leader. The team member is left to drive the project or task. High-performing team members will benefit from the use of this style.

Based on the descriptions of the four styles above, let's evaluate which styles are the most comfortable for you to use.

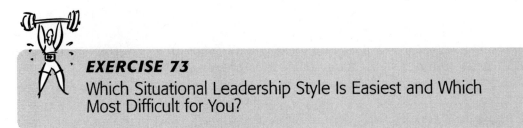

EXERCISE 73
Which Situational Leadership Style Is Easiest and Which Most Difficult for You?

For each of the four leadership styles, answer the following questions in the boxes below.

1. Which style is the easiest for you to use, and why?
2. Which style is the most difficult for you to use, and why?
3. What correlation, if any, do you observe between your temperament and working style and the Situational Leadership styles described?
4. To what extent are you able to adjust your leadership style depending on the person and the situation?
5. Moving forward, how can you ensure that you consider the situation and adapt your style accordingly?

Directing __________ __________ __________ __________ __________	**Coaching** __________ __________ __________ __________ __________
Delegating __________ __________ __________ __________ __________	**Supporting** __________ __________ __________ __________ __________

Coaching Point

Most team leaders tend to gravitate toward two of the four styles. This means that in a specific situation they may not be using the most effective one. Failure to adjust leadership style can result in a loss of team productivity and lower team member morale. The ability to use each style is fundamental for leading an effective team.

Team Dynamics from the Inside Out

There seems to be some correlation between temperament, cognitive processes, and preferred Situational Leadership style. Following are some general observations taken from a series of leadership development programs run for a large financial consulting company.

Directing: Most participants comfortable with Systematizing found directing to be their natural style (some Guardians and Rationals: STJs and NTJs). In addition, Analyzing Artisans (STPs) often gravitated toward this style as they pushed to achieve results. Many Idealists struggled with directing, as it seemed too one-way and they tend to prefer two-way interaction.

Coaching: This style is what is taught in most leadership/management training programs; therefore, many participants demonstrated some proficiency in this area. Idealists tended to gravitate toward coaching because of the empathy it involves. Additionally, the other temperaments with a Feeling preference (Guardians with Harmonizing [SFJs] and Artisans with Valuing [SFPs]) also tended to like the coaching style because of its relationship focus.

Supporting: Again, because the skills used in supporting can be learned behaviors, these styles tend to be more widely used. The only temperament group that seemed to struggle with this style was Rationals. They felt that if people were competent, they would not necessarily need the relationship support from their leader.

Delegating: Artisans tended to excel at delegating because it is pragmatic and it makes life easier. Some Rationals liked to delegate if they felt the person to whom they were delegating was competent. On the other hand, some Rationals expressed concern about the perceived loss of control that delegating inferred. Guardians seemed to struggle with delegating because, as one person put it, "There is a right way to complete the task. By the time I have explained this to someone else, I could have completed the task three times." Idealists tended to struggle with delegating because they wanted to remain involved with the people and their project. Idealists also struggled with letting go of something they see as being uniquely their own.

Coaching Point

Based on functions and temperament, certain working styles appear to gravitate toward certain Situational Leadership styles. The greater awareness you have of your innate preferences, the greater the possibility that you will be able to adapt according to the needs of the situation.

End of Exercise

Evaluate and Intervene As Needed

One of the more subtle aspects of the team leader's role in achieving the objective is serving as the bridge between the organization and the team. Leaders have the overall responsibility for evaluating team responsibilities and organizing extra support where barriers need to be overcome. These types of interventions can include

- Obtaining access to resources
- Making sure the team has the information it needs
- Publicizing the team results to the rest of the organization
- Communicating with other organizational teams
- Intervening in organizational politics

Let's identify the barriers your team might be facing.

EXERCISE 74
Barriers to Team Performance

1. In this exercise, have each team member complete the following steps:

- Looking at the list of interventions above, which of these factors, if any, are negatively impacting team performance? Write them down in the left-hand box below.
- Think about any possible challenges your team members have described in team meetings or when meeting one on one. What might this indicate about any other additional challenges facing the team? Write down these additional challenges in the left-hand box as well.

Barriers	Ideas for Reducing the Barriers

2. Then, as team leader, look at each barrier in turn and ask what you could do to overcome any of these challenges and increase the team's chances of success. Write your ideas in the right-hand box. Finally, ask team members, "What else could I do to help you succeed?"

Coaching Point

The team leader's role in terms of accomplishing goals is almost transparent when the team is performing effectively. However, the team leader's ability to indirectly influence team performance—by removing obstacles so that team members can continue getting the work done—is critical.

End of Exercise

Develop the People

Having reviewed the two leadership tasks in achieving the objective—lead when necessary and evaluate and intervene as needed—let's look now at the two techniques required in developing the people: appreciate team members and develop individuals by coaching.

Appreciate Team Members

What motivates your team? Whenever we talk about coaching and providing positive feedback to team members, the most frequent comment is, "Well, that's all very good, but if they are not paid enough, they are not going to stay!" Let's investigate that sentiment for a moment.

EXERCISE 75
What Motivates Your Team?

Have each member of your team complete the following steps:

- Rank the motivating factors in the list below according to how important they are to you. Mark 1 for the strongest motivator, 2 for the next strongest, and so on, until you reach 10, the least important factor in motivating you.
- Then, in the next column list those motivating factors you think would be important to your team members.

Motivating Factors

Motivating Factor	Ranking for You (1–10)	Ranking for Team Members (1–10)
Job security		
Interesting work		
Tactful discipline		
Loyalty of the company/supervisor		
Appreciation for work done		
Help with personal problems		
Good working conditions		
Promotion in the company		
Feeling of being in on things		
High wages		

- Determine the differences between your own ranking and the way you ranked the motivating factors for your team. To see how 3,000 employees in a study ranked these factors, see page 320.

Coaching Point

Appreciation for work done is a strong motivator for individuals at work. Plus, positive feedback is a lot easier to give than a high wage!

End of Exercise

Types of Feedback

Because appreciation for effort and work completed is a strong motivator, let's spend some time reviewing the skills necessary in providing feedback. The types of feedback described in *Turning Team Performance Inside Out* are reviewed in table 16.

Table 16 Types of Feedback

Type of Feedback	Definition
Positive	• Feedback is provided on strengths, what the person innately does well (known as unconscious competence—see pp. 4–6); this includes praise, recognition, attention, and interest • The goal for positive feedback is reinforcement of specific desirable behaviors demonstrated
Developmental	• Feedback is provided on what the person could do differently in order to improve (known as unconscious incompetence—pp. 4–6) • The goal for developmental feedback is improvement of behavior
Zero	• No feedback is provided, either because the team leader is too busy or because he or she does not think it necessary • The often unintentional outcome of zero feedback is lack of motivation
Negative	• Feedback is harshly critical and has no positive content or intent; the team leader may unintentionally provide negative feedback when stressed or upset • The outcome is reduction in self-esteem, reduced motivation, and often lower performance from the individuals affected

Providing Positive Feedback

Because positive feedback has such a morale-boosting effect on individuals, let's use an exercise to try out this valuable technique.

EXERCISE 76
Providing Positive Feedback

TEAM EXERCISE

The value of providing positive feedback is not restricted to the team leader. Complete this exercise with the whole team.

1. Divide your team into two equal groups: one group becomes the A's and the other group becomes the B's.
2. Form two circles, with the inner circle (A's) facing the outer circle (B's). Each A member in the inner circle faces a B partner in the outer circle.
3. Instruct the A's to give positive feedback to the B's. Remember, the positive feedback can be about talents, knowledge, approach, experience, personality, or skills. Be specific and provide examples.

Foul!

Don't focus on superficialities such as nice clothes or good hair! They are not related to behavior!

4. Instruct the B's to answer, "Thank you; I do think I'm good at..." (the sentence is completed with a repetition of the feedback they have just received).

Foul!

Make sure the B's don't block the positive feedback by:

- Using the Ping-Pong paddle: "Oh, you are too."
- Minimizing the importance: "No, it's really nothing."
- Closing their body language; for example, crossing their arms or turning away.

5. Have the two groups switch roles. The B's give positive feedback to the A's by the same standards and process outlined above (feedback given, feedback accepted, feedback repeated).
6. Now have the A's take a step to the left to meet new B's; the whole sequence begins again until all team members have provided feedback to every other member and received feedback from every other member.

Team Huddle!

Now discuss the exercise using the following questions:

- How did it feel to provide positive feedback?
- How easy was it to receive positive feedback?
- Which was easier: giving or receiving positive feedback?
- What happened to the energy in the team during that exercise?
- What are the benefits of doing this exercise?
- How can we ensure that we make time to provide each other with positive feedback?

Normally, individuals find it harder to receive than to give positive feedback.

Team Dynamics from the Inside Out

Remember, each temperament approaches positive feedback differently:

- *Artisans* will often provide quick, informal feedback, usually tied to more tangible rewards.
- *Guardians* will provide positive feedback usually accompanied by developmental feedback.
- *Rationals* may view positive feedback as somewhat redundant and tend to focus on areas for development as they look for ways to improve performance.
- *Idealists* will often be generous with positive feedback but may avoid the tougher developmental messages.

End of Exercise

Develop Individuals by Coaching

Coaching is a critical skill team leaders use to achieve the perfect balance between positive and developmental feedback. Following are instructions for a basic coaching session and checklist (see table 17).

1. Start with a positive to set an upbeat tone for the discussion.
2. Agree on an agenda to keep the discussion focused.
3. Get the person's input with open-ended questions and phrases beginning with "Who?" "What?" "When?" "Why?" "Tell me about," "Describe," "Explain," and so on.

Coaching Point

It is a good idea to ask questions because this helps those being coached diagnose their own behavior. By recognizing their own strengths and possible weaknesses, they are more likely to buy into developmental actions.

4. Give feedback, remembering to balance positive with developmental feedback.
5. Develop an action plan together with the person to guide further actions. As the purpose of a coaching session is to improve performance, the action plan is a critical tool for building on strengths and improving possible weaknesses.
6. Confirm actions and checkpoints by summarizing the actions that have been decided on and verifying that both parties agree with the course of action.

Table 17 Coaching Steps Checklist

Coaching Steps
1. Start with a positive.
2. Agree on agenda.
3. Get the person's input: • Skills being handled well ("What do you think you are doing well?") • Skills needing improvement ("What do you think you could do differently?")
4. Give feedback: • Skills being handled well • Skills needing improvement
5. Develop an action plan together.
6. Confirm actions and checkpoints.

Coaching Point

Before you wrap up the coaching session, always ask questions such as, "How does that sound, look, or feel?" or, "What do you think about this coaching session?" This can help ensure that the person has understood the feedback and that any remaining issues that might otherwise arise after the discussion are allowed to surface.

While the benefits of coaching are very clear, making the coaching session effective is not as straightforward, particularly when we also have to consider our own and our team members' working style.

EXERCISE 77
Coaching Using Working Style

The purpose of this exercise is to help you coach team members using your knowledge of their working style and temperament. For this exercise you will need to work with at least three other managers/team leaders from temperament groups other than your own.

1. Spend approximately fifteen minutes reviewing the four case studies on pages 293–94 and preparing coaching sessions using the Coaching Steps Checklist (table 17).
2. For each coaching case study, if possible, ask one of your co-managers who actually has that working style to play the role of the person being coached. For instance, try to pick a Guardian (ISFJ) to play Marie. That way you will get to see what it might really be like and whether or not your approach worked! If you cannot find a co-manager with that working style, at least make sure that the person is the correct temperament—for example, a Guardian for case study 1, an Artisan for case study 2, and so on.
3. Ask one of the other managers to play the role of *your* coach—he or she is to observe your role playing and give feedback on how working style and temperament show up in the coaching process.

4. Now read the case studies—based on the following scenario—below.

Scenario

You are responsible for the annual performance review of the four staff members listed below. They are all long-term team members. As you read about each member, remember that you want the outcome to be a positive one for both of you, but it needs to result in a behavior change. Think about the underlying issues that you need to address. What is driving the behavior from a temperament perspective? What functions are used by each team member to gather information and make decisions? What points do you want to emphasize and discuss? What would be your coaching points based on each member's temperament and working style?

Case Study	Approach
Case Study 1 Marie is an Introverted Guardian who uses Recalling and Harmonizing (ISFJ). She is an incredibly hard worker with excellent follow-through skills and the ability to manage a large number of projects. However, this is one of the reasons that she often ends up being overloaded. Not only does she do her own work, but she will often step into the gap and pick up others' tasks because she does not feel comfortable saying no. She hates for the team to miss a deadline. As a result, she sometimes snaps at people and can act irritably with her co-workers. This behavior is beginning to affect team morale.	• What are the underlying issues? • What areas do you want to emphasize and discuss with her? How will you adapt your coaching approach based on her temperament and working style?
Case Study 2 Jeff is an Extraverted Artisan who uses Experiencing and Analyzing (ESTP). He is an excellent technician, crisis manager, and problem solver. He has produced some significant results for your team by being able to recognize current options and taking advantage of them. However, he can occasionally appear to be somewhat of a rebel by going around processes without telling others. Recently, you also observed his increasing use of off-color humor and outrageous statements.	• What are the underlying issues? • What areas do you want to emphasize and discuss with him? How will you adapt your coaching approach based on his temperament and working style?

Case Study	Approach
Case Study 3 Theresa is an Introverted Rational who uses Visioning and Systematizing (INTJ). She brings a logical, independent perspective to team projects. She is very efficient at creating structured plans to achieve team goals. However, she appears to be unaware of the effect her constant critical questioning of ideas is having on the team. She also tends to hold to one vision of the outcome and is unwavering in its pursuit. She can frustrate team members because she is not open to new ideas and has trouble articulating her viewpoint.	• What are the underlying issues? • What areas do you want to emphasize and discuss with her? How will you adapt your coaching approach based on her temperament and working style?
Case Study 4 June is an Extraverted Idealist who uses Brainstorming and Valuing (ENFP). She contributes great energy and ideas to the group. She always has something positive to say to other team members and naturally helps build enthusiasm. However, she lacks follow-through and tends to reinvent the wheel when there is often a simpler approach. Team members are frustrated with her propensity to extend deadlines, plus she sometimes expresses her viewpoint too adamantly and abruptly for their liking.	• What are the underlying issues? • What areas do you want to emphasize and discuss with her? How will you adapt your coaching approach based on her temperament and working style?

Team Dynamics from the Inside Out

- *Artisans:* Make sure you don't communicate to Marie that she should be less responsible and forget the team deadlines!
- *Guardians:* Don't just tell Jeff to stick to the rules and behave in an adult way!
- *Rationals:* Don't tell June that she is not special and people don't like her!
- *Idealists:* Don't tell Theresa that she is incompetent and should be more approachable.

Suggested answers to the questions on approach can be found on pages 321–24.

Team Huddle!

Discuss the case studies with your co-managers using the following questions:

- How did you see temperament in action?
- To what extent were you able able to adapt your style to the needs of the staff?
- What were some specific words or phrases that you used to appeal to the person being coached?
- How can you improve your coaching skills with different types and temperaments?

Many team leaders find it hard to adapt their style to the team member they are coaching. As a result, the coaching session may not be successful. By adapting our style to the needs of our individual team members, we increase the likelihood of successful coaching sessions.

Coaching Point

If the team member you wish to coach is a certain working style, you may want to find colleagues who share the same style and practice your approach on them.

End of Exercise

Build the Team

Now that we have reviewed achieving the objective and developing the people, let's review the final set of skills and techniques for a team leader, which include building the team by engaging the team and reinforcing results.

Engage the Team

Team activities are essential to engage team member interest, build trust, and aid the team as it moves through the four stages of team development, as described in *Turning Team Performance Inside Out*. The stages are defined as follows:

- *Forming:* members are unclear about roles and goals and exhibit minimal trust and superficial communication
- *Storming:* there may be conflicts between team members as they disagree about tasks, processes, and goals
- *Norming:* procedures are beginning to be put into place, ground rules are defined, and standard operating norms are established
- *Performing:* the team is operating well collectively, and there is synergy between team members

Table 18 lists the types of activities you could use to build the team, the benefits of each type of activity, and the team stages in which the activity is best used. This chart will enable you to engage your team in a way appropriate to the benefit desired and the stage of team development.

Table 18 Team-Building Activities and Stages of Team Development

Ice-Breaker Activities	Benefits	Stages of Team Development
Use books such as *Games Teams Play* by Leslie Bendaly and *100 Training Games* by Gary Kroehnert	• Builds trust • Raises team energy • Breaks down barriers	• Forming • Storming • Norming • Performing
Use the role nouns exercise on pages 232–34 to introduce team members to each other	• Allows team members to see behind work personas to the person beneath • Surfaces common interests	• Forming • Storming

Team-Building Activities	Benefits	Stages of Team Development
Use the team purpose exercise on pages 168–69 to establish a written and three-dimensional representation of the team purpose	• Builds trust • Builds team cohesiveness • Establishes team direction	• Forming • Storming • Norming • Performing
Use the ground rules exercise on pages 174–76 to document the way the team wishes to work together	• Builds team norms and sets correct expectations	• Forming • Storming
Use the team values exercise on pages 177–79 to see how well your team is adhering to its values	• Builds team culture	• Forming • Storming • Norming

Table 18 Team-Building Activities and Stages of Team Development (cont'd)

Team Learning	Benefits	Stages of Team Development
Complete a working style and temperament assessment with a qualified administrator	• Provides a common language for discussing differences against an objective framework	• Forming • Storming • Norming • Performing

Team Responsibilities	Benefits	Stages of Team Development
Use the key result areas exercise on pages 186–87 to define the overall responsibilities for the group	• Clearly allocates responsibilities	• Forming • Storming • Norming • Performing
Have regular team meetings	• Builds relationships • Maintains communication and builds trust	• Forming • Storming • Norming • Performing
Use the objectives exercise on pages 212–13 to facilitate sessions to set team member objectives	• Sets goals and clarifies responsibilities	• Forming • Storming

Team Interaction	Benefits	Stages of Team Development
Review the information on temperament and working style (chapters 1–3) and diagnose any conflicts or issues against this backdrop	• Provides objective diagnosis of differences to detach emotions from the conflict	• Storming
Use the feedback exercise on pages 289–90 to raise team energy and trust	• Raises team energy • Builds trust	• Storming • Norming • Performing

Now let's review which of these activities you could use to build your team.

EXERCISE 78
Building Your Team

1. Review the list of activities in table 18. To what extent have you used exercises to establish and manage team cohesiveness?

____

____

2. Review the four stages of team development described earlier in this chapter: Forming, Storming, Norming, and Performing. Based on this data, what stage of team development do you perceive your team to be experiencing?

____

____

3. From table 18, identify two activities that you could use to build team cohesiveness and results.

____

____

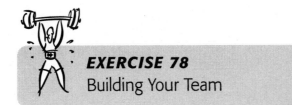

Coaching Point

Remember, building an effective team is a process, not an event! By constantly monitoring the team's effectiveness and intervening where necessary, it is possible to develop a cohesive and productive team. If you become submerged in the team's day-to-day operation and forget to consider building the team, by the time you do so it may be too late.

End of Exercise

Reinforce Results

One of the most important aspects of building your Dream Team is reinforcing and celebrating results. This contributes to effective teamwork in two main ways: (1) by raising individual morale—accomplishment is one of the key motivating factors; and (2) by contributing to a positive team culture.

Too often, teams view achievements as a completion of major milestones. Achievements can also consist of multitudes of "moments of truth"—small successes that occur every single day. These achievements and moments of truth can occur in both the task and group process elements of teamwork (getting the work done and effectively working together, respectively). Yet, instead of recognizing them and celebrating them, we tend to focus on what has not worked, thereby reducing team confidence and lowering motivation levels.

In our society we receive, on average, six pieces of negative feedback for every one piece of positive feedback. No wonder we sometimes feel we are not achieving our objectives! By recognizing and celebrating accomplishments, teams not only feel more positive, but also generate trust and better morale.

Time Out!

Achievements can include such things as:

- One team member providing genuine, meaningful feedback to another team member
- A team member offering to help another team member who is overloaded
- A difficult decision being made by consensus
- A moment of laughter between team members
- A short task being completed
- The team recognizing that there is a problem and beginning to work on it together
- A smoothly run, productive meeting
- Explaining the team purpose to someone outside the team
- Presenting team results to other organizational groups or senior management
- Achieving either a short- or long-term objective

Coaching Point

In the future, keep your eyes open for those positive "moments of truth" that you can use to build team spirit and, ultimately, team productivity. Awareness of these achievements is the first step in being able to celebrate successes.

Now that we have redefined our criteria for what we consider to be a success, let's look at some ways to celebrate achievements.

Celebrating Achievements

Celebrating achievements provides a sense of well-being and builds esprit de corps. It can be as simple as having a potluck or as sophisticated as organizing an off-site event for team members at an innovative location. Other ideas for celebrations are listed below. The list is by no means complete!

- Team dinner/picnic/barbecue
- Team training and learning
- Giveaways such as sweatshirts, T-shirts, water bottles, etc.
- Applauding achievements as they happen
- Awards
- Social events after work
- Complimentary time off
- Celebrating key milestones with cake, cookies, etc.
- New assignments—when the project is completed
- Certificates for project completion or outstanding efforts
- "Team Player of the Month" awards
- Team exercises that build communication and trust
- Outdoor experiential events

EXERCISE 79
Celebrating Team Achievements!

TEAM EXERCISE

To aid you in celebrating achievements, complete this exercise with the whole team. List some of your team's achievements in the past month.

____

____

____

____

- How did we celebrate these achievements?

____

____

____

____

- How can we ensure that we continually celebrate our successes?

____

____

____

____

- Our commitment to celebrating our successes is:

____

____

____

Signed (by all team members):

End of Exercise

Wrap-Up

As you can see, the role of team leader is critical in guiding the team to achieve its targets and objectives. An effective team leader is able to do the following:

L: Lead When Necessary—adjusting his or her style to the team member and the task the team member is accomplishing

E: Evaluate and Intervene As Needed—to remove barriers and obstacles

A: Appreciate Team Members—by providing positive feedback to build self-esteem and raise individual motivation levels

D: Develop Individuals by Coaching—using a dialogue to capitalize on team members' strengths and minimize weaknesses

E: Engage the Team—by using different team-building activities at each stage of team development

R: Reinforce Results—to maintain morale and momentum

SCORECARD

Before leaving this chapter, answer the following questions:

- ☐ How effective a "LEADER" do you think you are? What did you decide to do to increase your leadership effectiveness?
- ☐ Which was the Situational Leadership style you were most comfortable using? Which was the one you were the least comfortable using? To what extent were you able to adjust your style depending on the situation?
- ☐ What barriers were you able to remove that may have been hindering your team's performance?
- ☐ How aware were you of the factors that motivate individuals? What were the surprises? How did the team respond to receiving positive feedback? How can you ensure that you continue to provide positive feedback?
- ☐ When coaching, how easy was it for you to adjust your style to the needs of each specific temperament? How can you improve your proficiency in adapting your style?
- ☐ What activities did you decide to undertake to build your team process? How can you make sure you continue to smoothly move your team through the different stages of team development?
- ☐ How will you reinforce results more regularly? What commitment did team members make to each other to reinforce results?

Appendix 1

Answers to Exercises

Exercise 9: Identifying Temperaments in Case Studies (pp. 30–34)

Subcontract Trainers	
Jennifer's temperament: Rational *Clues:* • Values knowledge and competence • Enjoys autonomy and control • Enjoys research and gravitates toward logical data • Likes new theories and models • Enjoys being recognized as an expert in her field	**Tony's temperament: Artisan** *Clues:* • Is able to make an impact with the participants • Enjoys the flexibility and freedom inherent in the role • Can make the content relevant and hands-on for the group and tells great stories! • Sees immediate, tangible results from each program

Sales/Account Managers	
Karen's temperament: Idealist *Clues:* • Builds long-term relationships • Likes to help her customers make a difference in positioning their products • Gravitates to work with meaning and purpose • Uses empathy to understand customer needs	**Sharon's temperament: Guardian** *Clues:* • Is organized and follows up with customers • Values belonging and contributing to the team • Tunes in to past experience and information • Likes to see concrete results from her work

Exercise 9: Identifying Temperaments in Case Studies (cont'd)

<table>
<tr><th colspan="2">IT VP/Directors</th></tr>
<tr><td>
Tim's temperament: Guardian
Clues:
<ul>
<li>Establishes processes and procedures within a clear structure</li>
<li>Likes to define responsibilities for his team</li>
<li>Feels obliged to be responsible</li>
<li>Likes to question change before going along with it</li>
<li>Seeks program consistency</li>
</ul>
</td><td>
Adam's temperament: Idealist
Clues:
<ul>
<li>Likes to develop the people on his team</li>
<li>Has created a supportive and collaborative culture</li>
<li>Focuses on the future</li>
<li>Does not enjoy conflict and tends to invest in team-building activities as a preventative measure</li>
</ul>
</td></tr>
</table>

<table>
<tr><th colspan="2">CEOs</th></tr>
<tr><td>
Alison's temperament: Artisan
Clues:
<ul>
<li>Took advantage of the opportunity in the moment to start her business</li>
<li>Enjoys the sensory elements of her work: touch, look, smell, etc.</li>
<li>Creates a fun and flexible culture at her organization</li>
<li>Runs the business in an informal way</li>
<li>Tends to get bored when the work becomes repetitive</li>
</ul>
</td><td>
Bob's temperament: Rational
Clues:
<ul>
<li>Uses precise language</li>
<li>Enjoys the autonomy and independence of his role as CEO</li>
<li>Is good at setting strategy for team members to then implement</li>
<li>Tends to be uncomfortable when he perceives a lack of logic</li>
<li>Excels at developing models</li>
</ul>
</td></tr>
</table>

Exercise 10: Temperament Contributions to the Team (pp. 35–37)

Characteristics of a High-Performing Team	Artisans	Guardians	Rationals	Idealists
Cohesive Strategy	**Strengths** • Bring a realistic perspective of the current situation • Lighten up the planning process with humor **Challenges** • May think more in terms of current tactics and details • May want quick, tangible results	**Strengths** • Encourage team involvement toward organizational goals • Use past data as a tool in guiding future direction **Challenges** • May view setting a team purpose as impractical • May want to focus on improving weaknesses rather than capitalizing on new opportunities	**Strengths** • Bring a natural, strategic perspective to the planning process • Bring an excellent view of trends and future opportunities **Challenges** • May struggle with creating realistic time frames—everything is possible • May wordsmith purpose and mission statements too much	**Strengths** • Bring a natural focus on team purpose and identity • Will tend to focus on the strengths of the team **Challenges** • May be unrealistic in defining the team purpose and direction • May get offended if team members are not as committed to the process as they are
Clear Roles and Responsibilities	**Strengths** • Bring a flexible approach to defining roles • Have a clear focus on results **Challenges** • May resist an in-depth definition of roles • May want to work around processes where necessary	**Strengths** • Bring a natural affinity for defining roles • Will define outcomes and measures for each role **Challenges** • May be too rigid in defining roles • May pick up others' responsibilities rather than confronting others about lack of task completion	**Strengths** • Bring a natural affinity for defining roles • Will define outcomes and measures for each role **Challenges** • May want to stay focused on the big picture and may not be aware of the detailed tasks required • May set very high expectations	**Strengths** • Bring a natural ability to understand what roles others may enjoy (through empathy) • Will be flexible in adapting roles to individual abilities **Challenges** • May not consider detailed tasks • May focus too much on potential versus current ability required

Exercise 10: Temperament Contributions to the Team (cont'd)

Characteristics of a High-Performing Team	Artisans	Guardians	Rationals	Idealists
Open Communication	**Strengths** • Bring a positive energy and sense of fun to communication • Use direct, succinct communication—get to the point **Challenges** • May offend others with their no-nonsense style • May not frame the communication before sending the message—may just jump in	**Strengths** • Bring an organized, step-by-step communication approach • Provide data and examples to make key points **Challenges** • Under stress, may use words such as "should" and "ought to," which might seem too judgmental • May want to discuss only what is real and proven	**Strengths** • Bring precise language and have a full arsenal of words • Are able to present an abstract, logical argument or position **Challenges** • May frustrate others with their critical questioning as they try to clarify meaning • May appear arrogant as they focus on their concepts and ideas	**Strengths** • Bring an ability to connect diverse points of view • Are naturally empathetic and able to connect with others on the team **Challenges** • May use too many general words and communicate effusively • May talk about impressions without being able to link these to concrete data
Rapid Response	**Strengths** • Bring an ability to respond quickly to the needs of the moment • Can see creative options for resolving problems **Challenges** • May reinvent the wheel and appear to change for change's sake • May forget to consider future options as they respond expediently	**Strengths** • Bring an ability to institute processes for smoothing change when change is understood • Are able to use past data with a new slant for future creativity **Challenges** • May initially respond negatively to new ideas in which they have no prior experience • May appear hesitant in taking risks	**Strengths** • Bring an ability to foresee and anticipate future changes in team and organizational direction • Are able to view changes from a logical, independent perspective **Challenges** • May gravitate toward initiating major changes without consideration of status quo • May not be realistic about time frames and deliverables	**Strengths** • Bring an ability to understand how people may be affected by major transitions • Tend to be future focused and open to new ideas **Challenges** • May not evaluate logical criteria in deciding what to do • May not allow enough time for changes in implementation

Exercise 10: Temperament Contributions to the Team (cont'd)

Characteristics of a High-Performing Team	Artisans	Guardians	Rationals	Idealists
Effective Leadership	**Strengths** • Understand what team members want and help them achieve it • Are quick-thinking and resourceful **Challenges** • May not follow though on detailed implementation • May get frustrated in the early stages of team development, when time is spent on less tangible group process issues	**Strengths** • Build a strong team culture and uphold traditions • Nurture their team—support members in achieving results **Challenges** • May be too hands-on and struggle with delegating • May be too authoritative	**Strengths** • Bring an ability to help team members define goals • Challenge team members to achieve these goals **Challenges** • May neglect to provide positive feedback, as they might perceive this to be redundant • May not focus on some of the interpersonal aspects of leadership	**Strengths** • Bring an ability to facilitate interaction and development of a positive culture • Guide individuals in personal development **Challenges** • May not be comfortable providing developmental feedback • May not focus enough on the task at hand

Exercise 18: Thinking and Feeling (pp. 66–67)

Possible Objective Criteria (Thinking)	Possible Subjective Criteria (Feeling)
• Experience • Specific technical expertise • Degrees • Award	• Fit with team • Conflicts with team members • Potential versus current performance • Work ethic

Exercise 22: Identifying Cognitive Processes and Functions in Case Studies (pp. 81–86)

Subcontract Trainers	
Jennifer **Information-Gathering Function:** **Visioning (Abstract)** *Clues:* • Prefers abstract data: theories/models • Likes to absorb data and then step back to get the whole picture **Decision-Making Function:** **Systematizing (Objective)** *Clues:* • Starts with the end goal and then clearly defines steps to achieve it • Clearly articulates pros and cons; uses cause-and-effect logic to achieve an outcome	**Tony** **Information-Gathering Function:** **Experiencing (Concrete)** *Clues:* • Is able to notice small changes in body language to assess whether the audience is receptive • Acts in the moment and is adept at performing **Decision-Making Function:** **Analyzing (Objective)** *Clues:* • Is able to dissect a particular point of view in numerous ways • Normally has a point of view on a specific subject

Sales/Account Managers	
Karen **Information-Gathering Function: Brainstorming (Abstract)** *Clues:* • Enjoys exploring possibilities and opportunities • Excels at reading between the lines and recognizing patterns and themes that are not immediately discernible **Decision-Making Function: Valuing (Objective)** *Clues:* • Maintains integrity with clients in terms of confidentiality • Stops doing business with customers that behave unethically	**Sharon** **Information-Gathering Function: Recalling (Concrete)** *Clues:* • Goes back to previous clients with whom she has worked to gather data about similar projects • Possesses a strong, sequential sense of memory **Decision-Making Function: Harmonizing (Subjective)** *Clues:* • Has good empathy skills and understands customers' needs • Likes involving as many people as possible in decisions so that everyone is happy with the results

Exercise 22: Identifying Cognitive Processes and Functions in Case Studies (cont'd)

IT VP/Directors	
Tim **Information-Gathering Function: Recalling (Concrete)** *Clues:* • Uses past experience to plan for future contingencies • When problem solving, remembers details about a problem and how it was solved in sequential order **Decision-Making Function: Systematizing (Objective)** *Clues:* • Uses a clear-cut, sequential, detailed approach to planning • Is comfortable creating complex project plans	**Adam** **Information-Gathering Function: Visioning (Abstract)** *Clues:* • Was willing to undertake a new project without any prior experience; gathered information and then stepped back to allow the ideas to develop; came up with an innovative way of structuring the department • Sometimes struggles to articulate his clear mental picture to his team **Decision-Making Function: Harmonizing (Subjective)** *Clues:* • Is uncomfortable with conflict and prefers a nonconfrontational environment • Struggles with tough decisions where it is not possible to make everyone happy

<table>
<tr><th colspan="2">CEOs</th></tr>
<tr>
<td>
Alison
Information-Gathering Function:
Experiencing (Concrete)
Clues:
• Enjoys traveling and gathering data from firsthand experience
• Likes to be where the action is and prefers new challenges to running the company

Decision-Making Function:
Valuing (Subjective)
Clues:
• Places value on building a community and ensured that the company did what was right by listening to and responding to every piece of employee feedback
• When an employee criticized her means of gathering feedback, she restated her belief that people are important in business
</td>
<td>
Bob
Information-Gathering Function:
Brainstorming (Abstract)
Clues:
• Avoids "hands-on" implementation
• Is comfortable exploring new possibilities for the company, thinking as far outside the box as he can!

Decision-Making Function:
Analyzing (Objective)
Clues:
• Has created a new financial model that he believes will ensure profitability for the retail chain
• Enjoys testing logical assumptions and investigating alternative approaches
</td>
</tr>
</table>

Exercise 23: Trying On All Eight Functions (pp. 86–88)

Task	Experiencing	Recalling	Brainstorming	Visioning
Putting Together a Budget	• What are the current costs? • What are the current data?	• What were the costs? Overruns? • What does last year's budget look like?	• What could we do differently this year? • How can we use scenario planning?	• What is the end goal? • How does the budget help us to run the business?
Organizing an Off-Site Event	• What is the location? What about size? Facilities? Light? Accommodations? Go to location; try out equipment and facilities • How can we make it stimulating, exciting, and impactful?	• What worked last time? What do we want to change from last time? • What were the sequential steps that we used last time? What previous data can we find?	• What type of theme could we have? How might we weave this theme throughout? • How could we approach this off-site event completely differently?	• What should the theme be? • What is the ultimate outcome that we wish to achieve?
Writing a Report	• What information is in print? On the Web? • What are the sources for primary research?	• What information from previous reports could be relevant? • What are some secondary sources of information?	• What other sources of information might be relevant? • What are some new ideas from other industries that could be included in the report?	• What is the key information/summary we want to share with executive management? • Is there a completely innovative thesis that we could recommend?
Solving a Problem	• What are the symptoms of the problem? • How do we know there is a problem right now? What is the relevant information?	• What happened last time compared to this time? • What resolution worked last time?	• What are some different possible solutions? • What about…? What about…?	• What would the total solution look like? Feel like? • How else could we achieve that solution?

Task	Systematizing	Analyzing	Harmonizing	Valuing
Putting Together a Budget	• Do we have a template? • What are the timeline and schedule?	• What are the causes of variance? • How else could the figures be recategorized?	• How can we balance stakeholder needs? • How can we involve others to achieve consensus?	• How do we ensure the best use of resources? • What's important to the company/department?
Organizing an Off-Site Event	• What resources do we need? • What is the timetable for making this happen?	• How do we monitor progression against desired end results? • How could the program be adapted to better achieve the goal?	• How do we make people comfortable? • How can we create an open, welcoming environment?	• How do we ensure congruence between aims and methods of the event? • What types of food might offend attendees?
Writing a Report	• What is the end result? What goes first, second, etc.? • Where are the inconsistencies (capitalization, periods, commas, etc.)?	• What is the logical premise or point of view? • How could the content be resequenced? What paragraphs could be moved? How could data be moved under different headings?	• Who needs to be included so that no one is offended? • Will the information be well received?	• Do we include diverse viewpoints because they have value? • Does the report meet my standards?
Solving a Problem	• What action plan will best correct the problem? Who needs to do what when? • How can we create a flow chart for problem resolution steps?	• What is the root cause of the problem? • Have we reviewed the data from different angles?	• What is the appropriate solution for individuals and the company? • How will people be affected by the solution?	• How will the decision sit with you? How do I feel about this? • Will anybody have personal objections to the solution?

Exercise 28: Lost on the Moon (pp. 136–37)

Instructions:

1. Enter your rankings in the "Your Rank" column.
2. Calculate your "Error Points." Error Points are the absolute difference between Your Rank (or Team Rank) and NASA's Rank (disregard plusses or minuses).
3. Then, enter your team rankings and calculate your Team Error Points.

Item	NASA's Reasoning	NASA's Rank	Your Rank	Error Points	Team Rank	Team Error Points
Box of matches	No oxygen on moon to sustain flame: virtually worthless	15				
Food concentrate	Efficient means of supplying energy needs	4				
Parachute silk	Protection from sun	8				
Stellar map of moon's constellations	Primary means of navigation	3				
Two .45-caliber pistols	Possible means of protection	11				
One case dehydrated milk	Bulkier duplication of food concentrate	12				
Two 100-lb. tanks oxygen	Most pressing survival need	1				
Magnetic compass	Magnetic field on moon isn't polarized: worthless for navigation	14				
Self-inflating life raft	CO_2 bottle in military raft may be used for propulsion	9				

Item	NASA's Reasoning	NASA's Rank	Your Rank	Error Points	Team Rank	Team Error Points
Signal flares	Distress signal when office site is in view	10				
First-aid kit with injection needles	Needles for vitamins, medicines, etc., will fit special aperture in NASA space suits	7				
Five gallons water	Replacement for tremendous liquid loss on lighted side	2				
Solar-powered heater	Not needed unless on dark side	13				
50 feet nylon rope	Useful in scaling cliffs, tying injured together	6				
Solar-powered FM receiver/ transmitter	To communicate with office site: but FM needs line-of-sight transmissions and short ranges	5				

Scoring: Individual

Your individual score is the total of all the numbers in the "Error Points" column.

Scoring: Team

The team score is the total of all the numbers in the "Team Error Points" column.

Scale:

0–25	Excellent
26–32	Good
33–45	Average
46–55	Fair
56–70	Poor
71–112	Very Poor (suggests possible faking or the use of earthbound logic!)

Exercise 52: One- and Two-Way Communication (Round 1) (pp. 220–22)

Diagram 1

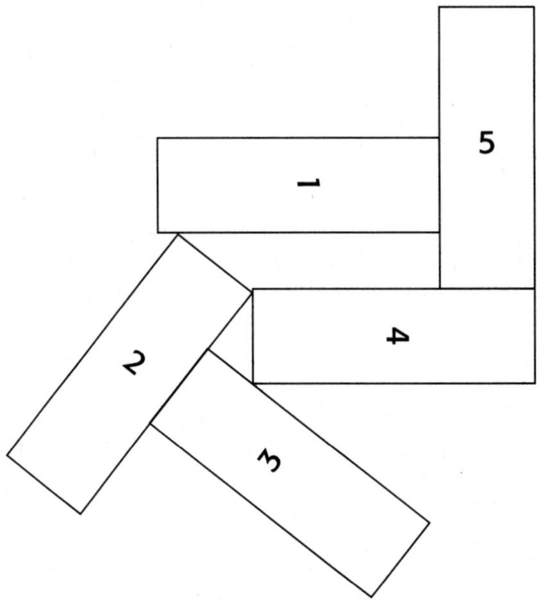

Exercise 52: One- and Two-Way Communication (Round 2) (pp. 220–22)

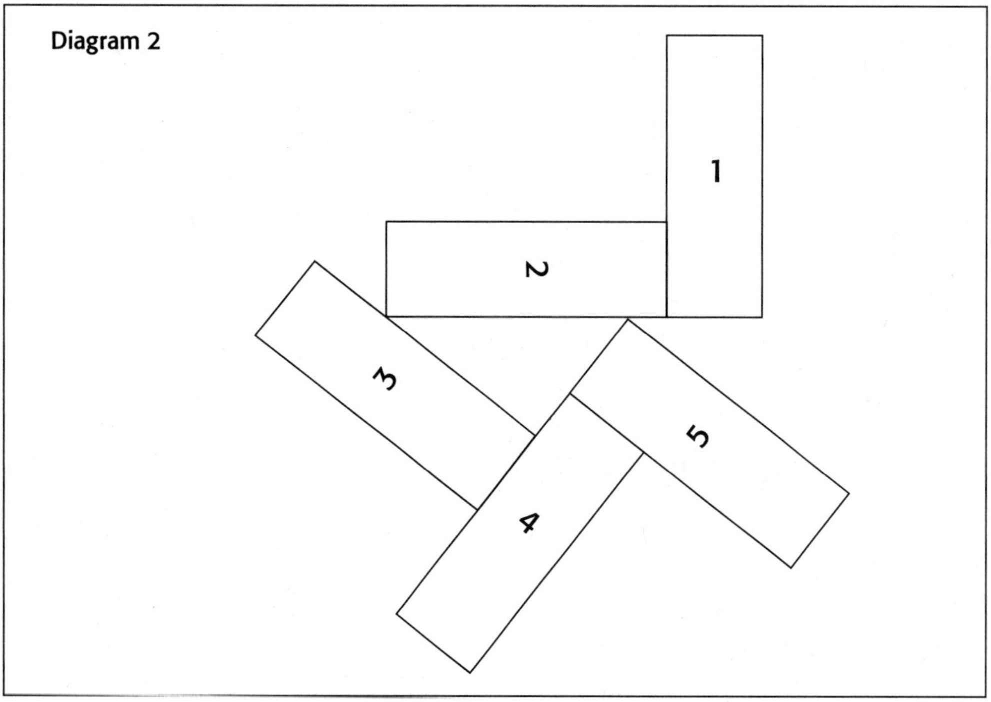

Exercise 53: Closed and Open-Ended Questions (p. 224)

Closed	Open-Ended
Do you watch TV?	Example: What do you like to do for fun?
Do you like to eat fish?	What food do you like?
Did you solve the problem?	How did you deal with this problem?
Can I help you?	What can I help you with?
Was this subject interesting?	What did you think about it?
Have you finished your project?	What is your current project status?

Exercise 54: Active Listening (pp. 225–26)

1. Q: Some months have 31 days. How many have 28?
   A: All months have at least 28 days.
2. Q: If there are three apples and you take away two, how many do you have?
   A: Two: you just took two apples.
3. Q: Why can't a man living in the USA be buried in Canada?
   A: Because he is living, and we don't bury living people!
4. Q: How far can a dog run into the woods?
   A: Half-way—then he would be running out.

Exercise 67: Creativity Quiz (pp. 260–63)

7	W of the AW	Wonders of the ancient world
1001	AN	Arabian nights
12	S of the Z	Signs of the zodiac
54	C in the D with the J	Cards in the deck with the joker
88	PK	Piano keys
13	S on the AF	Stripes on the American flag
18	H on a GC	Holes on a golf course
32	DF at which WF	Degrees Fahrenheit at which water freezes
90	D in a RA	Degrees in a right angle
200	D for PG in M	Dollars for passing "Go" in Monopoly®
9	P in the SS	Planets in the solar system
8	S on a SS	Sides on a stop sign
3	BM (SHTR)	Blind mice (see how they run)
4	Q in a G	Quarters in a game (quarts in a gallon)
1	W on a U	Wheel on a unicycle
5	D in a ZC	Digits in a Zip Code
57	HV	Heinz® Varieties
11	P on a FT	Players on a football team
1,000	W that a P is W	Words that a picture is worth
64	S on a CB	Squares on a checkers board
40	D and N of the GF	Days and nights of the Great Flood
29	D in F in a LY	Days in February in a leap year

Exercise 75: What Motivates Your Team? (pp. 286–87)

Research for Motivating Factors

The chart below shows how over 3,000 employees in a study ranked the motivating factors listed in exercise 75.

Ranking	Factor
1	Appreciation for work done
2	Feeling of being in on things
3	Help with personal problems
4	Job security
5	High wages
6	Interesting work
7	Promotion in the company
8	Loyalty of the company/supervisor
9	Good working conditions
10	Tactful discipline

Exercise 77: Coaching Using Working Style (pp. 292–95)

Case Study	Approach
Case Study 1 Marie is an Introverted Guardian who uses Recalling and Harmonizing (ISFJ). She is an incredibly hard worker with excellent follow-through skills and the ability to manage a large number of projects. However, this is one of the reasons that she often ends up being overloaded. Not only does she do her own work, but she will often step into the gap and pick up others' tasks because she does not feel comfortable saying no. She hates for the team to miss a deadline. As a result, she sometimes snaps at people and can act irritably with her co-workers. This behavior is beginning to affect team morale.	• **What are the underlying issues?** As a Guardian, Marie is driven by the responsibility and need to contribute to the team. This means she tends to take on other team members' duties so that team results are achieved. In addition, her use of the Harmonizing decision-making function means she tends to be uncomfortable delivering difficult messages such as saying no. • **What areas do you want to emphasize and discuss with her? How will you adapt your coaching approach based on her temperament and working style?** You will want to provide positive feedback on her ability to fulfill her responsibilities and contribute to the team. Additionally, you will want to recognize her ability to manage multiple projects. In terms of developmental feedback, it is important to emphasize the potentially negative effect her occasional irritability will have on team cohesiveness. As a Harmonizing Guardian, this will be very important to her. Plus, you can offer her guidance on using assertive communication to clearly communicate her wants and needs.

Exercise 77: Coaching Using Working Style (cont'd)

Case Study	Approach
Case Study 2 Jeff is an Extraverted Artisan who uses Experiencing and Analyzing (ESTP). He is an excellent technician, crisis manager, and problem solver. He has produced some significant results for your team by being able to recognize current options and taking advantage of them. However, he can occasionally appear to be somewhat of a rebel by going around processes without telling others. Recently, you also observed his increasing use of off-color humor and outrageous statements.	• **What are the underlying issues?** As an Artisan, Jeff is driven to be noticed and when bored may attract negative attention versus positive. His use of the Experiencing information-gathering function allows him to cue into current stimuli, but this may result in boredom when new sensory input is lacking. You may want to evaluate why he is making an impact in a negative way: Is he bored? Does he want more of a challenge? • **What areas do you want to emphasize and discuss with him? How will you adapt your coaching approach based on his temperament and working style?** You want to provide positive feedback on his ability to achieve results: emphasize how much his tactical problem-solving ability is respected in the organization. In terms of developmental feedback, make sure you do not lecture him—nothing would be more likely to escalate the situation! Trying to take away an Artisan's freedom is destined to produce the very result you are trying to avoid. Investigate his current level of challenge. Recognize that you like the positive impact he brings but refer to the organizational behavior norms that preclude his more nontraditional behaviors. Investigate ways you could provide him with more challenge.

Exercise 77: Coaching Using Working Style (cont'd)

Case Study	Approach
Case Study 3 Theresa is an Introverted Rational who uses Visioning and Systematizing (INTJ). She brings a logical, independent perspective to team projects. She is very efficient at creating structured plans to achieve team goals. However, she appears to be unaware of the effect her constant critical questioning of ideas is having on the team. She also tends to hold to one vision of the outcome and is unwavering in its pursuit. She can frustrate team members because she is not open to new ideas and has trouble articulating her viewpoint.	• **What are the underlying issues?** As a Rational, Theresa is driven by the need to be competent and create her own destiny. She uses critical questioning as a way of perfecting an idea or system, and she may not be aware of the effect her comments have on the team. In addition, her use of the Visioning information-gathering function can mean that she has a clear picture of the outcome she wants but may not understand why others do not buy into her vision. • **What areas do you want to emphasize and discuss with her? How will you adapt your coaching approach based on her temperament and working style?** You will want to provide positive feedback on the long-term strategic viewpoint that Theresa brings to the team. Emphasize how her competence in planning to achieve goals improves the efficiency of the team system. In terms of developmental feedback, don't tell her she is incompetent in dealing with people! Explain how critical questioning might be perceived by the team and discuss how these questions could be introduced in a more positive way with prefacing statements. Discuss how she might be more open to new ideas that might not be in agreement with her picture.

Exercise 77: Coaching Using Working Style (cont'd)

Case Study	Approach
Case Study 4 June is an Extraverted Idealist who uses Brainstorming and Valuing (ENFP). She contributes great energy and ideas to the group. She always has something positive to say to other team members and naturally helps build enthusiasm. However, she lacks follow-through and tends to reinvent the wheel when there is often a simpler approach. Team members are frustrated with her propensity to extend deadlines, plus she sometimes expresses her viewpoint too adamantly and abruptly for their liking.	• **What are the underlying issues?** As an Idealist, June is driven by making a difference and having a purpose. She naturally tunes in to the potential in team members. Her use of the Brainstorming information-gathering function means that she tends to want to explore new possibilities while sometimes neglecting current reality and processes. In addition, her use of the Valuing decision-making function can mean that sometimes she can be rigid with ideas that appear to go against her internal value system. • **What areas do you want to emphasize and discuss with her? How will you adapt your coaching approach based on her temperament and working style?** You will want to provide positive feedback to June on the difference she makes to the team with her positive energy and passion for people. Emphasize how her unique contribution of seeing possibilities aids team members. In terms of developmental feedback, make sure you focus on the potential challenges that her behavior can have on other individuals on the team. Discuss specific techniques to help her create more realistic plans and stick to them. Plus, you could discuss how she might soften her message when her value system is crossed.

Appendix 2

Consulting Resources for Help in Understanding Type and Temperament

Susan Nash
CEO
EM-Power, Inc.
1120 First Street
Coronado, CA 92118

www.em-power.com
619-522-6811
619-522-6833 (fax)
smnash@aol.com
susan.nash@em-power.com

Courtney Bolin
Behind the Bottom Line
1100 Adella Avenue, 11
Coronado, CA 92118

619-437-4620
cbolin@san.rr.com

Linda V. Berens
Temperament Research Institute
16152 Beach Boulevard, Suite 179
Huntington Beach, CA 92647

714-841-0041
800-700-4874
www.tri-network.com

CPP, Inc.
3803 East Bayshore Road
Palo Alto, CA 94303

800-624-1765
www.cpp.com

Situational Leadership Consulting and Training

Blanchard Training and Development
125 State Place
Escondido, CA 92909

800-728-6000
www.blanchard.com

Online/Written Assessments

Keirsey Temperament Sorter II: www.advisorteam.com/user/ktsintro1.asp

Personality Type Quiz: www.personalitytype.com/quiz.html

Online MBTI® Assessment: www.skillsone.com

Bibliography

Adair, J. *Action Centered Leadership*. N.p.: Ashgate Publishing, 1979.

Bendaly, L. *Games Teams Play*. New York: McGraw-Hill Ryerson, 1996.

Berens, L. V. *Dynamics of Personality Type: Understanding and Applying Jung's Cognitive Processes*. Huntington Beach, CA: Telos, 1999.

———. *Understanding Yourself and Others: An Introduction to Interaction Styles*. Huntington Beach, CA: Telos, 2001.

———. *Understanding Yourself and Others: An Introduction to Temperament—2.0*. Huntington Beach, CA: Telos, 2000.

Berens, L. V., L. K. Ernst, J. E. Robb, and M. A. Smith. *Temperament and Type Dynamics: The Facilitator's Guide*. Huntington Beach, CA: Temperament Research Institute, 1995.

Berens, L. V., L. K. Ernst, and M. A. Smith. *The Guide for Facilitating the Self-Discovery Process*. Huntington Beach, CA: Temperament Research Institute, 1998, 2002.

Berens, L. V. and D. Nardi. *The 16 Personality Types: Descriptions for Self-Discovery*. Huntington Beach, CA: Telos, 1999.

Berens, L. V., et al. *Quick Guide to the 16 Personality Types in Organizations: Understanding Personality Differences in the Workplace*. Huntington Beach, CA: Telos, 2002.

Blanchard, K., D. Zigarmi, and P. Zigarmi. *Leadership and the One Minute Manager*. New York: William Morrow, 1985.

Bridges, W. *The Character of Organizations*. Palo Alto, CA: Davies-Black Publishing, 1992.

Brownsword, A. W. *Type Descriptions*. Herndon, VA: Baytree, 1990.

———. *It Takes All Types*. Herndon, VA: Baytree, 1994.

Covey, S. *The Seven Habits of Highly Effective People*. New York: Fireside, Simon & Schuster, 1989.

Delunas, E. *Survival Games Personalities Play*. Carmel, CA: SunInk Publications, 1992.

Fitzgerald, C., and L. K. Kirby. *Developing Leaders*. Palo Alto, CA: Davies-Black Publishing, 1997.

Handy, C. *The Age of Paradox*. Boston: Harvard Business School Press, 1994.

———. *The Age of Unreason*. Boston: Harvard Business School Press, 1990.

———. *Beyond Certainty*. Boston: Harvard Business School Press, 1996.

Hersey, P., and K. H. Blanchard. *Management of Organizational Behavior: Utilizing Human Resources*. Upper Saddle River, NJ: Prentice-Hall, 1996.

Herzberg, F., B. Mausner, and B. B. Snyderman. *The Motivation to Work*. Piscataway. NJ: Transaction Publishers, 1993.

Hirsh, S. *MBTI Team-Building Program*. Palo Alto, CA: CPP, Inc., 1992.

———. *Work It Out: Clues for Solving People Problems at Work*. Palo Alto, CA: Davies-Black Publishing, 1996.

Hirsh, S., and J. Kummerow. *Life Types*. New York: Warner Books, 1989.

———. *Introduction to Type in Organizations*. 3rd ed. Palo Alto, CA: CPP, Inc., 1998.

Huszczo, G. *Tools for Team Excellence*. Palo Alto, CA: Davies-Black Publishing, 1996.

Isachsen, O. *Joining the Entrepreneurial Elite*. Palo Alto, CA: Davies-Black Publishing, 1997.

Isachsen, O., and L. Berens. *Working Together*. San Juan Capistrano, CA: Institute for Management Development, 1988.

Katzenbach, J., and D. K. Smith. *The Wisdom of Teams*. New York: HarperCollins, 1993.

Keirsey, D. *Please Understand Me II: Temperament Character Intelligence*. Del Mar, CA: Prometheus Nemesis Books, 1998.

———. *Portraits of Temperament.* Del Mar, CA: Prometheus Nemesis Books, 1987.
———. *Presidential Temperament.* Del Mar, CA: Prometheus Nemesis Books, 1992.
Keirsey, D., and M. Bates. *Please Understand Me.* Del Mar, CA: Prometheus Nemesis Books, 1978.
Kriegel, R. J., and D. Brandt. *Sacred Cows Make the Best Burgers.* New York: Warner Books, 1997.
Kriegel, R. J., and L. Patler. *If It Ain't Broke...Break It!* New York: Warner Books, 1992.
Kroeger, O., and Thuesen, J. M. *Type Talk.* New York: Delacorte Press, 1988.
———. *Type Talk at Work.* New York: Delacorte Press, Bantam Doubleday, Dell, 1992.
Kroehnert, G. *100 Training Games.* Sydney: McGraw-Hill, 1994.
Kummerow, J. M., N. J. Barger, and L. K. Kirby. *Work Types.* New York: Warner Books, 1997.
Lakein, A. *How to Get Control of Your Time and Your Life.* N.p.: New American Library, 1996.
Lawrence, G. *People Types and Tiger Stripes.* Gainsville, FL: Center for Applications of Psychological Type, 1995.
Myers, I. B., with L. K. Kirby and K. D. Myers. *Introduction to Type.* 6th ed. Palo Alto, CA: CPP, Inc., 1998.
Myers, I. B., and P. B. Myers. *Gifts Differing.* Palo Alto, CA: Davies-Black Publishing, 1995.
Myers, K. D., and L. K. Kirby. *Introduction to Type Dynamics and Development.* Palo Alto, CA: CPP, Inc., 1994.
Nash, S. *Dating, Mating and Relating.* Oxford: HowTo Books, 2000.
———. *Starting and Running Your Own Consultancy Business.* Oxford: HowTo Books, 2002.
———. *Turning Team Performance Inside Out: Team Types and Temperament for High-Impact Results.* Palo Alto, CA: Davies-Black Publishing, 1999.
Nash, S., and D. Nash. *Delighting Your Customers.* Oxford: HowTo Books, 2001.
———. *Deliver Outstanding Customer Service.* Oxford: HowTo Books, 2002.
Newstrom, J. W., and E. Scanell. *The Big Book of Team-Building Games: Trust-Building Activities, Team Spirit Exercises, and Other Fun Things to Do.* New York: McGraw-Hill, 1997.
———. *Even More Games Trainers Play.* New York: McGraw-Hill, 1994.
———. *Games Trainers Play.* New York: McGraw-Hill, 1980.
———. *Still More Games Trainers Play.* New York: McGraw-Hill, 1983.
Nichols, R. G., and L. Stevens. *Are You Listening?* New York: McGraw-Hill, 1957.
Pearman, R. R. *Hardwired Leadership.* Palo Alto, CA: Davies-Black Publishing, 1998.
Pearman, R. R., and S. C. Albritton. *I'm Not Crazy, I'm Just Not You.* Palo Alto, CA: Davies-Black Publishing, 1997.
Peters, T. J., and R. H. Waterman, Jr. *In Search of Excellence.* New York: Warner Books, 1988.
Quenk, N. *Beside Ourselves: Our Hidden Personality in Everyday Life.* Palo Alto, CA: Davies-Black Publishing, 1993.
———. *In the Grip: Our Hidden Personality.* Palo Alto, CA: CPP, Inc., 1996.
Russell, P. *The Brain Book.* New York: Routledge, 1979.
Segal, M. *Creativity and Personality Type.* Huntington Beach, CA: Telos, 2001.
Sharp, D. *Personality Types: Jung's Model of Typology.* Toronto: Inner City Books, 1987.
Thompson, H. L. *Jung's Function-Attitudes Explained.* Watkinsville, GA: Wormhole Publishing, 1996.
Tieger, P. D., and B. Barron-Tieger. *Do What You Are.* Boston: Little, Brown, 1995.
———. *Nurture by Nature.* Boston: Little, Brown, 1997.
Tuckman, B. W. 1965. "Development Sequences in Small Groups." *Psychological Bulletin* 63.
Waterman, R. H. *Adhocracy.* New York: Norton, 1993.
———. *The Renewal Factor.* New York: Bantam Books, 1988.
———. *What America Does Right: Learning from Companies That Put People First.* New York: Norton, 1994.